AF552377

ATLA Monograph Series
edited by Dr. Kenneth E. Rowe

1. Ronald L. Grimes. *The Divine Imagination: William Blake's Major Prophetic Visions.* 1972.
2. George D. Kelsey. *Social Ethics Among Southern Baptists, 1917-1969.* 1973.
3. Hilda Adam Kring. *The Harmonists: A Folk-Cultural Approach.* 1973.
4. J. Steven O'Malley. *Pilgrimage of Faith: The Legacy of the Otterbeins.* 1973.
5. Charles Edwin Jones. *Perfectionist Persuasion: The Holiness Movement and American Methodism, 1867-1936.* 1974.
6. Donald E. Byrne, Jr. *No Foot of Land: Folklore of American Methodist Itinerants.* 1975.
7. Milton C. Sernett. *Black Religion and American Evangelicalism: White Protestants, Plantation Missions, and the Flowering of Negro Christianity, 1787-1865.* 1975.
8. Eva Fleischner. *Judaism in German Christian Theology Since 1945: Christianity and Israel Considered in Terms of Mission.* 1975.
9. Walter James Lowe. *Mystery & The Unconscious: A Study on the Thought of Paul Ricoeur.* 1977.
10. Norris Magnuson. *Salvation in the Slums: Evangelical Social Welfare Work, 1865-1920.* 1977.
11. William Sherman Minor. *Creativity in Henry Nelson Wieman.* 1977.
12. Thomas Virgil Peterson. *Ham and Japheth: The Mythic World of Whites in the Antebellum South.* 1978.
13. Randall K. Burkett. *Garveyism as a Religious Movement: The Institutionalization of a Black Civil Religion.* 1978.
14. Roger G. Betsworth. *The Radical Movement of the 1960's.* 1980.
15. Alice Cowan Cochran. *Miners, Merchants, and Missionaries: The Roles of Missionaries and Pioneer Churches in the Colorado Gold Rush and Its Aftermath, 1858-1870.* 1980.
16. Irene Lawrence. *Linguistics and Theology: The Significance of Noam Chomsky for Theological Construction.* 1980.

MINERS, MERCHANTS, AND MISSIONARIES:

The Roles of Missionaries and Pioneer Churches in the Colorado Gold Rush and Its Aftermath, 1858-1870

by

ALICE COWAN COCHRAN

ATLA Monograph Series, No. 15

The Scarecrow Press, Inc.
and
The American Theological Library Association
Metuchen, N.J., & London
1980

Library of Congress Cataloging in Publication Data

Cochran, Alice Cowan.
Miners, merchants, and missionaries.

(ATLA monograph series ; no. 15)
Orginally presented as the author's thesis, Southern Methodist University.
Bibliography: p.
Includes index.
1. Missions--Colorado. 2. Frontier and pioneer life--Colorado. 3. Colorado--Gold discoveries. 4. Colorado--Church history. 5. Colorado--History--To 1876. I. Title. II. Series: American Theological Library Association. ATLA monograph series ; no. 15.
BV2803.C6C62 1980 978.8 80-16895
ISBN 0-8108-1325-4

Manufactured in the United States of America

CONTENTS

EDITOR'S NOTE

Since 1972, the American Theological Library Association has undertaken responsibility for a modest dissertation series in the field of religious studies. Our aim in this series is to publish two dissertations of quality each year at a reasonable cost. Titles are selected from studies in a variety of religious and theological disciplines nominated by graduate school deans or directors of graduate studies in religion. We are pleased to publish Alice C. Cochran's splendid study of merchants, missionaries and miners in the Colorado gold rush as number 15 in our series.

Following undergraduate studies in history *summa cum laude* at Rice University, where she was elected to Phi Beta Kappa, Alice Cochran took the M. A. and Ph. D. degrees in religious studies at Southern Methodist University where she served as a teaching fellow. She has published several articles and reviews in leading theological journals and has prepared several chapters for a college text on the history of Christianity which will be published by St. Martin's Press in 1980. Dr. Cochran currently serves as Educational Coordinator for the Episcopal Diocese of Kansas in Topeka.

Kenneth E. Rowe
Series Editor

Drew University Library
Madison, New Jersey 07940

FOREWORD

The all-important question in regional history, as in photography, is that of perspective. When close-ups are clear enough, their backgrounds tend to be blurred or blank; or, on the other side, there are distortions--like the over-sized feet in pictures of a man in a recliner. In _Miners, Merchants, and Missionaries_ we have a case-study of a thin slice of American frontier history, which focuses on a motley of people within the compass of a few thousand square miles over a span of a bare dozen years. But this makes for an impressive example of how a single piece within a larger mosaic may be set so as to achieve a clear and credible perspective.

Dr. Cochran's "close-up" is the wilderness region of Colorado around what came to be Denver during the peak years of a gold rush that began in 1858 and that was all but played out by 1870. Her organizing theme is the dramatic effort, during a chaotic decade, of a small corps of "civilizers" (merchants, teachers, missionaries) to bring a semblance of social order out of what had begun as a mere mad scramble. It is a drama with an abundance of plots and counterplots and with a wild jostling cast of characters. Its chief merit is that this confusion is contained within a steady view of what the drama meant to its various characters and what it still means for our own interpretation of American frontier history within the American experience as a whole. It breaks new ground with its rich documentation and use of primary sources. This means that it will be of nearly equal interest to historians of frontier history and also to historians of the expansion of Christianity. It is whithal richly readable--ample proof of its author's skill in narration _and_ interpretation, in balance.

Within the larger story, we are provided with fascinating vignettes of the "Wild West"--of men gripped with "gold fever" and of men and women whose heroism consisted largely in their stubborn determination to plunge live roots into an inhospitable "new land." There are analyses of economic forces in turmoil, of demographic and social developments, of local and national politics on the westward edge of a nation in the throes of civil war. It is a story of the primal evolution of a segment of the American West, from "howling wilderness" through a short-lived orgy of greed, toward the rudiments of an ordered society with an open future. But even more importantly, we are led through a careful analysis of the pioneer's fundamental views of "civilization" and its values, with special reference to the mission of the frontier churches in transplanting "American" social institutions and their values from their original culture bases in the East and mid-West to the new frontier.

Dr. Cochran's conclusions suggest an important modification of the famous "frontier hypothesis" of Frederick Jackson Turner, with its stress on the changes forced on pioneers by their new environments. Actually, as we are enabled to see from the evidence of their words and deeds, the Colorado pioneers were more interested in re-creating the patterns they brought with them than they were in innovation and were, moreover, more successful in this undertaking than the Turner hypothesis ever allowed for.

Miners, Merchants, and Missionaries is, then, a well-crafted, plausible narrative of the emergence and tumults of a "new" society in a "new" land. It is also an illuminating interpretation of an important social process set against a background broad enough so that the horizon never closes in. The problem of perspective comes as near to a satisfactory solution here as one might reasonably wish for.

The result is first-rate regional history in its own right, but something much more than that. One way or another, Dr. Cochran has managed to pose most of the typical issues that have confronted organized religion on any of its "frontiers," and her insights here are worth pondering in any long reflection on the perennial problem of the interactions of church and society in any epoch of rapid social change.

Albert C. Outler
Professor of Theology, Emeritus
Perkins School of Theology
Southern Methodist University
Dallas, Texas

PREFACE

"What do we want with this vast worthless area, this region of savages and wild beasts, of deserts, shifting sands and whirlwinds of dust, of cactus and prairie dogs?"[1] asked Daniel Webster in an 1838 debate over United States expansion into the Far West. Some applauded his opposition to westward movement, but others advanced even more substantial arguments for extending American dominion over the far western parts of the North American continent. No argument, however, answered Webster's question so well as events. Discovery of precious metals in California and the Rocky Mountains swept philosophical questions of nation building aside. "This vast worthless area" promised wealth and, beginning in 1849, attracted sufficient numbers of miners and merchants to promote the rudiments of civilization in the wilderness. Artisans, laborers, farmers, ranchers, and their families soon followed.

These people brought the civilization they had known with them into the wilderness. To them, civilization meant a relatively high level of cultural and technological development, characterized by social organisms based on productive and profitable labor, orderly republican government, regular religious observance, common school education, and easily accessible channels of trade and communication. They felt sure that the beliefs and practices of Christianity formed the base of civilization. They were convinced that stability of society depended upon the common acceptance of Christian moral principles. Beyond this, and equally necessary, was common assent to some sort of religious view of God, the world, and human life. To an extent virtually unrealizable by twentieth-century secularists, nineteenth-century Americans saw the establishment of church and society as necessarily linked in the expansion of civilization.[2]

The Colorado pioneers were no exception. The gold rush to Colorado furnishes an excellent example of social and religious growth during pioneer expansion into the nearly uninhabited regions of the American continent. Within a twelve-year period, the pioneers established and consolidated a complete society, thus creating something like a civilization in what had been wilderness. In 1858, the first large-scale migration of white Americans began. By 1870, when the railroad linked the area to the rest of America, their first main task had been accomplished. In this period, the missionaries and churches did much to shape the emerging society. The roles of clergy and churches (between 1858 and 1870, the terminal points as just indicated) in the creation of civilization in the wilderness that came to be Colorado, are the subjects of this study.

Although there has been no comprehensive survey or interpretation of the roles of churches in Colorado's pioneer society, primary sources for this subject are abundant. The contemporary documents present a kaleidoscopic view, with more factual data than any single or coherent overview. Interpretation requires ordering of these data and assessment of their significance for the social and institutional development of the territory. Some interesting questions arise from consideration of the primary sources. Though their information is neither sufficiently precise nor statistically abundant enough to answer the questions a sociologist might want to ask, the testimony of those who were there furnishes many of the elements from which a partial set of answers may be constructed. The conclusions drawn from these data and the answers advanced suggest different ways in which hypotheses may be framed and tested. It was in search for plausible hypotheses that I asked such questions as these: What kinds of people civilized the wilderness? What sort of society did they create? Did the people and their institutions change in the process? What roles did clergy and churches play? Corollary to these central queries is the question of how Colorado church people adapted to the frontier environment. Did they bring the practices and beliefs of contemporary American Christianity with them? Did they create new policies to deal with the new situation? How did they interact with church people of other denominations? How did the churches interact with society?

To discover the nature of Colorado frontier society and the churches' relationship to it, I have attempted to explore the pioneers' concept of civilization, their fundamental beliefs and practices in matters religious, and their actions in the creation of ordered society. Throughout the story, one finds overlappings and role-exchanges in the functions of church and civic leadership. Sometimes civic leaders and churches cooperated in joint ventures; sometimes they pursued common goals along parallel courses; sometimes they worked for different goals. The early chapters chronicling the civilizers' attempts to impose order point up the areas of cooperation and common goals. The later chapters contain an assessment of the impact on frontier society of practices current in American Christianity, especially revivalism, reformism, anti-Catholicism, education, and problems of doctrine and belief. A combination of narrative and analysis seems the most appropriate way to present these findings, for the society of Colorado unfolded progressively over the period under study. What is offered, therefore, is a congeries of the patterns of social growth in a territory of a nation that self-consciously proclaimed itself--or aspired to be--Christian.

Appended to the text are two essays on sources: one dealing with the works on Colorado's religious history and the other dealing with books devoted to analyses of patterns in American Christian development. These appendixes are intended to guide the reader in further search and interpretation. They also lay out some of the more useful hypotheses developed by American church historians. Naturally, my own work makes considerable use of these ideas. However, my findings led me to question some of the key concepts and to suggest some modifications. For example, scholars of the American Far West after Frederick Jackson Turner[3] have usually assumed that frontier environments forced pioneers to change their social organizations and to create unique social institutions. For decades many western historians have worked on the assumption that what is uniquely American was forged in the crucible of the frontier wilderness. My reading of the primary data about Colorado churches leads me to question this assumption, as far as religion in the Rocky Mountain West is concerned. In this instance, the pioneers set out to transplant the eastern and midwestern society that they admired, changing as little of it as possible. Though they made inevitable changes in technology (mining, farming, etc.), they did not alter their social institutions by any conscious intention or principle. The pioneers felt that they had a mission to recreate American civilization as they had known it "back East" to impose a familiar order on chaos. Innovative social organization would have been contrary to their purposes. More practically, they saw no reason to change institutions which already had worked well elsewhere.

The churches played a large role in this conservative

tendency. The first civic institutions to be transplanted in the wilderness were the churches. For some time, churches were the major institutions of social order. They served a vital function as the most effective bearers of moral order in the situation. Later, with the establishment of regular territorial government, the churches relinquished their near-monopoly but remained an important element in the creation and sustenance of orderly communities.

And yet, despite its original conservative intentions and policy, life in the pioneer West did come to have a different quality than life "back East." This resulted less from innovative social organization than from an intensification of certain traits of the American character. For example, Westerners have tended to be more optimistic and egalitarian than their cousins in the East and Midwest. The selectivity of migratory patterns and early economic egalitarianism help to account for this intensification. The pioneers did not hope to create a new kind of society; they transported what seemed the most important social elements for imposing order on a "howling wilderness." In conserving, the pioneers stressed some characteristics more than others. But the shifts in emphasis occurred less in the life of the pioneer churches than in other areas of life. From the first, clergy and laity worked together to create orderly and productive communities. Furthermore, the churches carried centuries-old traditions to this area. As communities of concern, they helped alleviate the loneliness and alienation which vexed frontiersmen but which are common, in varying measure, in all social settings. The preaching of the Word and the administration of the sacraments always remained the primary functions of the churches, but around this central core other roles developed. Most important, the churches served as the cohesive center of orderly life, the social center of pioneer society, and the bearer of moral order. The churches furnished continuity in a fluctuating social scene. Thus, the churches became the bulwark of conservative creation in this corner of the American wilderness.

NOTES

1. Quoted in Peter Winne, "Historical Gleanings," The Trail, Vol. VIII (June, 1915), p. 9.

2. See Robert T. Handy, A Christian America (New York: Oxford University Press, 1971).

3. For the basic formulation of Turner's hypothesis see the collected essays in Frederick Jackson Turner, The Frontier in American History (New York: Henry Holt, 1928).

For critical assessment of Turner's theories see Ray Allen Billington, America's Frontier Heritage (New York: Holt, Rinehart and Winston, 1966); George R. Taylor (ed.), The Turner Thesis (Boston: D. C. Heath, 1956); Billington, Frederick Jackson Turner (New York: Oxford University Press, 1973).

CHAPTER 1

THE COLORADO GOLD RUSH, 1858-1861

Gold found on the remote, western edge of the Kansas Territory brought thousands of white men to the Rocky Mountains between 1858 and 1861.[1] Like the migrants to the California coast a decade earlier, most came for gold. Some came to make new homes and to extend the culture they had inherited. Many hoped to build economic empires and personal fortunes; some wanted to help fulfill America's Manifest Destiny; some longed to tame the wilderness by cultivating the land; still others hoped to establish a Christian American civilization.[2] Less exalted motives spurred most, however. The Panic of 1857 had swept away entrepreneurs' paper fortunes and had left many workers jobless and bored. Financial depression acted as a catalyst in westward movement. The gold rush frontier, as had all other frontiers, attracted not only opportunists but also drifters and social misfits who did not live easily in "older and better regulated communities" and who "made the most of the total absence of all legal and social restrictions."[3]

Motives for migration were strong and needed to be, for the gold rushers had to travel more than six hundred miles from the line of stable settlement (on the Missouri River) to the Rocky Mountains that dominate Colorado's landscape. Those coming from the East (as most of them did) had to cross the Great American Desert, flat, arid, windy, treeless grasslands, through which sluggish rivers flow. The Great Plains,[4] as they are properly called now, were dotted with oases of cottonwood trees, regarded by pioneers as generally worthless. Before stage coaches and railroads traversed the plains, winter travel was practically impossible. Snow covers the grasses on which pack animals feed, and storms reach blizzard force minutes after they begin. Summer travel was easier but still dangerous for the inexperienced since water, food, and fuel were scarce. The eastern third of Colorado consists of plains, and the western two-thirds of mountains.

Gold hunters camped on the plains of Colorado and established trading centers, the most important of which was Denver. West of Denver are the foothills of the Rockies. When men climbed upward in search of gold, they thankfully left the heat and dust of the plains behind and breathed cool, thin air among the aspens and evergreens. Huge boulders often blocked their ways as they climbed beside streams of cold, usually clear, water. Miners built the first Colorado boom towns perched on the sides of gulches cut by such streams.

Some restless men did not stop in the environs of Denver but pushed further west toward the crest of the Continental Divide itself. The high passes and peaks are above the timberline and almost bare of vegetation, but scattered in the central region are a series of grassy parks, the largest of which early cartographers called North, Middle, and South Parks. Lush grasses watered by small streams and lakes flourish in these parks. They furnished camp sites for prospectors and miners. The few who moved beyond the parks and crossed the Divide in the late 1850's found the western slope similar to the eastern, though more rugged and rocky. Within the western range, explorers discovered larger, drier parks, the largest of which they called San Luis.

Seasonal changes in the mountains produce spectacular beauty. In summer, aspen and evergreen cover the forested part of the range. Light filters through the trees and speckles the gulches. On the peaks, vistas broaden; the sky seems to loom larger. In autumn, the days shorten; trees turn into a sea of red, gold, green, copper, and silver leaves. Snows begin early and move to the plains in blizzard force. The peaks hide the sun except at midday in the valleys and gulches. When sunlight brightens the snowscape, the air is crisp and the colors dazzling. When spring comes, the snowbanks thaw; water pours from the peaks through gulches and canyons. Creeks, dry for the rest of the year, briefly become rivers. Leaves, grasses, and flowers spring up. The cycle of the seasons begins again.

This harsh land with its grace notes of beauty became part of the United States in two diplomatic transactions. America's President Thomas Jefferson had bought the Mississippi River Valley from France's Napoleon in 1803. The Louisiana Purchase included Colorado's eastern plains and much of the eastern slope of the Rockies. Forty-three years later, Americans went to war with Mexico--the primary issue was the United States' annexation of Texas. But expansionists wanted to extend the United States to the Pacific Ocean. The fighting lasted two years and ended when President James K. Polk announced the Treaty of Guadalupe Hidalgo on July 4, 1848. Under the peace provisions, the United States annexed 529,000 square miles of territory, which included not only Texas but also present-day California, Utah, and Nevada and parts of Colorado, New Mexico, Arizona, Oklahoma, Kansas, and Wyoming. John Charles Fremont, explorer, soldier, and adventurer, publicized California; Senator Thomas Hart Benton gave his sanction to Fremont's exploits; many Americans applauded acquisition of land on the Pacific Coast. But few, except government surveyors, had seen the Pike's Peak region.[5] When prospectors found gold in California in 1849, miners and entrepreneurs crossed the plains, but most avoided routes through the high passes near the Continental Divide. Thus, before the 1858-61 gold rush, "Anglo" settlers showed little interest in future Colorado.

But Indians, Mexicans, and "mountain men" already lived there. A small number of Cheyennes and Arapahoes roamed the high plains in search of buffalo. Bands of Utes hunted in central mountain parks. The various tribes competed for the existing food supply, colliding occasionally in battle. Would-be Mexican colonists feared Indian attacks and refused to settle in land grants on the Rio Grande and Arkansas rivers until the early 1850's when a handful of families moved into the San Luis Park. They built villages, raised sheep, and farmed the land watered by the Upper Rio Grande River. Their settlements were so small that they proved no threat to the Indians.

A few white fur traders, called "mountain men," led solitary lives in the hills, where they bartered with the Indians for beaver pelts and buffalo robes. Several lived with Indian women at fortified trading posts, which became way stations for explorers and travelers. Some of them experimented with farming and prospecting for precious metals. They disliked conventional social organization and avoided civilization. Still they maintained useful and mutually rewarding relations with the Indians. Mexican settlers and white "mountain men" rarely met. Since the fur trade had tapered off at least a decade before the gold rush, only a few "mountain men" remained in the gold regions in 1858.

Wandering prospectors, akin to the fur traders in social attitudes, inadvertently began the "civilizing" of the

Pike's Peak region by finding gold. William Green Russell, a veteran prospector in California and Georgia, uncovered a pocket of gold at the mouth of Dry Creek in July, 1858. In February, Russell had left Georgia for the Rockies, convinced that he could build a mineral empire there. With his two brothers and a number of Cherokee Indians, he explored the tributaries of the Platte River.[6] An adventurer returning from a trading venture in Utah heard of the discovery and eagerly carried the news to Kansas. His story grew with each retelling. Newsmen seized on rumors and printed them as facts. Many of the stories demonstrated what Albert D. Richardson spoke of as the "well-known proclivity of lumps to increase in size the further they roll."[7] For example, a few days after Russell's small discovery, a Leavenworth, Kansas, journalist reported that five hundred Pike's Peak miners were recovering gold worth $6,000 each day. A rival newsman wrote that miners were finding nuggets worth as much as $250 and pearls the size of peas.[8] In fact, Russell and about a dozen miners found approximately $300 worth of "flour gold," exhausted the "lode," and set out to explore other branches of the river for new diggings.[9]

Newspapers in towns along the main routes to the gold fields continued to create "gold fever." When in August, 1858, men appeared in eastern Kansas with samples of gold dust from Russell's diggings a Kansas City paper reported the story under this headline:

> THE NEW ELDORADO!!
> GOLD IN THE KANSAS TERRITORY!!
> THE PIKE'S MINES!
> FIRST ARRIVAL OF GOLD DUST AT KANSAS CITY!!![10]

Encouraged by tangible evidence, journalists printed increasingly optimistic stories. Throughout autumn, headlines appeard daily proclaiming:

> GOLD--PIKE'S PEAK
>
> PIKE'S PEAK--GOLD EXCITEMENT IN THE CITY--A NEW CALIFORNIA
>
> GOLD! GOLD! GOLD!
>
> GOLD WITHIN OUR REACH
>
> THE GOLD FEVER
>
> HO! FOR PIKE'S PEAK

GOLD FEVER INCREASES

As journalists, eager for sensational news, blazed headlines of each new discovery, no matter how meager, merchants began advertising mining equipment of all kinds. Handbooks, broadsides, and newspaper articles vaunted the rich prospects and lured men to try their luck supplied with goods bought in towns where the publicists lived.[12] Henry Villard, who tried to write a reliable guidebook, warned prospective miners against believing what they read in the newspapers.[13] He recalled:

> It was difficult to glean a few grains of fact from the piles of chaff of exaggeration and outright fiction that I found everywhere. All of the river points, from Kansas City to Omaha, which had suffered more than other parts of the country from the subsidence of the speculative fever of 1855-57, saw a chance for a rapid revival in the Pike's Peak excitement, and all were working with might and main to feed it, through their local papers and by every other means.[14]

While the Kansas papers were reporting gold discoveries, they also claimed that large numbers of miners were heading out to the gold fields. One journalist (among many) said that "trains after trains continue to throng the road... bound for the new El Dorado."[15] The truth of the matter is, however, that only a few groups did journey to the gold fields in 1858.

Along with the miners were entrepreneurs who hoped to make fortunes in real estate as well as in mining. In 1858, more men laid out towns on paper than discovered gold mines. Promoters established at least ten towns: Montana City, Auraria, Boulder City, Colona, Arapahoe City, Golden Gate, Fountain City, El Paso, and St. Charles (later Denver City). These men were, indeed, practitioners of what Henry Villard spoke of as "the popular Anglo-American art of town-making."[16] The founding of Denver, future capital of Colorado, best illustrates the town-builders' craft. In summer, 1858, forty-five young men, itching for some excitement, left Lawrence for the gold fields. They dug at the base of Pike's Peak and in New Mexico; failing to find gold, they trekked to Cherry Creek, where they panned some gold in September. Eager to secure their claims, they laid out Montana City, which they abandoned when another site looked more promising. Thus, they moved and established

St. Charles on Cherry Creek. Other prospectors arrived, settled in, and built a rival town, Auraria, across the creek.[17] The promoters envisioned both towns as business ventures; they drew up charters, platted the land, elected officers, and applied to the Kansas territorial legislature for legal sanctions.

Denver's founder, William Larimer, an experienced town-builder, waited until gold samples arrived in Leavenworth. Once he had visible proof of the discoveries, he gathered a group of thirty-two and left, via the Santa Fe Trail. Richard Whitsitt, a young but eager land trader, and George Fisher a retired Methodist preacher, agreed to accompany Larimer. In a small settlement on the Arkansas River (probably Fountain City), they met officials of Arapahoe County, recently appointed by James Denver, Kansas territorial governor. The county officials had decided to spend the winter on the river but changed their minds when they met Larimer's party bound for Cherry Creek. In November, 1858, they arrived in St. Charles, took possession of the site, and renamed it Denver City. Possession proved nine points of the law in a minor controversy between the "owners" of St. Charles and Denver City. The Larimer group took charge, selected officers and directors, and organized the Denver Town Company.[18] The town builder's activities proved significant because the miners and entrepreneurs assembled in these towns served as the vanguard for the great rush of 1859 and as sources of information for promotors along the Missouri River and the trails further west. Even more significantly, these towns, at first centers of rowdiness, soon became focal points in the settlers' attempts to create an orderly society.

When town-builders and miners settled in for the winter, promoters made much of their reports. Enterprising men compiled guidebooks for hopeful miners. D. C. Oakes, a veteran of the California gold rush, made a quick survey of the region and penned a cursory but widely-read account of its resources. William N. Byers, a surveyor, wrote a popular guide even though he had never been to the area.[19] Newsmen in Kansas, Nebraska, Illinois, Missouri, and Iowa reported thousands preparing for the journey. The Omaha *Times* told of the departure of two large caravans even before the snow melted. Eastern newsmen expressed skepticism. Others predicted (and thereby encouraged) heavy emigration. Horace Greeley expected at least fifty thousand men to start for the mines.[20] John B. Miege, a Roman Catholic bishop living in Leavenworth, anticipated the departure of 100,000 young men and accused the press of leading them astray.[21] In the spring of 1859, the gold rush began in earnest. Contemporary observers estimated that about 100,000 people started the trip to Pike's Peak and that nearly half of them reached their destination.[22] Adventurers left in companies, in pairs, or alone with high hopes and little else. In March they came to the border towns in steamboats and set off across the plains in ox wagons, in dog carts, on foot, on horseback, and on mules. One man made a wind wagon, a sailboat on wheels. The atmosphere, at the beginning of these adventures, was that of a holiday. One journalist described the prospective miners as "enthusiastic, merry, with light hearts and a thin pair of breeches."[23]

The journey proved arduous along the three main routes to the Pike: the Platte, Smoky Hill, and Sante Fe trails.[24] Few took the Smoky Hill route, which was the shortest overland trail from the Missouri River to Cherry Creek. Following no main river for several hundred miles, the path attracted only the rash and inexperienced, many of whom died along the way. The northern route paralleled the South Platte River, and the Santa Fe Trail lay along the Arkansas River. These streams, although unnavigable, created natural highways. With mule-drawn wagons, travelers could journey from embarkation points along the Missouri to the gold fields in about a month. They found little grass but passable water and adequate fuel for fires. Some marveled at the novelty of using buffalo chips instead of wood for their fires. Dust, high winds, sudden storms, extremes of heat and cold plagued the inexperienced.

To reach the gold fields, adventurers turned from the main river roads at the sites of Pueblo (on the Sante Fe Trail) and Greeley (on the Platte River Trail) to follow lesser streams.[25] Though their spirits rose as they approached the gold fields, travelers found the land more forbidding than they had expected. William H. Goode called Colorado's eastern plains "unfit for cultivation or residence... an arid, sterile desert, producing no sustenance for man, and scarcely any for beast."[26] But the mountains begin to rise a few miles west of Cherry Creek. And the adventurers were headed for the mountains.

In March and April, 1859, when the first miners reached the mountains, however, they discovered no rich lodes. Instead, they encountered disappointed and hungry gold seekers described by Villard as "a promiscuous crowd that spent their days in gloom and distress."[27] Some set out to prospect; others turned back. The latter returned to the border towns "destitute of provisions or means of conveyance, disappointed and utterly disheartened, with broken hopes and blasted fortunes, toil-worn, and heart-weary."[28] They felt duped and angrily called the enterprise a "humbug."

Still the mad rush continued; wagon trains passed one another along the way.[29] In one week, an Iowa reporter counted 584 wagonloads of miners on the way to Pike's Peak.[30] Those who persisted were not disappointed. In May, 1859, miners uncovered three lodes, the richest of which was John R. Gregory's placer deposit, about 30 miles west of Denver. Hundreds swarmed from the new towns to Gregory Gulch and staked claims on every available inch. Almost everyone deserted Denver. As the news spread, even disgruntled men on the way home turned around.

Headlines across the country once more proclaimed:

PIKE'S PEAK--GOLD IN ABUNDANCE

UNPARALLELED RICHES

GOLD! GOLD! GOLD![31]

This time the journalists came closer to the truth than they had the year before. Miners had found significant quantities of gold, which they could dig with rudimentary equipment. Horace Greeley, Albert D. Richardson, and Henry Villard visited the fields in June and composed glowing reports, which eastern papers printed and reprinted. Though the trio warned against migrating without money and mining experience, they touted the area's potential for commerce, agriculture, and manufacturing.[32]

Eager to believe, thousands of hopeful miners and merchants flocked into the new towns and crowded the old gulches. Gold hunters made several new strikes, and entrepreneurs built more towns--Golden City, Colorado City, Mountain City (later Central City), Black Hawk, Breckenridge, Alma, Tarryall, Fairplay, and Nevada City (or Nevadaville). Villard observed the "town-making was with many a perfect mania. Some traveled from point to point for many weeks, searching, like the hunter for game, for town sites."[33]

Newcomers found life in the towns crude and manners

among the miners vigorous and rowdy. Even though the living conditions were primitive and the work grindingly hard, optimism and enthusiasm filled the air. One man recalled, "Everything was astir."[34] In June, 1859, Denver and Auraria consisted of about two hundred log cabins, with dirt floors, sod roofs, and glassless windows.[35] Horace Greeley estimated that a fourth of the buildings were unfinished, a third were uninhabited, and two-thirds were not fit to live in.[36] Scattered tents and covered wagons housed those on their way to the mines. Denver was "unsightly," and visitors lamented that it offered few of the amenities of civilized life.[37] Worse, according to a Vermont correspondent, every "third building was a groggery."[38]

In the early days of the gold rush, speedy creation of an ordered society appeared unlikely. Cut loose from the restraints of mannered life, many lusty young men drank, cursed, whored, and fought. Saloons and gambling houses tempted them constantly. A soberer citizen recalled unscrupulous men "who toiled not, nor did they spin" as they themselves fattened on "the industry of the mining pioneers, whom they beguiled of their hard-earned dust, through the enticements of the gaming table, or the fascination of the music hall."[39] Criminals and social misfits drifted to frontier villages. Libeus Barney noted the abundance of "ravenous human bloodhounds, preying upon the unsophisticated innocence of the trusting and unwary."[40]

Fearful of each other and also of the nearby Indians, most men went about armed.[41] The combination was explosive; shootings and robberies occurred almost daily until alarmed residents created a vigilance committee to aid Arapahoe County's harried sheriff, appointed the year before by the Kansas governor.[42] Rowdy high spirits caused much of the turmoil. Richardson reported:

> When the great gaming saloon was crowded with people, drunken ruffians sometimes fired five or six shots from their revolvers, frightening everybody pell-mell out of the room, but seldom wounding any one.[43]

But the shootings, theft, and almost casual violence constituted a serious problem for settlers and transients alike.

All, however, had great expectations for Denver and the other boom towns. They remembered the mushroom-like growth of California mining towns and trading centers and expected the same in Colorado. And their expectations were not to be disappointed. Indeed, houses, shops, hotels, and restaurants sprang "into being as if by enchantment."[44] Such magic produced fifty frame buildings in Denver each month; young laborers who found no gold eagerly sought work in the burgeoning town.[45] Richardson and Villard marveled as Denver grew into a real town almost as if overnight. Early in 1860, they returned to Denver and found a busy metropolis with streets, brick buildings, and many urban amenities. Richardson recognized only two of the cabins there in June, 1859. Villard counted over five hundred buildings, which included thirty-nine stores, five commission houses, eleven restaurants, twenty-three bars, three billiard saloons, two livery stables, an express office, a newspaper and printing company, two schools, four lumber yards, and two theaters. Many people (Villard guessed two thousand) had settled in Denver, and thousands passed through.[46]

The population of Denver and surrounding towns fluctuated as miners came and went.[47] Many, finding the mines less than advertised, drifted away when rich strikes were made in Nevada and British Columbia in 1859. The transients and settlers came from all sections of the country, according to the United States census takers who toured Colorado towns and camps in June, 1860. Over 2,500 Europeans (but no Africans and few Asians) joined the gold rush. A few Mexicans and a large number of Indians mingled with the white majority. Few, if any, slaveholders brought their chattels with them, but a small number of free blacks came. Almost all were men under thirty.[48]

Among the thousands who clustered around the mines were a small core of settlers--agents of civilization. They, too, were young adults in search of opportunity in the new land. Many came to mine but discovered richer rewards in merchandising, freighting, banking, insurance, real estate, building, and the professions. Though almost all--shop keepers, doctors, lawyers, actors, bankers, waiters, and bartenders--staked claims and carried specimens of blossom rock in their pockets,[49] many of them applied their best efforts to the speedy creation of a settled society in this wilderness. Their confidence knew no bounds. In one instance, Richardson asked a miner if the townsmen had a church. The man replied that they did not, but would by the next Sunday. "Erecting a temple of worship in a week was in thorough accordance with the prevailing spirit," Richardson explained.[50]

Confidence in their ability to transplant American civilization in western soil swelled as more prospective settlers joined the migration. Throughout 1859 and 1860, "traders with extensive stocks of goods, speculators with capital, industrious artisans, and thrifty and steady men with their families" crossed the plains with the gold diggers.[51]

Early in 1860, Denver men and women enjoyed the services of fourteen lawyers, thirteen doctors, seven surveyors and architects, four building contractors, and nine real estate agents. Artisans--cabinetmakers, carpenters, watchmakers, shoemakers, blacksmiths, masons, barbers, tailors, and butchers--all plied their several trades.[52] By June, 1860, over 34,000 lived in Colorado's gold regions. Of these about five thousand settled, at least for a time, in Denver. Almost 90 percent of Colorado's people were native-born, white, young men; over 22,000 of them claimed to be miners. But about 4,500 men engaged in trades and professions; two hundred farmers produced food for local consumption. The ranks of tradesmen and professionals increased substantially after the first of the year. Eighty-nine lawyers, 116 doctors, 4 surveyors and architects, and 24 contractors claimed residence in the gold regions. The number of artisans mushroomed.[53]

Most of the eager miners found little gold. The Pike's mines yielded about three-quarters of a million dollars worth of gold in 1859, far less than California's mother-lode in 1849.[54] So, on average, each miner recovered $15 worth of gold. This is no indication of actual income, since not all mined and not all earned equally. But few, if any, amateur miners got rich. Disappointed, many of the '59ers returned to the States.[55] Some stayed and entered other occupations in the new land. New migrants took the places of those departed. All who came encountered an exciting environment; they saw a new society unfolding before their eyes.

The mercantile development described in preceding paragraphs was supplemented by the establishment of such important social and cultural institutions as newspapers, theaters, schools, fraternal lodges, and, of course, churches. By the end of 1859, Denver had such amenities, even before formal government had been proclaimed. By 1861, the other mining towns did too.

Newspapers came into being quickly. The first in the

territory was William N. Byers' Rocky Mountain News. Byers bought a used press in Omaha and carried it to Denver in an ox cart in April, 1859. The day after his arrival, he issued the first edition of his newspaper on brown wrapping paper. A rival, John Merrick, issued the Cherry Creek Pioneer. Finding themselves in competition, the two editors raced to be first on the street with their paper. Byers won by twenty minutes, winning both the battle and the war, for Merrick left town shortly thereafter. Byers soon faced other competitors though. A former associate, Thomas Gibson, began the Rocky Mountain Herald in 1860. The rivals exchanged almost daily insults in their editorial pages and seemed naturally to take opposing stands on every issue great or small. The mining town papers also entered the field. Soon Central City had the Miner's Register (est. 1862); Golden City residents read the Western Mountaineer (1859); Black Hawk citizens bought the Journal (1862); Mountain City journalists issued the Gold Reporter (1859); and farmers and miners north of Denver read the Boulder Valley News (early 1860's). This was an era of highly personal journalism, in which editors clearly voiced their views and challenged all comers. The journals served not only as a source of news but also as a public arena for controversial issues. The newspapers also took every chance to act as community "boosters." They mirrored not only the events but also the aspirations of their era.[56]

Schools came quickly to Denver. The first in Denver was that founded by Oscar J. Goldrick in the summer of 1859. Goldrick, a flamboyant Irishman, drove into town dressed in broadcloth suit, stove-pipe hat, and yellow kid gloves, addressing his mules in Latin and Greek. Dick Wooten, an early store-keeper, thought him the most imaginative swearer he had ever heard. Goldrick opened an academy and enrolled thirteen children the first day. His school was a success but did not afford him a full living. Indeed, Goldrick also worked as part-time journalist and eventually gave up teaching for editing. Other private school owners included Marietta Ring, Indiana Sopris, and Iris Sopris. Their private academies had limited curricula and lacked physical comfort. But they filled crucial needs until the churches established schools and until the public schools came into operation.[57]

Theater often served as the school of the illiterate. Colorado's pioneer actors set out to entertain but were not insensitive to the educational and hortatory uses of the stage.[58]

The first theatrical companies arrived in 1859. They included Charles Thorne's group from New York and Mademoiselle Haydee's troupe from the Missouri River circuit. Both were eclipsed in 1860-61, by the Jack Langrishe Company. Langrishe and his wife enjoyed life-long popularity in Denver and the mining camps. They are regarded as the founders of theater in Denver and honored as such. Their establishments were described with pride by most residents and always played a prominent part in efforts to boost the city and its image.[59]

Fraternal lodges, most of which were devoted to the improvement of community morals, formed in Denver and the mining camps, in 1859 and 1860. The Masons wielded the most public influence and drew many of the influential men into their brotherhood. However, the Good Templars, the Odd Fellows, the Fenians, and the Turners also found plentiful support in Denver and the mining camps. Often, the first solid buildings in a town were the lodge halls.[60]

The first important lodge in the territory was organized in Denver. The Masons began activities early on. When John M. Chivington, about whom we will hear more later, arrived, he added new zest to their activities. During his residence in Denver, the Masons completed their spacious hall and engaged in temperance work. Chivington served as a Grand Master and other prominent men in the city succeeded him.[61]

The Central City Masonic organization began informally in 1858. Formal organization took place the following summer. They soon built their first "temple" from stripped logs. Other fraternal groups also formed. In 1860, Nevada City men gathered into the Order of the Sons of Malta, a secret, semi-military society. At about the same time, the Odd Fellows began meeting in the Central mining region. The Good Templars promoted temperance in Central City and in the gulches. Next to the Masons, the Good Templars attracted the most members of all the lodges.[62]

Lodges not only performed community services and brought about reform but also served as the center of mining-camp social life. Lodge members held balls and entertainments regularly, and they insisted on a reasonable standard of behavior. Thus, the balls proved very popular with the civilizers. Even those formerly opposed to dancing found the lodge parties decorous enough either to attend or to condone.[63] In towns where saloons served as the main social gathering places, such lodge affairs were welcome alternatives.

Early social organization filled many needs for the settlers and civilizers. But "an irrepressible conflict between the industrious sterling citizens and the desperadoes"[64] continued. Laws and a political order were, of course, essential to the orderly operation of the gold regions. However, establishing regular governmental authority proved difficult. By the Treaty of Laramie concluded in 1851, the Arapahoes and Cheyennes had legal claim to the gold regions and, in fact, the whole eastern slope between the South Platte and Arkansas Rivers. White settlers, however, ignored the Indians' right to the land and acted on the principle of squatters' rights on the theory that since the Indians did not farm the land, they had no right to it. Town companies blithely applied to the Kansas legislature for charters and received them.[65] Even though such documents were not technically valid, they served as the functional authorization for early governing bodies.

Of more lasting importance were the early mining laws designed to regulate mining claims and water rights. Miners copied laws from the mining districts of California and modified them slightly to meet the needs of an arid region.[66]

The mining towns and camps became "instant cities" and overcrowded ones at that. Squeezed together around the mines, greedy for riches, and naturally suspicious of one another, the gold diggers realized the pressing need for self-imposed and self-enforced laws. In each district opened in 1859 and 1860, the miners held mass meetings, where they agreed on rules for the staking, registering, and working of their claims. They also adopted standards for community behavior, sometimes banning gaming houses, prostitutes, and saloons from the district. They created miners' courts and elected judges for them. If violators did not accept the judgments, miners assembled in mass and acted as a jury. Claim jumping, working a plot belonging to another, was the most frequent crime. Mining law required that an owner work a registered claim at regular intervals to retain title. Miners' courts often settled disputes among men who had claimed the same plot, at one time or another, worked it unsuccessfully, and abandoned it. If later someone found gold or silver on or near the claim, the previous holders would rush to re-establish ownership. In settling such cases, the miners' courts worked well, in spite of rowdiness and disorder.

In commercial centers, residents created people's courts. In cases of murder and theft, they acted as judge, jury, and executioner. They banished most offenders but hanged a few, some too hastily. Their over-zealous prosecution of felons stemmed from what Charles Shinn called the pioneers' "passion for regulation."[67]

Kansas officials could not satisfy the '59ers desire for regulation. First, the settled portions of the territory were so far away from the gold region that effective government was impossible, Second, the battles over slavery in eastern Kansas made peaceful governing impossible even in the territorial capital.[68] Third, Americans moving west wanted local autonomy under federal sanction. Richardson exaggerated only a little when he boasted:

> Congregate a hundred Americans anywhere beyond the settlements, and they immediately lay out a city, frame a state constitution and apply for admission into the Union, while twenty-five of them become candidates for the United States Senate.[69]

In the spring of 1859, miners voted to apply for territorial status. During that summer, a convention drafted a petition to Congress and wrote a preliminary constitution. Congress, unwilling to aggravate the controversy over the extension of slavery into the territories denied the request. Undaunted, the frontiersmen took unilateral action and created the Territory of Jefferson.

On October 24, 1859, residents elected R. W. Steele as governor, Lucien W. Bliss as secretary, C. R. Bissell as auditor, and G. W. Cook as treasurer. They elected a legislature, which convened in Denver on November 7. The legislators passed necessary laws and ordinances modeled on those of other territories and states. They levied modest taxes. Meanwhile, they paid their bills with warrants, collectable when taxes should be collected. But many in the camps refused to pay taxes, and the government almost failed. This forced concerned citizens to rely on a committee of public safety. Vigilante justice did not suit most.

In July and August, 1859, yet another group met in Mountain City and Golden to badger Congress for admission to the Union as a state. They failed to make an impression on Washington politicians, and they decided to support a provisional government as better than none. Meanwhile they continued to press Congress for action.

Two main problems delayed Congress: the slavery controversy and Indian-white relations. Though Colorado lay outside the area likely to support a slave economy, southern legislators consistently blocked moves to admit Kansas as a free state. They objected to formation of the Colorado Territory, because it would be another brick in the wall of free states and territories. Civil conflict, which had been building for decades, seemed inevitable when Abraham Lincoln won the presidential election in November, 1860, and seven states led by South Carolina subsequently seceded from the Union.

Uneasy peace followed for several months. During these tense days, Congress took up several measures heretofore opposed by southern Congressmen. Among other things, they voted to admit Kansas as a free state late in January, 1861; shortly thereafter they agreed to allow the creation of the Colorado Territory as soon as the Indians consented to abandon claim to the gold regions. A few days later, federal officials met with Indian chiefs and extracted an agreement that the Indians not only would move to an area between the Arkansas River and Sand Creek but also would relinquish claims to the gold regions, in exchange for cash and food. Indians and whites misunderstood one another. The whites understood that the Indians had abandoned hunting rights as well as residence rights. The Indians thought they had agreed to live between the two waterways but to continue hunting wherever they wished. Though this inconclusive agreement caused friction later, it satisfied Congressmen and lame-duck President James Buchanan, who signed the act creating the Colorado Territory.

Buchanan deferred to the president-elect in appointment of territorial officials. Shortly after his March 4 inauguration, Lincoln appointed William Gilpin as governor, Charles Armour, Newton Pettis, and Benjamin Hall as judges, Lewis Weld as secretary, and Copeland Townsend as federal marshal. Lincoln instructed Gilpin to leave as soon as possible and to do whatever seemed necessary to secure Colorado for the Union. Gilpin spent some weeks arranging his affairs and took a stagecoach to Denver in mid-May. Gilpin reached Denver on May 17, 1861, and immediately began establishing a territorial government which would be loyal to the Union. His task, as we shall see, proved relatively easy, since so many Coloradans welcomed the establishment of a federally sanctioned political order.

Once law came to the territory, order could be and was enforced. The civilizers, armed with social institutions and a functioning government, set out to consolidate their gains. However, they could not have come so far so quickly had it not been for the missionaries and pioneer churches.

NOTES

1. Colorado Territory came into legal existence in 1861. Until that time, Colorado was technically a part of the Kansas Territory. However, the gold rush population established _ad hoc_ governing units separate from and independent of Kansas.

2. For illuminating discussions of the ideas of Manifest Destiny, wilderness, and Christian American civilization see, for instance, Frederick Merk, _Manifest Destiny and Mission in American History_ (New York: Vintage Books, 1963); Roderick Nash, _Wilderness and the American Mind_ (New Haven: Yale University Press, 1967); Handy, _A Christian America_.

3. Henry Villard, _The Past and Present of the Pike's Peak Gold Regions_ (Princeton: Princeton University Press, 1932, first publ., 1860), p. 121.

4. For a thorough description and analysis of the plains region see Walter P. Webb, _The Great Plains_ (New York: Grosset & Dunlap, 1931).

5. The gold regions are not near Pike's Peak but about 100 miles north of it. However, gold rushers and eastern observers called the gold rush region near Denver the Pike's Peak region after the familiar landmark. This contemporary usage will be employed here.

6. E. D. Russell Spencer, _Green Russell and Gold_ (Austin: University of Texas Press, 1936).

7. Albert D. Richardson, _Beyond the Mississippi_ (Hartford: American Publishing Co., 1867), p. 136.

8. (Leavenworth) _Kansas Weekly Herald_, July 24, 1858; (Leavenworth) _Times_, Aug. 21, 1858, in LeRoy R. Hafen (ed.), _Colorado Gold Rush: Contemporary_

Letters and Reports (Glendale, Calif.: Arthur H. Clark Co., 1941), pp. 25, 27-28.

9. William Greever, The Bonanza West (Norman: University of Oklahoma Press, 1963), pp. 157-58.

10. (Kansas City) Journal of Commerce, Aug. 26, 1858 in Hafen, Colorado Gold Rush, pp. 30-32.

11. (Brownsville) Nebraska Advertiser, Sept. 9, 1858; (Leavenworth) Times, Sept. 11, 1858; (Leavenworth) Kansas Weekly Herald, Sept. 11, 1858; (Omaha) Times, Sept. 16, 1858; Nebraska Advertiser, Sept. 23, 1858; (Kansas City) Journal of Commerce, Sept. 24, 1858; (Kansas City) Metropolitan, Sept. 29, 1858, in Hafen, Colorado Gold Rush, pp. 46-47, 49-50, 55, 63-64, 67-68. Hafen writes that these same stories appeared in many river town journals.

12. Several rare handbooks are reprinted or summarized by LeRoy R. Hafen in Pike's Peak Gold Rush Guidebooks of 1859 (Glendale: Arthur H. Clark Co., 1941).

13. Villard, Past and Present ..., p. 19.

14. Villard, Memoirs, Vol. I (New York: Houghton, Mifflin Co., 1904), p. 103.

15. (Lawrence) Republican, Nov. 4, 1858, in Hafen, Colorado Gold Rush, pp. 95-96.

16. Villard, Past and Present ... p. 11; William H. Goode asserted that "the great game of the time was town-building." He described it: "A few men associated; laid a claim upon a plat of vacant prairie; had a load of stakes hauled from some grove near or remote; employed a surveyor, and run off streets and lots, with park, public square, college or seminary lots, grounds for railroad depot and other public uses; set the stakes, gave sounding titles to the streets, and still more to the city itself, had the plat lithographed; and forthwith dispatched a competent agent in the direction of sunrise to gull the orientals [i.e., eastern American purchasers] with corner lots." Outposts of Zion (Cincinnati: Poe and Hitchcock, 1864), p. 378.

17. Auraria is not the predecessor of Denver's section called Aurora. Auraria is now an indistinguishable part of downtown Denver.

18. For Larimer's own account see William Larimer, Jr., and William H. H. Larimer, Reminiscences (Lancaster, Pa.: New Era Printing Co., 1918). Until 1860, when Denver City and Auraria merged under the name of Denver, the towns competed with one another. For clarity, I refer to the two as Denver, even though the name is not strictly apt until the date of the merger.

19. Oakes' guide, written in collaboration with prospector Luke Tierney, is printed in Hafen, Pike's Peak Guidebooks, pp. 89-145; Byers' is summarized on pp. 212-24.

20. (Omaha) Times, Feb. 3, 1859; (New York) Tribune, Jan. 29, 1859, in Hafen, Colorado Gold Rush, pp. 256-57, 254-55.

21. John B. Miege, "Letters," Mid-America, Vol. XVIII (Oct., 1936), p. 267.

22. Statistics in gold rush society pose several problems. First, miners came and went so much that even reliable population figures stayed reliable only for a while. Second, many observers simply guessed; the accuracy of these estimates varies according to the acuteness of the observers' perceptions. Third, as we have already seen, newspapers and entrepreneurs sometimes exaggerated the numbers of men en route to the gold fields and later the numbers of disgruntled, returning adventurers. The most reliable source for gold rush population figures is the 1860 United States census, which is analyzed on pp. 10-11. The estimate that 100,000 men started for the gold fields in 1859 and that half reached the region appears in many contemporary sources, including Villard, Past and Present ..., p. 116 and Goode pp. 402-403.

23. (St. Louis) Missouri Republican, March 27, 1859, in Hafen, Colorado Gold Rush, pp. 285-87.

24. See map of the overland routes in LeRoy R. Hafen (ed.),

Overland Routes to the Gold Fields, 1859, from Contemporary Diaries (Glendale: Arthur H. Clark Co., 1942), p. 323.

25. For travel accounts see Miege, pp. 267-69; Goode, pp. 401-19; Hafen (ed.), Overland Routes to the Gold Fields.

26. Goode, p. 416.

27. Villard, Past and Present ..., p. 27.

28. (St. Louis) Missouri Republican, May 11, 1859, in Hafen, Colorado Gold Rush, pp. 310-11.

29. Goode, pp. 401-404; Hafen, Colorado Gold Rush, pp. 305-29.

30. (Council Bluffs) Bugle, May 18, 1859, in Hafen, Colorado Gold Rush, p. 312.

31. Hafen, Colorado Gold Rush, pp. 326, 329.

32. Rocky Mountain News, June 11, 1859. For a more readily accessible copy see Hafen, Colorado Gold Rush, pp. 376-82, and T. M. Marshall, Early Records of Gilpin County (Boulder: University of Colorado Press, 1920), pp. 4-10.

33. Villard, Past and Present ..., p. 139.

34. Henry L. Pitzer, Three Frontiers (Muscatine, Iowa: Prairie Press, 1938), p. 96.

35. Villard, Past and Present ..., p. 130.

36. Horace Greeley, An Overland Journey (Ann Arbor: University Microfilms, 1966, orig. ed., 1860), pp. 139-48, 157-65; Autobiography (New York: E. B. Treat, 1872), p. 365.

37. Francis C. Young, Echoes from Arcadia (Denver: Pub. privately, 1903), p. 3; Richardson, pp. 177-292; Villard, Past and Present ..., pp. 121-22.

38. Libeus Barney, Early Day Letters from Auraria, 1859-1860 (Denver: Pub. privately, 1907), p. 28.

39. Young, pp. 3-4.

40. Barney, pp. 36-37.

41. Villard, Past and Present ..., p. 121.

42. Rocky Mountain News, 1859-1860, passim; Richardson, p. 305.

43. Richardson, p. 186

44. Barney, p. 36.

45. Miege, p. 270.

46. Richardson, p. 279; Villard, Past and Present ..., pp. 131-32.

47. Greeley, p. 139. Greeley guessed that about one-third of the '59ers were from California. There is no way to verify his estimate; but it is unlikely that the proportion was so high. Silver in the Comstock Lode in Nevada almost certainly drew more Californians than Pike's Peak, which was quite hard to reach from California. British Columbian mines also drew many from that state. 1860 census figures show few emigrants native to California, but this is scarcely conclusive, since all of the '49ers had been born elsewhere.

48. U. S. Department of Interior, Bureau of the Census, Eighth Census of the United States, 1860, pp. 546-49. Hereafter cited as United States Census, 1860.

49. Bayard Taylor, Colorado: A Summer Trip (New York: G. P. Putnam & Son, 1867), p. 59.

50. Richardson, pp. 197-98.

51. Villard, Past and Present ..., pp. 122, 131.

52. Ibid., pp. 130-31.

53. United States Census, 1860, pp. 546-49.

54. Villard, Past and Present ..., p. 92; Greever, p. 54.

55. Greever, pp. 161, 167.

56. William N. Byers, "The Newspaper Press of Colorado," ms., Bancroft Library, 1884.

57. Nolie Mumey (ed.), O. J. Goldrick and His Denver (Denver: Sage Books, 1959).

58. See pp. 140-42.

59. Alice C. Cochran, "Jack Langrishe and the Theater of the Rocky Mountain Mining Frontier," M. A. Thesis, S. M. U., 1968; "Jack Langrishe and the Theater of the Mining Frontier," Colorado Magazine, Vol. XLVI (Fall, 1969), pp. 324-37; "Jack Langrishe's Mining Town Theaters," Montana, the Magazine of Western History, Vol. XX (April, 1970), pp. 58-69.

60. Lynn Perrigo, "A Social History of Central City, Colorado, 1859-1900," unpubl. Ph.D. dissertation, Univ. of Colorado, 1936, pp. 237-48.

61. Reginald Craig, The Fighting Parson (Los Angeles: Westernlore Press, 1959), pp. 52, 237.

62. Perrigo, pp. 237-48.

63. Julia Lambert, "Plain Tales of the Plains," The Trail, Vol. VIII (March, 1916), p. 9.

64. Richardson, p. 292.

65. Calvin W. Gower, "Kansas Territory and the Pike's Peak Gold Rush: Governing the Gold Region," Kansas Historical Quarterly, Vol. XXXII (Autumn, 1966), pp. 289-313.

66. Charles G. Shinn, Mining Camps, A Study in American Frontier Government (New York: Alfred A. Knopf, 1948; orig. pub. 1885).

67. Ibid., p. v.

68. Gower, "Kansas Territory and the Pike's Peak Gold Rush...."

69. Richardson, p. 177.

CHAPTER 2

MISSIONARIES IN BONANZA LAND: THE CHURCHES RESPOND TO THE GOLD RUSH

Part I

Far from home with its normal social restraints, many of the pioneers felt a need for the speedy establishment of a sound moral order. Preachers and priests were the most important bearers of the morality and a sense of group identity. In the antebellum gold rush, people in search of orderly life flocked to the infant churches, the first and most firmly grounded social institutions. The pioneer preachers, who hoped to Christianize and civilize the frontiersmen, created small centers of order and identity in an environment plagued by considerable disorder. They brought the gospel and historic traditions to a raw frontier. In this mission, the preachers formed church organizations identical (or as nearly identical as possible) to those in New England, the Middle Atlantic region, the South, or the Midwest. As we will see, they made little effort to adapt their institutions to the new land.

The major Christian denominations dominated the missionary scene in frontier Colorado. Small groups of recent origin which displayed some sectarian characteristics did not flourish during the pioneer period.[1] Frontiersmen who looked to the churches for stability and group identity, approved the fact that their preachers brought age-old tradition without alteration. The pioneers chose to join those churches which had strong public support back East. Roman Catholic and Methodist missions gathered the most adherents because their organizations were geared to ready expansion. Other major denominations--Episcopal, Presbyterian, Congregational, and Baptist--established themselves solidly in Colorado though with fewer members.

Smaller groups, many of recent origin and with some sectarian characteristics--Quaker, Unitarian, Universalist, Seventh Day Adventist, United Brethren, and Mormon--did not gain favor among Colorado gold hunters. Since the frontiersmen looked to the churches for stability and continuity, they found innovation unhelpful. In frontier days, no splinter groups broke away from the large popular denominations. The settlers clung to workable, accepted forms in their attempt to cope with the social dislocation involved in their westward trek.

Eager lay preachers and adventurous free-lance ministers preceded the denominational agents and prepared the ground for them. George Fisher, a Methodist local preacher,[2] arrived in the gold fields along with Denver's founder, William Larimer, in the autumn of 1858. Fisher, a carpenter, wheelwright, and would-be gold miner, held preaching services for miners and town-builders alike. He preached his first sermon in the gold fields in a double log cabin on Cherry Creek. "There were no church bells to ring, no finely draped ladies, no choir, no pews," Will Larimer reported. Instead a small group of travel-weary men, sitting on buffalo robes, sang hymns, prayed, and listened to Fisher's exhortation. They attended as closely as possible and tried to ignore a dice game at the other end of the cabin.[3] Fisher preached almost every Sunday though he searched for gold during the week. He found a handful of loyal Methodists among the miners and entrepreneurs who attended classes and mid-week prayer meetings in Denver throughout the winter of 1858-59. When the 1859 mining season began, Fisher took to the hills with the rest of the miners. After a fruitless summer's digging, he gave up mining and returned to preaching.[4]

In Spring, 1859, Lewis Hamilton, a "New School" Presbyterian minister, journeyed to the gold fields hoping to recuperate from an illness by enjoying a vacation in the mountains. In June he preached in the streets of Denver. He joined the stampede to John Gregory's diggings in early summer and held preaching services for the miners. Hamilton gathered a union congregation[5] and applied to his home mission board for financial support. The agency denied his petition. Disappointed but not defeated, Hamilton opened a grocery store to earn his living and held regular Sunday services without pay. He liked the vitality of the gold fields and thrived on the mountain air. His union congregation remained small but loyal throughout the gold rush. When full-time, paid Presbyterian and Congregationalist ministers established churches in the towns near Gregory's Gulch in 1861, Hamilton's union church disbanded.[6]

Many wandering preachers drifted through the busy gold fields in 1859 and 1860. They prospected, mined or vacationed, preaching whenever they had the chance. William Goode found "a number of preachers--miners--of the different persuasions serving... the many church members" at Gregory Gulch. At other camps and towns, he met "quite a respectable proportion of clergy of different churches, who, though engaged in secular pursuits are generally respected as ministers."[7] Miners remembered the preaching of the Reverends Porter, Hammond, Steele, Mann, Wood, Bunch, Hewett, and Hildreth, though their records tell us nothing else about these preachers.[8]

These men made significant contributions to the early missionary effort, by creating a base on which home mission authorities built. Perhaps more important, they helped the miners, many of whom were lonely and adrift. Furthermore, services, classes, and prayer meetings came as a welcome alternative to saloon sociability. Finally, the churches furnished an element of social stability. Without recognized and effective government, people worried that they might sink into barbarism. The existence of small congregations and the promise of more to come assured the miners and settlers that they had not lost civilization and did not need to become barbarians in the wilderness.

Lay people, in several instances, took the initiative in establishing religious institutions. A group of Baptist miners and entrepreneurs formed a congregation in Central City in September, 1860. They worshipped together for several months under the leadership of Brother James Ripley. When the mining season ended, most returned to the States, and the church disbanded.[9] Congregationalists in the Boulder Valley established an assembly in 1864, and managed without a clergyman for a year.[10] Roman Catholics in Golden gathered, requested a priest, and survived for some time with the help of Joseph Machebeuf, future bishop of Colorado, who made frequent visits from Denver. During this period, they erected a church building. When a clergyman came, the parish was stable and active.[11]

Lay persons from several Protestant denominations created a union Sunday school in Denver on November 5, 1859. The school's founders included Denver's most influential lay civilizers: O. J. Goldrick, schoolmaster and journalist; Thomas Bayaud, Samuel Cushman, Lewis Tappan, merchants; David Collier, lawyer, politician and newspaper editor; Indiana Sopris, school teacher; Clara Brown, ex-slave and laundress; George Fisher, local preacher; and Jacob Adriance, Methodist circuit rider.[12] This venture is a good example of both the interaction of church and society in the task of civilizing and the early cooperation of denominations. Of those founding the school, at least three were Methodists; two claimed Congregational membership; one was a Presbyterian; and one was an Episcopalian. Though their cooperation faltered when missionaries established regular denominational bodies, the joint action served an important purpose. For some, it was a substitute church. For others, it supplemented Methodist worship services. For many, it was a place for moral instruction. It was another alternative to saloon sociability--a place to meet like-minded people.

Though the small groups gathered by lay people and vacationing ministers filled a crucial need in gold rush life, the missionaries sent by home mission societies and denominational hierarchies established the stable and lasting religious structures that many pioneers wanted. For more than half a century, the major Christian denominations in America had been moving west with restless pioneers. Though frontiersmen might boast that there was no law west of Kansas City and no God west of Fort Scott, frontier ministers moved quickly and kept abreast of population expansion in the densely populated mining camps and towns of Colorado and other territories. Roman Catholics, Methodists, Presbyterians, Congregationalists, Episcopalians, and Baptists had developed various home missionary techniques that worked with varying degrees of success. The denominations with congregational polity (Presbyterian, Congregational, Baptist) had established voluntary societies, the purpose of which was to recruit and support home missionaries. The denominations with episcopal polity (Roman Catholic, Protestant Episcopal, Methodist Episcopal) incorporated home mission projects into their general church programs; bishops assigned ministers to serve as missionaries in frontier provinces, districts, and conferences. Lay persons in these denominations formed voluntary societies to raise money for missions but did not direct the missions. A more detailed analysis of the historical development of mission policies can help to bring into focus the contributions of missionaries to gold rush society.

Roman Catholic missionary policy has a long and complex history. From the European rediscovery of the western hemisphere in 1492, Roman Catholic missionaries had an enormous influence on the growth of civilization in the Americas. Monastic orders--Franciscans, Dominicans, Augustinians, and Jesuits--played a role in the sixteenth-century conquest of Latin America. Catholic missions, especially through education and amelioration, contributed much to life in the United States and the other countries in the western hemisphere.

Monastic missionaries continued to contribute to Christian outreach in the Americas as the centuries passed. But Roman Catholics developed other agencies to help in the task. The most important agencies for missions in the United States during the nineteenth century were the Congregation for the Propagation of the Faith, established in 1622, for the purpose of papal supervision of the overseas missions, the Society for the Propagation of the Faith, founded in 1822 by French lay persons for the purpose of supporting missionaries in the field, and the Austrian _Leopoldinen Stiftung_, another lay organization created in 1829. The papacy exercised close supervision of American churches and missions, which retained their missionary status until 1908, much longer than population, resources, and piety required. Even so, the missionaries on the American scene helped develop expansion policies and church practices which suited life in an increasingly diversified society. The way was neither easy nor smooth; nevertheless, American Roman Catholics (under fire from suspicious Protestants at home and a defensive hierarchy in Europe) created a workable church system as one denomination among many.[13]

Though able to work beside their Protestant brethren on the frontier, Roman Catholic missionaries in Colorado differed from their colleagues in at least four ways. First, most Roman Catholic missionaries came to the frontier from Europe. Though efforts to train Catholic clergy in the United States had progressed significantly by 1859, the supply of native clergymen was far too small to fill the needs of the West. Thus, many European missionaries came to the American West. Coincident with American expansion to the Pacific were a series of revolutions in Europe. Priests, who became political exiles during these wars and their aftermath, were natural candidates for missions in North America. Italian, French, Spanish, and German priests migrated to the United States. Others, not in exile but enthusiastic about the missionary enterprise, responded eagerly to the appeals made by vicars apostolic visiting European seminaries. The potato famine and political upheaval in Ireland also caused large emigrations to North America, especially to the United States. A quick look at the list of Roman Catholic clergy in Colorado from 1858 to 1870 shows foreign born clergy in the majority. The Roman Catholic laity also contained a high proportion of foreign born or second generation Americans. Most Mexican-Americans joined Roman Catholic congregations, as did most Irish immigrants. 14

Second, frontier Roman Catholic clerics at first expressed skepticism or dismay about the rampant expansionism accompanying the gold rushes. They did not share their Protestant colleagues' enthusiasm for extending American Christian civilization beyond the Missouri River. John Miege grumbled that souls would be lost in the headlong race for riches. Jospeh P. Machebeuf hopefully predicted that Colorado would become depopulated as soon as the placer gold was gone. 15

Third, the Roman Catholic missionary outreach depended on orders of nuns and priests as well as on secular parish clergy. Normally, secular clergy established mining town parishes as the first stage in missionary advance. Then, they created parish schools and begged for nuns to staff them. A next stage usually included the creation of hospitals, orphanages, and other benevolencies staffed by nuns and clergy. Last, frontier prelates established colleges in which to train a native clergy. These, too, depended on monks and nuns for staff. In some areas, religious orders took over the entire evangelization task. The achievements of frontier Roman Catholics in education and amelioration would have been almost impossible without nuns, monks, and friars.

Fourth, Roman Catholic missionaries emphasized administration of the sacraments as the principal mark of the true church, while the evangelical Protestants emphasized preaching of the Word as the main sign of the true church. For Roman Catholics, ordained priests empowered to administer the sacraments were absolutely necessary for church establishment and survival. Lay leadership was important in raising money for missions and benevolencies, but lay people alone could not sustain a congregation. The Roman Catholic hierarchy quickly dispatched resident priests to the gold fields and established parishes in the main centers of population.

The Episcopalians lacked a well-defined mission policy; they had few priests to send, and no orders of religious clergy prepared for educational and mission work. Before

1835, their plans for missions were haphazard. The church sent neither missionaries nor money to frontier parishes. Priests who wanted to go west went on their own. Since such a venture required apostolic poverty or independent wealth, few priests followed the moving frontier across the Appalachians into the Mississippi River Valley. As many Americans migrated westward, the denomination lost ground to churches with more efficient missionary organizations. Clinging precariously to the eastern seaboard, the Episcopal Church seemed indifferent to expansion.

In 1835, tardily realizing that they had missed the huge missionary opportunites in the Mississippi River Valley, the House of Bishops began to create a missionary policy. They declared the whole church a missionary body and provided for the appointment of missionary bishops to oversee the westward expansion. Jackson Kemper and his successor Joseph C. Talbot set the procedural patterns for the Plains and Rocky Mountains.[16]

The Episcopalians did not evangelize as widely as did the Roman Catholics and the Methodists; nor did they attract as many members. Several factors explain this. First, each parish needed a resident priest; educational requirements precluded the use of unschooled clergy; and no army of exiled Europeans was at hand.

Second, from 1859 to 1866, Colorado Episcopalians had no resident bishop. Only a bishop could increase membership by the rite of confirmation; only he could do the business of the church; he was the primary fund raiser; and he had no intermediate official, such as the Methodist presiding elder, to whom he could delegate some of these tasks. Prior to 1865, the Colorado area was part of Bishop Talbot's diocese which extended over three-quarters of a million square miles; he could not visit often enough to do even the minimum of jobs properly.[17]

Third, many westerners accustomed to the seemingly more democratic polities of Methodist, Presbyterian, Congregational, and Baptist groups, found Episcopalians too formal. This dislike was not so serious as it had been in early national days when Episcopalians suffered from the stigma of Toryism as well, but it remained a barrier to successful evangelizing.[18]

The Methodists easily outdistanced all other Protestant

denominations in frontier evangelizing. From their origins, Methodists had been a missionary body with an efficient polity for expansion. John Wesley had been influenced by reports of earlier revivals in the British American colonies.[19] The Great Awakening, as these revivals were called, began in the 1720's and achieved real momentum in the 1730's through Jonathan Edwards, a great American Congregational minister.

All this played its part in the spread of Wesley's "connection" in the British colonies. Wesley did not intend to leave the Church of England; he hoped to breathe new life into it. But the American Revolution separated American Methodists from their parent organization. Francis Asbury, Wesley's deputy in the colonies, remained in America throughout the war for independence and secured a place for Methodism as a separate denomination. Asbury's itinerancy during the conflict actually strengthened Methodism when other churches declined. Further, his activities set a model for later missionaries.

With the Peace of Paris in 1783, American independence seemed assured. American Methodists' independence from the Church of England seemed equally secure. Wesley, assuming his continued control late in 1784, sent Thomas Coke to join Asbury and named them both to be general superintendents. But the American Methodist preachers (prompted by Asbury) established their own sovereignty not by accepting Wesley's appointments but rather by electing both Coke and Asbury as superintendents of the newly organized Methodist Episcopal Church of the United States of America. Presently, Asbury assumed the title "bishop" without Wesley's authorization or approval.

Using Wesley's model, Asbury and Coke created a tightly knit organization which combined close supervision of missions with a high degree of local autonomy.[20] Bishops directed presiding elders of mission districts. Presiding elders guided the work of circuit riders and lay preachers. The itinerants watched over and fostered the growth of churches, classes, and Sunday schools. Lay leaders managed the classes and schools. Itinerants, local preachers and lay exhorters kept the churches running smoothly. The vital link in this chain of command was the circuit rider, who assumed charge of several congregations. This "friar on horseback" visited as often as he could, riding or walking enormous distances. Quarterly meetings of the minister, his presiding elder, and the members of the churches relieved the loneliness of the circuit rider's life as did the annual conferences of all the preachers. The Methodists required regular circuit changes, as often as once a year in the mid-1800's. This insured the mobility necessary to meet the challenge of constantly moving frontiers.[21]

Frequent ministerial changes required active lay leadership, which provided institutional continuity in settled areas. Such a flexible system succeeded in mining frontiers, even though early towns had transient populations. Local preachers and lay exhorters preached from town to town until circuit riders could be found to minister to the flocks. Even then, when a circuit was very large, lay leaders sustained regular preaching, prayer meetings, and Sunday schools. This Methodist system worked so well that even schism in 1844 over the slavery question did not blunt the force of Methodist missions on the Colorado frontier.

Schism of a different kind did effect Presbyterian and Congregational missions. In 1803, the Presbyterians and Congregationalists agreed under the Plan of Union to cooperate in missionary expansion. In 1862, they formed the American Home Missionary Society (A. H. M. S.), a voluntary society for the purpose of evangelizing the West. The society achieved a major victory in a missionary campaign in the Mississippi River Valley between 1828 and 1830.

Often working hand in hand with agents of the American Bible Society and the American Sunday School Union, the society's ministers formed an important part of the "benevolent empire."[22] During the early decades of the 19th century, these voluntary societies acted as articulate, influential, effective agents in the campaign to extend Christian influence over the whole of America. However, during the late 1830's and early 1840's, the Presbyterians and Congregationalists lost their sense of mutual purpose, squabbling over theology and polity.

Dissension in the Presbyterian ranks made things worse. Westward expansion exacerbated a long-time quarrel between the conservative, tradition-minded Old School and the more innovative New School. Led by such theologians as Archibald Alexander and Charles Hodge, the Old School looked suspiciously at the Plan of Union and the voluntary societies as dangerous departures from the _jus divinum_, which determined church order and polity. They became even more alarmed with the revivalists in their ranks who seemed to flaunt the Westminster tenets. The very success of the missionaries working under the plan of Union through the A. H. M. S. and other voluntary societies seemed cause for even greater concern. When Nathaniel Taylor's theology began to give theological weight to their opponents' practices, the Old School scions withdrew from the Plan of Union. Unwilling to allow other denominations to win all the West, the Old School men formed their own missionary society.

The New School, on the other hand, recognizing the effectiveness of revivalism, rethought its theology. Further, they regarded the voluntary societies as mighty instruments for good. Last, they cast out the older Calvinist insistence on double predestination and adopted a theory of redemption grounded in the doctrine of universal grace.

Heresy trials, contentious assembly meetings, and academic division rent the denomination until the controversy reached a crescendo in 1838, when the Old School domination of the assembly finally pushed New School members to set up a separate organization of synods. Litigation failed to heal the schism, and finally the two became, in effect, separate denominations.[23]

The Home Missionary Society lost much support when the Old School left but the final blow to its far-reaching effectiveness came when the New School left as well and formed a rival missionary society in 1852. Though it remained active, the A. H. M. S. had lost most of its forceful zeal by the time of the Colorado gold rush.

Presbyterians and Congregationalists suffered other disabilities in the race to evangelize the West. Both insisted on an educated clergy. Thus, they had fewer available missionaries than did the Methodists. Presbyterians on the frontier also insisted on congregational stability before a minister could be called. Both denominations needed but could not legislate centralized control. Late in 1869, Presbyterians appointed a missions superintendent to cope with this difficulty in the Rocky Mountains; Colorado Congregationalists tried to do likewise, but eastern opponents of the scheme thwarted their efforts.[24]

Colorado lay persons played a vital role in establishing Presbyterian and Congregational churches. Early in the gold rush, William Larimer and his friends asked eastern mission authorities to send an Old School minister. Congregationalists also requested that the A. H. M. S. send a preacher.[25]

Few Baptist missionaries joined the Colorado gold rush. The Baptists claimed their greatest strength in the South, from which only a handful of miners migrated to the Rocky Mountains. The Baptists' loyalty to congregational polity and local autonomy retarded missions in the West. Furthermore, the denomination demonstrated a certain anti-mission ideology. Fearing that centralization, even in missionary effort, might undermine local congregations' independence, the Baptists adopted a missionary program quite grudgingly. Their missionary society did not send many missionaries to Colorado or to other far western regions.[26]

Ministers of other denominations--Lutheran, Disciples, Reformed, Universalist--visited gold rush Colorado, preaching along the way; but none of them stayed to establish congregations among the miners during the period under review, because too few people wanted to join their churches.[27]

Part II

Back east, church officials and missionary organizations quickly responded to frontier needs. The Methodists, Roman Catholics, and Presbyterians sent advance scouts to reconnoiter. Typically, the Methodists arrived first. In April, 1859, Bishop Levi Scott and members of the Kansas-Nebraska Conference created a Pike's Peak district and sent William Goode and Jacob Adriance, both of Nebraska, to the area. In May Goode, the presiding elder of Nebraska City, and Adriance, a twenty-three-year-old circuit rider, set out along the Platte River, which Goode described as "a beautiful natural highway, linking the two halves of our continent." Both men enjoyed the journey, marveling at the miners' stampede and such novelties as the great buffalo herds and the comical prairie dogs. Each Sunday they preached to groups of travelers taking Sabbath rest. Late in June, they reached Denver and found to their relief that "the general state of society is orderly and quiet; no civil man need fear interruption." Even though miners drank and gambled (some of them "unemployed and vicious"), most of the residents appeared "worthy and reliable" to the missionaries.[28] Adriance felt awed by the "great work to be done."[29]

They set about it immediately. Goode rented a hotel for Sunday services; Adriance posted advertising handbills on rocks, trees, and cabins; both knocked on cabin doors in search of prospective members. On July 3, a handful of

Denverites attended services. Since most of the hopeful miners were digging near Mountain City, the ministers left Denver for the mines. For four weeks they toured the camps, preaching wherever they could--in tents, cabins, gambling halls, saloons, hotels, and in the streets. Everywhere they found Methodists, organized classes and quarterly conferences and held revivals. Goode organized a church at Mountain City and appointed George Fisher as supply preacher and circuit rider for the camps near the town.

Goode and Adriance did not expect all of the churches to be permanent. Mining communities grew and withered as quickly as spring flowers. The missionaries ministered to congregations as they could be gathered and moved on when the groups dispersed to new mining fields. The mobility of circuit riders and the flexibility of Methodist polity made this easy.

Their survey complete in early August, Goode and Adriance returned to Denver where pioneer leaders were writing constitutions for the State or Territory of Jefferson. Both men served as chaplains of the convention.

Confident that some of the new towns would draw permanent settlers, the missionaries decided that Adriance should stay to ride circuit in the environs of Denver.[30] The young man gathered hay and rented a small, dirt-floored cabin while Goode composed his report to mission authorities. On August 8, Goode preached and celebrated the Lord's Supper in Adriance's cabin, packed his bag, and said good-bye. Adriance felt lonely and anxious when his friend left.[31] He wrote that he felt "like a stranger in a strange land; more strange among a still stranger people, surrounded with circumstances and conditions still more strange."[32] For, he lamented, "None of them cared for religious things. Trading, trafficking, drinking, and gambling were the order of the day, seven days a week--interspersed with the occasional shooting of a man."[33]

Throughout the mining season of 1859, Adriance and Fisher preached, taught, and ministered to the spiritual needs of the miners. Adriance often walked to his appointments to spare his overworked mule. He slept in dug-outs, on the ground, under wagons, and in haystacks. He had no trouble attracting miners to his sermons but was frustrated by the comings and goings of his flock. He complained, "During the summer, my congregations were nearly all newcomers, every time."

Late in October, 1859, winter snows drove most of the miners out of the mountains. Many returned to the States, but a sizable number wintered in Denver. George Fisher joined the exodus to the plains city and moved into Adriance's cabin. Denver's population stayed almost stable throughout the winter. Adriance and Fisher preached to large crowds each Sunday. They tried to raise money for a church building but found few able or willing to give, since money was scarce. Nevertheless, Methodist miners demonstrated a religious responsiveness in classes, quarterly conferences, love feasts, and prayer meetings that kept Adriance and Fisher from becoming discouraged.

When the spring thaw began, the gold rush resumed. New mines in South Park attracted thousands of miners. Fisher returned to the mountains; Adriance journeyed to his annual conference in Leavenworth, to report on his work and to receive his appointment for 1860. The young man almost bubbled with joy. The meeting seemed to him an oasis in the desert. Furthermore, he entertained his colleagues with tales of his adventures and basked in the glow of his accomplishments: planting outposts of Zion in the Colorado wilderness.[34]

In May, 1860, John B. Miege, Roman Catholic vicar apostolic of the Indian Territory, journeyed grimly from Leavenworth to investigate "the truth or falsity of the reports of the richness of the discoveries." He was angry about the invasion of Indian land by greedy white men. He had no interest in establishing missions for miners and hoped that none of them were Catholics. Nevertheless, he dutifully made his investigation, which revealed at least a hundred Catholics in Denver and more at the camps. "Poor unfortunates!" he lamented, "If they would give to our Divine Master but a little of the energy which they show for wordly riches what a rich and real harvest they would gather."[35]

Miege established a parish in Denver, where members immediately began constructing a church. He promised them a priest and returned thankfully to Leavenworth. Unable to spare a man for that mission, he asked Rome to transfer jurisdiction of the gold regions to the province of New Mexico. Much to his relief, Roman officials agreed. Bishop Jean B. Lamy soon learned of the transfer and, in October, 1860, he sent his close friend Joseph P. Machebeuf and young Jean Raverdy to Denver.[36]

Near the end of October, they reached Denver. The arrival of Machebeuf, a missionary on American frontiers for over two decades, and Raverdy, a recent seminary graduate, delighted Denver Catholics, who had become discouraged with their building project as the months passed without the priests' arrival. When the two came, they encouraged their charges to complete work on the "foundation and pile of bricks out on the prairie." Catholics in Denver cheerfully resumed work and finished the thirty by forty-six-foot structure in time for Christmas Eve mass.[37]

At first, Machebeuf did most of the visiting and preaching, while Raverdy struggled to learn English. The priests found ten Catholic families in Denver, though about two hundred people, including non-catholics, usually attended mass each Sunday. Early in 1861, when church affairs seemed well begun in the city, Machebeuf left Raverdy to say masses (for which he needed no English) and set out for a tour of the mining camps. He traveled in a well-worn buggy that functioned as a movable rectory and chapel. He carried camping equipment, vestments, and a portable altar, which he assembled on the buggy's tailgate for outdoor services. Machebeuf visited the principal mining camps and towns and established congregations at Arapahoe City, Golden, and Central City. He and Raverdy, who had at last begun to conquer the English language, took turns itinerating to these places.[38]

The Catholic congregation at Central City, the largest of the mining towns, numbered about two hundred. Machebeuf shared available assembly space with several other ministers. After a few months he decided that Central City residents could easily afford to build a church. When his requests for pledges did not come up to the mark, he locked his congregation in the city hall one Sunday and refused to open the doors until members had pledged enough money. His tactic worked; Central City Catholics soon had a small church.[39]

Early on, Machebeuf bought a great deal of land, which he planned to use for benevolencies. War, Indian troubles, and scarce money delayed implementation of his plans. Meanwhile, the priest irrigated some of his land and planted vegetables and grain. He had learned how to farm nearly arid lands in New Mexico and introduced the techniques in Colorado. Despite a bout with typhoid in the summer of 1861, Machebeuf, with Raverdy's aid, successfully established Roman Catholicism in the gold fields of Colorado.[40]

Old School Presbyterian Alexander T. Rankin, another denominational surveyor, arrived in Denver in 1860. Rankin disliked his errand almost as much as Miege had, though for different reasons. A long-time resident of upstate New York, Rankin had grudgingly accepted an assignment to survey Kansas for his missionary society. He had finished his task and looked forward to going home, when word came that Denver residents had asked for a preacher. The society directed Rankin to assess the area's potential and to establish congregations if necessary.[41]

He reached Denver in July of 1860, during the worst outbreak of crime and violence in the city's short history. On his first day in town, Rankin visited the News office. As he chatted with editor William Byers, six angry, armed men burst in, grabbed Byers, and threatened to kill him. They shouted that the editor had slandered them in a series of editorials urging Denverites to rid the town of "bummers." Byers' assistants drew pistols, and Rankin tried reason. The gang dragged Byers to a nearby saloon, where the bartender diverted the gunmen and hustled Byers out a back door. Byers ran to his offices and barricaded the door; the outlaws returned and opened fire; the newsmen retaliated; the gunmen fled, pursued by a large crowd of merchants, who shot one of the gang and formed a vigilance committee to capture the others.

Angry citizens met that evening and vowed to rid the town of outlaws and gamblers. The vigilance committee returned with one outlaw (the other four got away), and the crowd almost lynched him. Leaders calmed the mob by promising a citizens' trial the next day.

The judge called Rankin as a witness. Frightened by the mob spirit and fearful that his testimony might "affect" his "mission unfavorably," he hid, but a determined posse found him and brought him to court, where he gave his testimony. The jury voted eleven to one for conviction. The judge referred the decision to the crowd, which voted overwhelmingly for conviction and sentenced the culprit to banishment. Thus was Rankin initiated to the rough justice of the frontier.[42]

Violence continued to plague Denver throughout Rankin's four-month tour of exploration and organization. Drifters, outlaws, and misfits flocked to the town, avoiding the mining camps for the most part. Rankin decided to establish churches at once so that the gospel might act as a civilizing influence on the wild and wooly town. Presbyterian mission authorities preferred to organize churches after settlements showed signs of permanence. Rankin organized a church in Denver because "public morals are bad,"[43] even though the town did not seem permanent to him.

To Rankin's surprised delight, Denver citizens packed the meeting hall whenever he preached. Many in the small core of civilizers eagerly supported his mission. Most of Denver's women, viewed by frontiersmen as key agents of the civilizing process, attended Rankin's services. He expressed amazement at "the numbers in attendance, the decency, order and decorum that prevailed." His success "was unexpected and unprecedented," for he had "not supposed there were so many churchgoing people here." Despite duels, horse thefts, murders, and public hangings, Rankin could boast in November, 1860: "Our efforts to propagate the gospel in this city have exerted a very apparent effect on public morals."[44]

Rankin finished his tour, submitted a report with recommendations to the mission board, and received word that a regularly appointed missionary was on his way to Denver. Rankin concluded that Presbyterians should form a mountain presbytery, including mission churches in Denver, Central City, Boulder, and Pueblo. He warned the board not to underestimate the pioneers' intelligence and education when selecting preachers for the job. The Colorado pioneers were not ignorant backwoodsmen but "a very shrewd people."[45]

When denominational authorities read Goode's, Miege's, and Rankin's reports recommending that missionaries be sent to the miners, they took action. The Methodists, who already had Adriance in Colorado, assigned John Chivington as presiding elder and appointed several circuit riders for the area.[46] The Catholics and Presbyterians sent resident clergy to lead the organizations created by the surveyors. In addition, Episcopalian John Kehler and Southern Methodist William Bradford joined the ranks of church builders in Denver.

Episcopalian John Kehler, at sixty-two, voluntarily left a comfortable Maryland parish to move west. Recently widowed, Kehler arrived in Denver on January 17, 1860, accompanied by four of his eleven children. His son Jack, sheriff of Arapahoe County, heartily welcomed them.[47]

Kehler began work immediately. He canvassed the town and urged citizens to attend an organizational meeting. An enthusiastic group of Episcopalians and a few members of other Protestant denominations met with Kehler, who appointed a committee to find a place to hold services. Several laymen suggested that another committee apply to the town company for a donation of building lots. Kehler announced services for the next Sunday.[48]

Both committees accomplished their tasks, and on January 29, 1860, Kehler read morning prayer in the union Sunday school cabin. He noted with awe, "Then and there, doubtless, for the first time since the creation were the solemn and befitting words uttered. "The Lord is in his holy temple; let all the earth keep silence before him." With less awe, he wrote that the collection totalled $8.85.[49]

Kehler held services each Sunday for increasingly larger congregations. Within a few weeks, the congregation had grown too large for the school house and had moved to the Apollo Theater, which seated about three hundred people.[50]

In his first weeks in Denver, Kehler called on almost everyone in town and addressed the newly-formed Denver and Auraria Library and Reading Room Association.[51] The <u>News</u> dubbed his lecture "a feast of good things." Byers wrote, "His subject--'Great Men of the Ages'--was ably handled, and no one speaks of the entertainment but with praise."[52]

By mid-February, Kehler had gathered enough followers for a formal organization. On February 19, he met with his congregation; they adopted by-laws and elected a vestry. The vestry included several of the town's leading young merchants, politicians, doctors, and lawyers: Thomas J. Bayaud, Samuel S. Curtis, Amos Steck, Richard E. Whittsitt, Charles A. Lawrence, Edmund S. Waterbury, Thomas G. Wildman, David C. Collier, C. E. Coaley, and A. F. Peck. Vestrymen then called Kehler as their rector and voted to name their parish St. John in the Wilderness. The vestry solicited enough money to support the expenses of the parish though they paid their rector in grants of land rather than cash.[53]

Kehler pursued his pastoral duties in Denver and the mining camps. He preached and celebrated the eucharist; he baptized, married, and buried his parishoners. Early on, funerals outnumbered baptisms and marriages. A distressing number of young miners died of diphtheria, typhoid, mountain fever (either a form of typhoid or Rocky Mountain spotted fever, carried by ticks), consumption, brain fever, bloody flux, dropsy, accident, murder, and suicide. Kehler practiced neither revivalism nor social reform, but he encouraged his parishioners in their civilizing activities and cheerfully donated his time and talent to the library association, the literary society, the Episcopal Mite Society, and other organizations aimed at improving the quality of life on the frontier. When the Civil War broke out, Kehler assumed double duty, ministering to his flock in Denver and also to the militia quartered at Camp Weld, several miles outside of Denver.[54]

Though Kehler and his vestrymen managed to establish and maintain services in Denver, they owed allegiance to the missionary bishop in the enormous diocese in which Denver lay. Elected in 1859 to serve as "bishop of all outdoors," Talbot journeyed to Colorado in 1860 and found Kehler's work progressing satisfactorily. While in Denver, he preached, celebrated the eucharist, and confirmed eight people. He visited church members in Denver and toured the mining camps. Talbot then returned home and left church business to Kehler.[55]

William Bradford of the Methodist Episcopal Church, South, journeyed to the gold fields from Kansas, in summer, 1860, gathered a congregation, and built a small brick chapel. Denver's citizens took enormous pride in the building which they regarded as a badge of civic permanence and social stability. Though a minority of Pike's Peak miners were southerners, Bradford's sermons attracted many Denver residents for a time.[56]

Denver's Methodists were polarized over the slavery issue, when in May, 1860, John Chivington, a fire-breathing abolitionist presiding elder of the Methodist Episcopal Church, took up residence. Chivington dominated any gathering by his imposing presence, great size and booming voice. He had earned the nickname "fighting parson" during border warfare in Missouri and Kansas between free soilers and proslavery advocates. Once, when border ruffians threatened to tar and feather Chivington if he preached on the slavery question, he mounted the pulpit, calmly placed pistols on either side of his Bible, and announced that he would speak by the grace of God and the power of his firearms. He tended to view himself as a soldier in the war between God and the Devil. He chose preaching of the gospel and temperance reforms as weapons to be wielded under the twin banners of Methodism and Masonry.[57]

As soon as Chivington reached Denver from Nebraska City, he launched a vigorous campaign to order social and religious life. He began by drafting local preachers and vacationing ministers to supply new churches. Within a few weeks, he had assigned A. P. Allen, H. H. Johnson, Joseph Canon, William Howbert, and Landon Taylor to mining camp circuits. Chivington assessed the situation and wrote, "The preachers were alert, diligent, devoted, and the Methodist Episcopal Church was in a forward state of organization at all points where we had been able to occupy the field." He assigned his band of preachers to circuits touching California Gulch (later Leadville), Hamilton, Tarryall, Breckenridge, Mountain City, Golden, Boulder, Gold Run, Blue River, Fairplay, Buckskin Joe, Georgia Gulch, and Colorado City. Chivington, as presiding elder, took the pulpit in Denver. He and his colleagues organized new congregations at almost every camp in the gold regions, collecting funds to build small log cabin churches in three of the camps.[58] Methodist membership increased dramatically from sixty-two in the spring of 1860, to 391 in the following spring.[59]

Chivington's style of evangelizing took four forms: vigorous revival preaching, ardent temperance advocacy, encouragement of education, and anti-slavery reform.

When Abraham Lincoln was elected in 1860, and several southern states tried to leave the Union in protest, Chivington naturally opposed secession. He and his subordinates supported the cause of Union but discovered that open advocacy offended enough men and women to cause concern. Some circuit riders tiptoed around the controversy, but Chivington remained outspoken. When war broke out, the elder immediately volunteered his services. Governor William Gilpin offered him a position as chaplain of the volunteer regiment then forming. Chivington declined, asking for a chance to fight. Gilpin assigned him as major in charge of recruiting and training the militia volunteers. Chivington accepted; he immediately began a tour of the camps alternating recruitment speeches and sermons.[60]

The Civil War caused serious disruptions in the Methodist missions in Colorado. Chivington's commission left his fellow missionaries without a leader for several months. Membership declined, but evangelization did not cease; circuit riders of the Methodist Episcopal Church, North, carried on as before in spite of the uproar.[61] Bradford, leader of the Methodist Episcopal Church, South, however, saw his congregation dwindle as southerners left the territory--many to return home to fight, others forced out by dominant unionist sentiments. A few months after the outbreak of hostilities, Bradford sadly closed his mission and turned his brick church over to a board of trustees for sale.[62]

Despite national schism, Coloradans found that they could live reasonably well in their outpost. By the opening of the war, they had achieved a tenuous balance of order and found that the consolidation of their society proceeded quickly thereafter.

By the opening of the Civil War, Roman Catholic, Methodist, Southern Methodist, Episcopalian, and Presbyterian churches staffed by resident clergy could be found in Denver. Resident clerics at once entered a partnership with the town-builders to both Christianize and civilize the miners. A survey of their work in the ante-bellum period shows how the churchmen helped tip the balance away from social chaos toward social order.

NOTES

1. See Sidney Mead, The Lively Experiment (New York: Harper & Row, 1963), pp. 106-107.

2. Local or "located" preachers were ordained ministers who had resigned their regular conference appointments and taken secular employment. These semi-laymen preached often, especially in frontier settlements where full-time ministers were scarce. They also held services in communities where circuit riders visited but could not hold services every Sunday. In pioneer Colorado, local preachers were far more numerous than circuit riders and made regular Sabbath observance possible for many who would otherwise not have had the opportunity for regular worship.

3. Larimer, Reminiscences, pp. 117-18.

4. Records of Membership of the Auraria and Denver City Mission, within the bounds of the Kansas and Nebraska Conference of the Methodist Episcopal Church, 1859-65, ms., Denver Public Library, n.p.

5. Union congregations were composed of members of two or more denominations. The practice of holding union meetings probably arose when Presbyterian and Congregational groups initiated corporate missionary endeavor under the Plan of Union in 1801. In the Colorado frontier setting union churches and Sunday Schools usually combined Presbyterians, Congregationalists, and Methodists.

6. Alexander T. Rankin, Alexander Taylor Rankin: His Diary and Letters, ed. Nolie Mumey (Boulder: Johnson Publ. Co., 1966), p. 138; Arthur B. Cooper, The Story of Our Presbytery of Denver (Denver: priv. pub.), pp. 7-8.

7. Goode, pp. 427-33, 438.

8. Cf. references in Jacob Adriance, Diary, 1859-61, passim; William Howbert, Diary, 1860.

9. Olaf Olsen, "A History of the Baptists of the Rocky Mountain Region," Ph.D. dissertation, University of Colorado, 1952, p. 140; Eugene Parsons, "History of Colorado Baptists," ms., Colorado State Historical Society, Denver, p. 2.

10. Walter S. Hopkins, et al. The Bible and the Gold Rush (Denver: Big Mountain Press, 1963), pp. 26-27.

11. William J. Howlett, Life of the Right Reverend Joseph P. Machebeuf (Pueblo, Colo.: Franklin Press Co., 1908), p. 328.

12. Adriance, Diary, November 19, 1859; Letter, The Trail, Vol. IV (January, 1912), p. 24.

13. Kenneth S. Latourette, Three Centuries of Advance, Vol. III, and The Great Century, Vol. V, in History of the Expansion of Christianity (New York: Harper & Row, 1937-45); John T. Ellis, American Catholicism (Chicago: University of Chicago Press, 1969).

14. William Howlett, "The Diocese of Denver," ms., Chancery Office, Denver; Gilbert Garraghan, The Jesuits of the Middle United States, Vol. II (New York: America Press, 1938), pp. 526-28; Howlett, Life of Machebeuf; J. M. Espinosa (ed.), "The Opening

of the First Jesuit Mission in Colorado," Mid-America, Vol. XVIII (Oct., 1936), pp. 272-75.

15. John B. Miege, "Letters," Mid-America, Vol. XVIII (October, 1936), pp. 267, 269; Howlett, Life of Machebeuf, p. 269.

16. William W. Manross, The Episcopal Church in the United States, 1800-1840 (New York: Columbia University Press, 1938); Hugh L. Burleson, The Conquest of the Continent (New York: Columbia and Foreign Missionary Society, 1911).

17. See Joseph C. Talbot, Diaries, 1859, 1862-1865.

18. George M. Randall, First Report to the Board of Missions (New York: Sanford & Harroun, 1866), p. 16.

19. Albert C. Outler (ed.), John Wesley (New York: Oxford University Press, 1964), pp. 15-16.

20. Methodist polity and constitutional organization is much like that of the United States. Elected executives (bishops) head the church; assembled clergy at General Conferences constitute a legislative body; elective committees adjudicate disputes and discipline. Checks and balances, divided authority, and local autonomy in matters not specifically delegated to central governing bodies are included in the Methodist Discipline as they are in the United States Constitution.

21. William W. Sweet, Methodism in American History (New York: Abingdon Press, 1961), pp. 27-121; E. S. Bucke (ed.), The History of American Methodism, Vol. II (New York: Abingdon Press, 1964); Charles Ferguson, Organizing to Beat the Devil (New York: Doubleday, 1971).

22. A host of voluntary societies directed to some specific purpose grew up in the wake of the Second Great Awakening. They derived their impetus from the Awakening but drew upon British models. The societies included the American Bible Society, the American Tract Society, the American Sunday School Union, and the American Home Missionary Society. For an excellent discussion of the societies and their

work see C. Z. Foster, An Errand of Mercy (Chapel Hill: University of North Carolina Press, 1960).

23. Sydney Ahlstrom, A Religious History of the American People (New Haven: Yale University Press, 1972), pp. 462-68.

24. Colin Goodykoontz, Home Missions on the American Frontier (Caldwell, Idaho: Caxton Press, 1939); Maurice W. Armstrong (ed.), The Presbyterian Enterprise (Philadelphia: Westminster Press, 1956).

25. Cooper, p. 8; Amos Bixby to Mr. Reed, Letter, April 25, 1859, A. H. M. S. Correspondence, Amistad Research Center, New Orleans.

26. T. Scott Miyakawa, Protestants and Pioneers (Chicago: University of Chicago Press, 1964), pp. 145-58.

27. Rocky Mountain News, December 21, 1865, December 30, 1865, October 26, 1866.

28. Goode, pp. 401-421.

29. Adriance, Diary, June 28, 1859.

30. Goode, pp. 420-51.

31. Adriance, Diary, June 28-August 8, 1859.

32. Adriance, Letters, Northern Christian Advocate, Jan. 25, 1861, p. 13, Feb. 1, 1861, p. 17.

33. Adriance, quoted by Isaac H. Beardsley, Echoes from Peak and Plain (Cincinnati: Curtis & Jennings, 1898), p. 232.

34. Adriance, Diary, Jan.-June, 1860.

35. Miege, pp. 268-69.

36. Miege, p. 271; Howlett, "Diocese of Denver," p. 7.

37. Howlett, Life of Machebeuf, pp. 289-90.

38. Ibid., pp. 289-96.

39. Ibid., p. 296.

40. Ibid., pp. 298-308.

41. Rankin, pp. 4-6, 37.

42. Ibid., pp. 85-87, 90.

43. Ibid., pp. 99, 117, 92.

44. Ibid., pp. 88, 91-92, 132.

45. Ibid., pp. 138-40.

46. Minutes of the Annual Conferences of the Methodist Episcopal Church for the Year 1860, p. 46 (hereafter cited as Annual Conference Minutes of the Methodist Episcopal Church). Each year the minutes for all of the conferences in the church are bound together for publication. The citations in this essay are from the Kansas and Nebraska Conference (1858-60), the Kansas Conference (1861-63), and the Colorado Conference (1864-72).

47. John Kehler, Diary, December 25, 1859-January 17, 1860, ms., Colorado State Historical Society, Denver.

48. Ibid., January 23, 1860.

49. Ibid., January 29, 1860.

50. Ibid., February-June, 1800.

51. Ibid., February 17, 1860.

52. Rocky Mountain News, February 22, 1860.

53. Kehler, February 19, 1860; Allen Breck, The Episcopal Church in Colorado (Denver: Big Mountain Press, 1963), pp. 4-14; Amos Steck, Untitled ms., Colorado State Historical Society, Denver, pp. 1-4; Minute Book, St. John in the Wilderness, ms., Denver Public Library, 1860-1862; Joseph C. Talbot, Diaries, Church Historical Society, Austin, Texas, 1859, 1862.

54. Kehler, Diaries, 1860-62, passim.

55. Talbot, Diary, 1859; Breck, pp. 9-13.

56. Rocky Mountain News, August 26, 1861; E. J. Stanley, Life of Rev. L. B. Stateler (Nashville: Pub. House of the Methodist Episcopal Church, South, 1916), pp. 166-67; Minutes of Annual Conferences of the Methodist Episcopal Church, South (Nashville: Southern Methodist Publishing House, 1878), 1856, pp. 667-68; 1858, p. 18; 1859, pp. 111-13; 1860, pp. 209-210.

57. In this period, the Masons functioned as moral reform societies, advocating temperance and education as solutions to about all social problems. Many Protestant ministers supported their efforts by joining the organization. See Rocky Mountain News, Dec. 30, 1861.

58. John Chivington, "Footprints of Methodist Itinerants in Colorado," Rocky Mountain Christian Advocate, Sept. 26, 1889, p. 2; Craig, The Fighting Parson, pp. 46-52; Clarence Lyman, "The Truth about Col. John M. Chivington," ms., Western History Dept., Denver Public Library, Denver, Colo., pp. 74-116.

59. Annual Conference Minutes of the Methodist Episcopal Church, 1860, p. 48; 1861, p. 41.

60. Chivington, Rocky Mountain Christian Advocate, Oct. 24, 1889, p. 2; Rocky Mountain News, Oct. 14, 1861.

61. John Dyer, Snow-Shoe Itinerant (Cincinnati: Cranston & Stowe, 1890), pp. 121-201.

62. Stanley, pp. 166-67; Minutes of Annual Conferences of the Methodist Episcopal Church, South, 1862-65, indicate that the Kansas Conference, in which Colorado had been included, sent no reports. In 1866 and after, no such conference appears in the records at all.

CHAPTER 3

COLORADO'S POLITICAL, SOCIAL, AND ECONOMIC DEVELOPMENT IN THE AFTERMATH OF THE GOLD RUSH: 1861-1870

In the aftermath of the gold rush, Coloradans worked to achieve stability in their political and economic affairs.[1] Each year they tipped the balance a bit farther away from chaos and toward political order and economic prosperity. Near the end of 1861, dramatic changes began to take place. Many of the adventurers left, and Colorado assumed an orderliness unknown before. With the core of solid citizens enlarged and the rowdy element diminished, order was much, much easier to impose. Eruptions of sporadic violence and disorder, however, reminded civilizers that their task was not complete. Sometimes they seemed to take two steps forward only to be pushed one step backward. The overall tendency though was toward increasing orderliness under the laws and increasing adherence to norms of moral behavior.

In the political realm, offical territorial government made political order more nearly possible. Even though appointed officials had to contend with the vagaries of the spoils system, they could govern far more authoritatively than could the members of the provisional government. Colorado citizens joyfully greeted Territorial Governor William Gilpin when he arrived late in May, 1961. In Denver, bands played while fifteen hundred citizens gathered to hear Gilpin speak in the street.[2] Next day, he left to assess Union strength in the gold fields. Stopping in each settlement and camp, he shook hands, slapped backs, made patriotic speeches, and looked over the state of society. After completing his swing, he estimated that about 25,000 people lived in the territory; he warned of "a strong disloyal element and many friends of the rebellion."[3] Gilpin exaggerated the rebel strength; but since his commission was to keep Colorado safely in the Union, he could not afford to be complacent about the few southerners who remained after secession.

War-time panic periodically seized Colorado residents

who thought that rebels would attack in order to seize gold and supplies.[4] Their fear was not without basis, for some secessionists did remain and Texas troops did march into New Mexico. But fear exceeded the actual danger.

Gilpin decided that Colorado could be counted in the Union column and turned to other matters as well. He declared that mining and municipal law codes already in force needed no changes. For the moment, he cheerfully authorized the ad hoc codes and congratulated miners and merchants on their sound political instincts.[5]

Shortly, the various branches of territorial government went into effect. Judges Newton Pettis, Benjamin Hall and Charles Armour reached their posts soon after Gilpin, and they held terms of court in Denver, Central City, and Canon City late in the summer of 1861. Colorado citizens welcomed this step by regularly constituted civil authorities and rightly predicted a decline in acts of violence.[6] Next, Gilpin ordered election of legislators and a territorial delegate to Congress. Coloradans duly elected thirteen representatives to the lower house and nine council members to the upper house; and they chose Hiram P. Bennett (nicknamed "Garden Seed" because of a campaign promise to distribute free vegetable seeds) as delegate to Congress. The legislature convened on September 9. The members created seventeen counties, passed reams of civil and criminal laws, and authorized a sorely needed charter for Denver.[7]

Citizens of Denver then elected city and county officials, establishing local ordinances and agencies for law enforcement. Even though policies laid down in 1858 by the town company had provided a nearly adequate set of laws for protection of life and property, no one had had authority to enforce them. Between August and December, 1861, a shooting occurred in Denver about once a week. Fist fights, duels, claim jumping (city dwellers "jumped" cabins and lots rather than mining sites), building on street rights of way, and reckless riding plagued Denver's citizens. In November, 1861, Denverites elected officials who established courts. The city police courts eventually proved effective in reducing the civilian crime rate. The magistrates met almost daily, levying fines and jail sentences for disorderly behavior. Shortly, crime declined dramatically except among the soldiers over whom city police had no control. Order improved in other towns as well, and county governments functioned in the same way where city governments did not exist.[8]

The political and legal order established by the territorial, county, and city officials, with the ardent support of many merchants and miners, functioned smoothly within a little over a year. In 1863, Maurice Morris, a British visitor, complained that he had "heard much of the primitive manners and customs of the far West," and that "it is disappointing to find merely a variation of the civilized world located here." He observed that "people of all classes behave with decorum and self-respect." He saw "nothing approaching to turbulence or disturbance of any kind. Indeed, I have not seen a drunken man yet." In fact, "One feels inclined to think that, now-a-days, what Byron said of a small privileged class is true of a far larger one,

Society is now one polish'd horde
Found'd of two mighty tribes, the bores and bor'd."[9]

Congregationalist William Crawford felt relieved rather than disappointed when he observed, shortly after his arrival in July, 1863, "Violence and bloodshed are not common. There has been a great improvement, the people tell me, within a year."[10]

Though pioneer politicians and civilizers had created orderly communities, wars, fires, floods, grasshopper plagues, disease, and occasional crime continued to disrupt life in Colorado. The Civil War and Indian wars reduced migration to the gold fields and made travel on the plains dangerous.

After Gilpin had set the judges and law-makers to work he turned his attention to what he thought to be his primary task: the defense of Colorado against rebel and Indian attack. On August 29, 1861, he proclaimed the formation of a volunteer regiment and opened recruitment offices all over the territory. Hundreds of men swarmed to enlist. They included such leaders as John Chivington, lawyer John Slough, merchants Samuel Tappan, Richard Whitsitt, Edwin Wyncoop, and Richard Sopris. Young miners eagerly enlisted in the ranks, exchanging the excitement of gold hunting for that of war. Gilpin authorized construction of barracks at a newly created post named Camp Weld and ordered guns, bullets, cannons, uniforms, and other military necessities. He had neither money nor federal authorization for these expenses. He issued promissory drafts to thousands of merchants, workers, and militiamen, who ultimately collected from the United States Treasury but only after considerable delay. Workmen hurriedly built the camp, which proved to be too small. Some volunteers billeted in Denver.

Major Chivington and others, with little or no military experience, undertook to train the volunteers. Discipline proved difficult. The excited and restless men were especially hard to control when they spent evenings in Denver. Shootings, fist fights, drunkenness, and brawling involving soldiers drove Denver's civilizers to near distraction. Leaders tried to prohibit sale of alcohol to soldiers, confident that sober militiamen would behave better than tipsy ones. As leaders improved discipline, the problem diminished but did not disappear.[11]

The volunteer regiment, despite its problems, protected Colorado's towns, and few civilians were touched by actual warfare. Occasional alarms went out. In September, 1861, Denver citizens arrested and banished a handful of southerners for treasonable utterances. The News editor declared, "In dangerous times such as these even free speech is sometimes a dangerous privilege." Most Colorado citizens agreed and proudly cheered the volunteers whenever they rode through Denver's streets in parades headed by Major Chivington. But regimental members waited restlessly for action.[12]

Early in 1862, they gladly responded to Colonel Edward Canby's orders to march south. Canby needed reinforcements to stop the Confederate advance up the Rio Grande. Before the Colorado volunteers reached Fort Union in northeastern New Mexico, Texans under the command of General Henry Sibley captured Albuquerque and Sante Fe. The rebels threatened to seize Fort Union and a cache of military supplies kept there. If the fort fell, the rebels could easily march on Colorado itself. Union forces surprised a portion of the rebel troops in Apache Canyon several miles south of Fort Union on March 26. Major Chivington commanded his troops with skill in this short but furious skirmish, executing a flanking maneuver that forced a hasty Confederate retreat.

Three days later, Confederate and Union forces numbering about one thousand and eight hundred, respectively, met in Glorieta Pass. The federals planned a direct assault by the center column and a flanking attack by about four hundred thirty men under Chivington's command. The rebels advanced more quickly than Canby had anticipated, and Chivington's flanking force missed its objective. The battle raged all day and ended without a clear-cut victory for either side. Near midnight, Chivington and his troops returned to the Union camp. They jubilantly reported that they had surprised the Confederate supply train in the canyon far to the rear of the main force and destroyed it. Next day, the southern soldiers began a retreat down the Rio Grande and abandoned their attempt to capture western territories.

Chivington became the hero of the campaign. When Colonel Slough resigned his commission in mid-April, 1862, the men of the First Colorado Regiment elected Major Chivington as colonel, passing over Lieutenant Colonel Samuel Tappan. Under Chivington's leadership, the Colorado volunteers moved down the Rio Grande harassing the retreating Texans. To guard against further Confederate movement along the river, Canby stationed the Colorado troops at Fort Craig. In January, 1863, a group of California volunteers relieved Chivington's men who returned to protect Colorado settlements.[13]

While his volunteer troops were in New Mexico, Governor Gilpin lost his office. Angry merchants, holding unredeemed warrants for material at Camp Weld, shouted for his removal. President Lincoln complied, removed Gilpin, and at Methodist Bishop Matthew Simpson's suggestion appointed John Evans, Illinois physician, financial wizard, and Methodist lay leader to the post.

After the federal victory at Glorieta Pass, no more Civil War battles threatened Coloradans. War panic flared briefly in the summer of 1864. Outlaws, thought to be Confederate renegades planning an assault on Denver and Central City, committed a series of highway robberies. Coloradans lived briefly in "anxious suspense." Citizens armed and began militia training. Reverend William Crawford wrote that "the loyal men and muskets were counted--and even your servant loaded his rifle, to be in readiness for an attack." However, authorities soon captured most of the guerrillas and shot the rest while they were "attempting to escape."[14]

Coloradans' other main concern during the war was protection against hostile plains Indians. Before the Civil War, federal troops stationed on the main overland routes did all they could to protect travelers and settlers from Indian raids. When war broke out, many federals transferred to the eastern front and left western forts lightly garrisoned. Westerners feared that in the absence of large Union forces Indians would raid more freely and unite with the rebels in Confederate attempts to seize western territories.

Few Indian raids occurred between 1858 and 1862. The

Arapahoe and Cheyenne generally avoided the whites. This was easy when miners clustered around the mines. But as farmers and ranchers spread out on the plains, contact increased, and Indians felt that whites were invading their hunt-grounds. In 1863 and 1864, Indian raids on ranches and wagon trains increased. The Indians stole stock, killed some men, and carried off some women and children. The Indian raids stopped overland trade and mail service for several weeks in the summer of 1864. Food became scarce, and prices skyrocketed. No one knows exactly how many white people the Indians killed and abducted, but angry whites claimed that seventy-five persons died in Indian attacks during 1863-64.[15]

Furthermore, the whites feared a massive attack on their towns by a confederation of Cheyenne, Arapahoe, Sioux, Kiowa, and Comanche. According to Indian sources, no such alliance or plan existed. Whites, however, suspected that the Indians lied and intended to drive the whites out of the settlements in order to reclaim their land. The Sioux of Minnesota had, in 1862, waged vigorous war with the avowed intent of forcing white settlers out of their hunting grounds. Though they had not succeeded, Colorado whites expected them and the other plains Indians to try again in Colorado.[16]

Both Indians and whites declared that they wanted peace. Governor John Evans tried to negotiate a settlement. Cheyenne head chief, Black Kettle, often expressed his peaceful intentions. But neither leader had sufficient control over his subordinates to prevent a tragic encounter in late 1864. Negotiations in 1862 and 1863 proved fruitless. Panic mounted on both sides throughout the summer of 1864. Both whites and Indians committed murders. For example, in June, 1864, Indians raided the Van Wormer Ranch twenty-five miles east of Denver and murdered the ranch foreman and his family. In April, 1864, white soldiers summarily shot a party of Indians peacefully driving some cattle along Bijou Creek, north of Denver.[17]

Colorado settlers urged Evans to exterminate the Indians. Black Kettle's younger chiefs refused to accept any policy of pacification and favored war on the whites. In June, Evans saw war to be inevitable; in an attempt to separate peaceful and hostile Indians before he ordered attack, he advised all peaceful Indians to go to Fort Lyon on the Arkansas River. He then began raising a regiment of volunteers to serve for one hundred days and authorized civilians to arm and fight hostile Indians. The Indians may have misunderstood Evans' offer, or they may have tried to manipulate him. In any case, no Indians appeared at Fort Lyon until September, 1864. By this time, Evans contended, his offer had expired; he assumed all plains Indians to be hostile. The Indians' arrival at the fort just as winter began looked suspicious. In previous years, Indians had hunted and made war in summer and rested in winter. Their peaceful approach at the end of the hunting and raiding season convinced most whites of the insincerity of Black Kettle's statements about peace.

Edwin Wyncoop, commander of Fort Lyon, believed that the Indians wanted peace. He met with chiefs at their hunting camp on the Smoky Hill River. He convinced seven Cheyenne and Arapahoe chiefs to accompany him to Denver and urged Evans to reopen negotiations. Evans agreed reluctantly. The council did no good; Evans did not trust Indian promises. At the end of the conference, army officers suggested that the Indians return to their reservation on Sand Creek. Thinking themselves at peace with the whites and under Wyncoop's protection, several hundred Cheyenne and Arapahoe followed Black Kettle to the Sand Creek camp. A large number of the young men, however, did not agree and refused to leave the Smoky Hill. On November 2, Major S. J. Anthony relieved Wyncoop of his command at Fort Lyon.

Meanwhile, Chivington recruited and trained the one-hundred-day volunteers; Evans traveled to Washington to plead for more regular troops. While Evans was away, Chivington decided to attack the Indians at Sand Creek. He hoped, by one swift surprise blow, to force the Indians into unconditional surrender. He led his troops from Camp Weld to Fort Lyon in late November. Anthony, whose garrison force consisted of fewer than two hundred, joyfully greeted Chivington and the volunteers. Anthony assured the colonel that he thought the Indians encamped at Sand Creek to be hostiles and that he himself would have attacked sooner but for insufficient troop strength.[18]

During the night of November 28, Chivington and about seven hundred fifty soldiers marched the forty miles from Fort Lyon to Sand Creek. At dawn they attacked the Indian camp, composed of about one hundred thirty lodges believed to hold about one thousand people. Reports of the battle vary. Indian survivors said that Black Kettle raised a white flag in his lodge as soon as the Indians were awakened by the sound of horses' hooves; Chivington's soldiers declared that they saw no flag of surrender; each side claimed that the other fired the opening shots; the Indians maintained that the camp contained many women and children and almost no warriors; whites asserted that they allowed time for women and children to flee, that the majority of the encamped Indians were warriors, and that the women who remained fought as fiercely as braves; Indians claimed that they were totally unprepared for the attack; whites insisted that the Indians had dug battle trenches (called rifle pits) and were well-prepared for battle.

Testimony regarding the opening shots and other parts of the battle was contradictory. Even so, we do know that once the shooting started, whites and Indians fought desperately for several hours. At the end of the fighting, many Indians lay dead. Estimates of Indian casualties ranged from one hundred fifty to five hundred. Nine white soldiers died in the assault. We also know, from white testimony, that several soldiers scalped their fallen foes, thinking it necessary to fight Indians in their own style. Indian sources reported and white witnesses denied extensive and brutal mutilation of corpses.[19]

Denver residents greeted the news of the Indian massacre with undisguised delight. Editors headed an early report, "Bully for the Colorado Boys!" On the next day, Byers echoed citizen opinion when he wrote,

> The members of the Third, and First, and the First New Mexico, who collectively "cleaned out" the confederate savages on Sand Creek, have won for themselves and their commanders, from Colonel down to corporal, the eternal gratitude of dwellers on these plains. This brave beginning will bring down the hauteur of the treacherous tribes, all round, so that, should there not be even another similar defeat enacted on them through this season, our people may rest easy in the belief that outrages by small bands are at an end, on routes where troops are stationed. Having tested the "bitter end," the news of which will quickly be dispatched among the others, the supremacy of our power will be seriously considered, and a surrender or a sueing for peace be perhaps very soon proclaimed. This plan of attacking them in their village is the only one available while it is certainly as advantageous to the Indians as they justly dare desire, if they're in for a fair fight.[20]

The Indians suffered a staggering defeat. The surviving remnant fled to Smoky Hill. Aware of the superior arms and persistence of the whites, they knew that they could not wage a winning war, but they decided to launch attacks of reprisal and revenge for the Sand Creek massacre.[21]

Full scale warfare erupted as Indians struck back in revenge throughout 1865. Chivington's theory that one decisive blow would end Indian raids proved false.

Reports of the Sand Creek affair aroused curiosity in Washington. Congressmen investigated; the Committee on the Conduct of the War and the Committee on the Condition of Indian Tribes both held hearings in 1865; a military tribunal in Denver also looked into the matter; all three groups condemned Chivington's actions and pronounced Sand Creek a massacre. Such censure enraged many Coloradans, who approved almost anything leading to Indian removal or extermination. Chivington supporters railed against eastern critics and even formed a political party called the Sand Creek Vindication Party. Some Coloradans, however, deplored the affair. Colonel Samuel Tappan concluded, "Nowhere could anything be found to justify the massacre." Bitter controversy over the engagement continued for decades.[22] Shortly after the storm erupted, Chivington resigned his commission, and Lincoln fired Evans and replaced him with Alexander Cummings. After defending themselves in the public arena, both Chivington and Evans turned to private concerns, though Evans continued active in Republican Party affairs.[23]

After the Civil War ended at Appomattox Court House on April 9, 1865, federal troops once more guarded western settlements and trade routes. The intensity and frequency of Indian attacks diminished in 1866 and in October, 1867, Cheyenne and Arapahoe agreed to the Medicine Lodge Treaty, under which they moved to Indian Territory (now Oklahoma). Small bands of Cheyennes made sporadic forays outside Indian Territory for another decade, but Coloradans saw little more of the plains Indians.[24]

While the Indian troubles were brewing, Colorado's politicians led by Evans and Henry M. Teller of Central City began the long battle for Colorado's statehood. As always in territorial politics, the outcome depended on national as well as local opinions. In 1864, Republicans in Congress passed acts providing for Nevada's, Nebraska's and Colorado's statehood, so that the additional electoral votes would help re-elect President Lincoln. Statehood was contingent upon the writing and public acceptance of state constitutions. Colorado leaders quickly wrote the required document, drew up a slate of officers, and submitted both to voters. Coloradans turned both down by a margin of four to one. Voters seemed to have objected not to the constitution but to the unopposed slate of officers. They wanted to elect them, not simply endorse the convention delegates' favorites.

The following year, even though the enabling act had expired, Coloradans wrote another constitution which was accepted. They elected officers: William Gilpin as governor and George Chilcott as delegate to Congress. The legislature appointed Evans and Teller as senators. Coloradans also voted to deny suffrage to blacks. Congress flatly refused to pass another enabling act; the election was over, and Republicans did not need Colorado's electoral votes. Further, Radical Republicans working for Negro suffrage objected to the referendum.

In 1866 and 1868, again election years, Coloradans and sympathizers in Congress tried to gain statehood. Both attempts failed, however. Colorado finally achieved statehood in 1876, making it the Centennial State. From 1864 to 1876, Colorado politicians had fought bitterly over the question of statehood. The issues are not clear, but the perennial question of who shall have the spoils seems to have been foremost.[25] It was a mark of political and social stability that Colorado's civilizers could address themselves to such a question. Between 1858 and 1864, most of their energy had gone into their struggle to overcome social and political chaos.

Colorado's economic history between 1861 and 1870 is a story of diversification with slow but rather steady growth. Mining continued even though miners uncovered no new bonanzas.[26] Agriculture, commerce, and transport increased, while mining production remained at 1859-1860 levels until 1868. In that year, Nathaniel Hill developed an efficient process for removing gold and silver from Colorado quartz. Mining profits increased steadily thereafter.[27] Even though production levels remained stable from 1859 to 1868 and rose in 1869 and 1870, the number of miners dropped dramatically over the decade. A small group of efficient, experienced miners replaced the hordes of amateurs who joined the gold rush. While in 1860 over twenty-two thousand Coloradans were miners, in 1870 only twenty-two hundred men dug in Colorado mines.[28]

Commerce, speculation, and real estate development contributed as much to Colorado's economic growth as did mining. Albert Richardson estimated that by 1866 Coloradans had developed properties greater in worth than the profits realized in gold production. The merchants and financiers, of course, depended upon mining in the pre-railroad days. Without the mines, Colorado had little reason for being. But as the years passed, other industries developed to create auxiliary economic bases.[29]

In the first decade, the most important of these were agriculture and transportation. From 1858 to 1867, Coloradans imported much of their food from midwestern farms. However, throughout the sixties more and more farmers migrated to the Colorado plains in spite of nearly arid land and grasshopper plagues. They dug irrigation ditches, often in cooperative companies, and planted their fields with grain and vegetables. Ranchers found the high plains good for stock grazing. By 1867, farmers and ranchers were producing enough foodstuffs to feed the citizens of Colorado. By 1870, the number of workers on farms and ranches had increased as dramatically as the number of miners had decreased. In 1860, 220 Coloradans worked on farms; in 1870, Colorado farmers and ranchers totalled nearly 6, 500.[30]

Freighting over the plains which separated Colorado towns from the line of dense settlement constituted a necessary service industry in the territory's economy. Freighters carried minerals back east to the States and returned westward with wagons loaded with food, building supplies, and other necessities. Freighting attracted hardy adventurers because it was a risky and lucrative trade until the railroads supplanted it.

Railroads created a genuine economic revolution in America during the middle of the 19th century. As the network of rail lines expanded from east to west, people spread across the continent building new towns, farms, ranches, and factories. Sparsely populated frontier areas such as Colorado suddenly mushroomed.[31] Towns dependent on mining developed other economic bases. Linked by rail to established communities, frontier isolation ended. (As we have seen, this is the reason for the _terminus ad quem_ of this study.)

The complex story of railroads in Colorado is told ably elsewhere.[32] Throughout the pioneer period, however, energetic Colorado entrepreneurs, including John Evans and William Palmer, lobbied incessantly for rail development in the territory. They worked hard to convince Congressmen to route the first transcontinental railroad through Colorado but failed. When, in 1867, the Union Pacific reached Cheyenne, Wyoming, eighty miles north of Denver, entrepreneurs quickly began a spur line from Cheyenne to Denver. Workmen completed construction of the Denver Pacific in June, 1870. That day, crowds cheered as officials drove a silver stake into the last tie. The first train puffed into Denver, and a new age had begun. In the same year, workers completed the Kansas Pacific linking Denver with Kansas City.[33]

By the beginning of the railroad era, Colorado had changed from a rip-roaring mining frontier to a staid midwestern village society, as reflected by contemporary observers and analytic comparison of the 1860 and 1870 census reports. The almost casual violence of gold rush days vanished by mid-decade. Whereas in the last four months of 1861 shootings occurred in Denver about once a week, not one shooting was reported in the same period in 1866.[34] Bayard Taylor, whose observations we have heard before, wrote in 1866, "The degree of refinement I have found in remote mining districts of Colorado has been a great surprise." On approaching Denver, he said,

> Suddenly I perceived, through the dust, a stately square Gothic tower, and rubbed my eyes with a sense of incredulity. It was really true; there was the tower, built of brick, well-proportioned and picturesque. Dwellings and cottages rose over the dip of the ridge, on either side; brick blocks began to appear, and presently we were rolling through gay, animated streets, down the vistas of which the snowy ranges in the west were shining fairly in the setting sun.

Taylor admired Denver's "brisk and lively air." There was "constant movement in the streets," and the people were "brimful of cheerful energy." Goods and services could be readily and cheaply obtained. He was amazed that the city was there at all, considering the floods, fires, Indian wars, and Civil War.

When Taylor visited Central City, he found the town

full of "men of culture and education." The audience attending his lecture "might have belonged to New York or New England."[35] Taylor's remarks verify Francis Young's assertion that Central City was "absurdly decorous for a mining town--a steady-going industrious community, easily controlled, and generally quiet and law-abiding."[36]

Demographic study based on census reports give substance to Taylor's and Young's descriptions. Federal census marshals visited Colorado in June, 1870. They found that Colorado's aggregate population (excluding the Indians) had increased over the previous decade from 34,277 to 39,864, an increase of only 16.2 percent. Indian population had increased from about 6,000 to 7,480 in spite of removal and heavy loss of life during the wars. The only Indians remaining in Colorado were the few who had left their tribal connection and the mountain dwelling Utes, who seem to have prospered in the decade between 1860 and 1870.[37] Colorado's population grew less than the national average and far less than California's during a comparable period. Between 1860 and 1870, the population of the country increased by 22.6 percent. Between 1850 and 1860, California's population mushroomed from 92,597 to 379,994 or 321 percent.[38]

Though numerical increase in population in Colorado was slight, especially compared with that of the California gold coast, the character of the population changed significantly. Indicators may be found in the statistics of race, age, sex, native origin, and occupation. In 1860, 46 blacks lived in Colorado, whereas in 1870, 456 lived there. The increase is statistically significant and an indication of a minor social change. The same is true for Orientals: in 1860 none lived in the territory, and in 1870, seven did. Colorado began as and continued to be overwhelmingly white.[39]

By 1870, the proportion of women had risen from 4 percent to 37.5 percent, indicating a marked change in the social scene. Even more dramatic is the increase in the number of children. In 1860, census takers counted 770 children under ten. A decade later, they found 9,515, an increase of 1,236 percent. Children between ten and fifteen increased from 298 to 3,885. Many of the children had been born in the territory during the decade; 7,579 births were recorded. It is likely that few of the families who bore these children left the area. Older people increased in number, too. In 1860 only 86 persons over sixty could be found; in 1870 census takers found 747. Between the two census years, those between fifteen and fifty-nine had declined from 32, 583 to 25, 417.[40]

Over the decade, the proportion of foreign born grew from 7. 5 percent to 16. 6 percent. The slight rise in the national average, from 13. 3 percent to 14. 2 percent, did not account for this increase. Also, the number reporting one or both parents born abroad totalled 10, 707. This suggests that Colorado had become a heterogeneous society, but it had not. The largest part of the immigrants and first generation Americans sprang from northern European and mainly Irish and English stock. In 1860, 98. 1 percent of the foreign born came from the British Commonwealth countries or northwestern Europe. By 1870, 96. 6 percent came from these same areas. Over two-thirds came from England, Ireland, and Germany. A large number came from Canada and other parts of British America. More than half of the foreign born lived in the emerging urban areas of Gilpin and Arapahoe Counties. Over 66 percent of the Irish lived in these counties, though less than 30 percent of the aggregate population did.[41]

Birth places of Americans resident in Colorado are also revealing. Though 19th-century Americans were a notoriously restless people, the places of birth probably indicate where they spent their childhoods. In 1860, over half of the Coloradans had been born in Ohio, New York, Illinois, Missouri, Indiana, and Kentucky. In 1870, more than half had been born in New Mexico, Colorado, New York, Ohio, and Illinois. Only 14. 9 percent in 1860 had been born west of the Mississippi, whereas 86. 1 percent had been born east of the great dividing river. By 1870, natives of the trans-Mississippi West constituted almost half, or 46. 1 percent. This suggests that large numbers of easterners joined the gold rush, stayed a while, and returned home. Many attracted by mining were there and counted in 1860. By 1870, most of the eastern gold diggers had been replaced by farming and town building pioneers and their offspring. During the decade, natives of eastern and midwestern states decreased dramatically. New Yorkers, though still of significant number, had dropped from 3, 942 to 2, 778. Ohioans, who had numbered 4, 125 in 1860, totalled 2, 057 in 1870. In 1860, New Englanders made up about 10. 5 percent of the population, in 1870, 4. 5 percent. Natives of mid-Atlantic states dropped from 17. 5 percent to 11. 9 percent in the ten years. The percentages of midwestern born men and women decreased from 38 percent to 14. 9 percent. In 1860, 12. 5

percent of Coloradans were native to the Deep South; ten years later, 5.4 percent claimed southern birth. The percentage of natives of the trans-Mississippi West rose, as we have seen, from 14.9 percent to 46.1 percent.[42]

Analysis of occupational distribution reveals a dramatic change in social patterns. In 1860, 26,741 of the 34,277 residents were gainfully employed. Of these 220 were in agriculture, 1,608 worked as professionals and service people, 1,374 traded and transported goods, and 23,539 engaged in mining and manufacturing. Of the last, only 1,453 worked in manufacturing whereas 22,086 mined. By 1870, 17,583 held paying jobs. Not only was the work force much smaller, but the distribution had changed: 6,462 men farmed or ranched (one may assume that large numbers of women and children also labored on the farms but were not counted among those gainfully employed); 2,815 traded and transported goods; and 4,681 dug for minerals and manufactured goods. A scant 2,200 listed miner as their occupation, as we have seen above.[43]

Though the work force was smaller in 1870 than it had been a decade before, there were fewer unemployed. Among men between the ages of fifteen and sixty, 4,742 were unemployed in 1860, whereas only 802 held no jobs in 1870. A fair number of these were school boys. Thus, in the halcyon days of the gold rush, 15 percent of the labor force did not work. In 1870, a mere 4.5 percent did not, and most of these were in school.[44]

Detailed analysis of Coloradans' occupations in 1860 and 1870 shows social change. An obvious category for comparison is that of "saloon keeper." In 1860, 192 men ran saloons. In 1870, the category is not even listed, though 17 men ran billiard saloons. This suggests dramatic reduction of the number of saloons over the decade.[45]

Other comparisons further suggest the extent to which this portion of the Wild West had been tamed by 1870. In the first decade, the number of Colorado clergymen increased from eleven to fifty-four. The ranks of teachers swelled seven-fold, from ten to seventy-two. Surprisingly, fewer doctors lived in Colorado in 1870 than in 1860. 122 medical men resided there in 1860, whereas 70 did in 1870. The legal profession gained a few new members: their number increased from 89 in 1860, to 99 in 1870. More than three times as many domestic servants worked in the territory in the latter year; the number grew from 110 to 357, indicating the presence of more affluent families as well. In 1860, journalists numbered nine, in 1870, twenty-three. While in 1860, eleven men had handled pioneers' banking needs, twenty-nine men were needed in 1870.

Perhaps the most striking change in the occupational picture (after the increase of farmers and decrease of miners) was the rise in the number of railroad company employees from zero in 1860, to 962 in 1870. In 1870, Colorado was on the verge of a virtual revolution in the realms of transportation and manufacturing. With the help of a good transport system and improved technology, manufacturers began to build their empires. In 1870, however, manufacturing consisted mainly of the labors of bakers, blacksmiths, shoemakers, brewers, masons, brickmakers, butchers, wagon builders, weavers, tailors, saddle makers, lumbermen, millers, painters, plasterers, plumbers, printers, saw mill operators, and wheelwrights. Most manufacturing was of hand-made items, and as one would expect in a growing frontier area, much manufacturing activity was in the service of the building trades. The age of the machine began in the Rocky Mountains in the 1870's, as it was beginning in the eastern cities. Although the number of men and women occupied in manufacturing rose from 1,453 in 1860 to 2,481 in 1870, the character of the manufacturing changed little over the decade, even though the quantities of shoes, clothes, bricks, finished lumber, and similar commodities increased.[46]

By 1870, it was clear that the civilizers had triumphed. The institutions which they had established had attracted large numbers of new settlers. The main catalyst in the migration had, of course, been the enlarged opportunites in the new land; but settlers would not have moved to an area without the added attraction of rather orderly communities where civilized life was possible. The social history of Colorado between 1861 and 1870 is not a story studded with the foundation of institutions. By the end of 1861, most of the basic social institutions had already been founded. After that time new newspapers, new theater companies, new literary societies sprang up in the mining towns and elsewhere to compete with those already established. But those who moved to the Colorado frontier after 1861 found the rudiments of civilized life on hand and ready for use. They enlarged, embellished, and polished; but they did not found.

The dramatic change of Colorado's society was a result both of migration patterns and of concerted efforts to impose order on the miners and merchants. The civilizers in Colorado leaned heavily on the support of frontier missionaries. Many of the civilizers felt the need of spiritual community and turned readily for encouragement and comfort to the churches. We now turn to the story of missionaries and churches during the Civil War and its wake.

NOTES

1. For a more detailed account of Colorado's history from 1861 to 1870 see James Smiley, History of Denver (Denver: Denver Times-Sun Publishing Co., 1901) and Frank Hall, History of the State of Colorado (Chicago: Blakely Printing Co., 1890). For a concise narrative see Carl Ubblelohde, A Colorado History (Boulder: Pruett Press, 1965).

2. Amos Billingsley, "Journal," Colorado Magazine, Vol. XL (October, 1963), pp. 242-70, May 27, 1861 entry. Hereafter references will be to Billingsley's dating entries.

3. Thomas Karnes, William Gilpin, Western Nationalist (Austin: University of Texas Press, 1970), pp. 251-98; quotation in W. B. Vickers, History of the City of Denver (Chicago: O. L. Baskin & Co., 1880), pp. 435-40. His count indicates the population to be much smaller than in June, 1860. Heavy migration to the gold fields seems to have ceased after the 1860 mining season.

4. Rocky Mountain News, August 29, September 5, October 1, 1861.

5. Karnes, pp. 251-98.

6. Rocky Mountain News, August 26, September 4, 1861.

7. Ibid., August 26, 27, September 9, 1861.

8. Ibid., August 26, September 10, 14, October 28, November 4, 9, 11, 13, 14, 15, 24, 26, 29, December 13, 14, 23, 1861; January 14, 1862.

9. Maurice O. Morris, Rambles in the Rocky Mountains (London: Smith, Elder & Co., 1864), p. 78.

10. William Crawford to Dr. Badger, July 13, 1863, Letter, A. H. M. S. Correspondence.

11. Rocky Mountain News, September 9, 23, 1861.

12. Ibid., October 1, 1861.

13. Craig, The Fighting Parson, pp. 99-144.

14. Crawford to Noyes, Sept. 25, 1864, Letter, A. H. M. S. Correspondence.

15. Rocky Mountain News, April, 1863-September, 1864, passim.

16. Craig, p. 152; Dee Brown, Bury My Heart at Wounded Knee (New York: Bantam Books, 1971), pp. 81-82, 39-65.

17. Rocky Mountain News, July 18, 1864; Brown, pp. 70-74.

18. John M. Chivington, "To the People of Colorado: Synopsis of the Sand Creek Investigation," (Denver: printed privately, 1865), pp. 5, 12-14.

19. See Contrasting accounts of the affair in Brown, pp. 86-91; Craig, pp. 177-202; Irving Howbert, Memories of a Lifetime in the Pike's Peak Region (New York: G. P. Putnam's Sons, 1925), pp. 95-162; Chivington, "To the People...," p. 15.

20. Rocky Mountain News, December 7 and 8, 1864.

21. See Rocky Mountain News, December 12, 1864, for a poignant speech delivered by Bear Rib, explaining the Indian attitude.

22. See Craig, pp. 9-11.

23. Ibid., pp. 231-38; Edgar McMechen, Life of Governor Evans (Denver: Wahlgreen Pub., 1924).

24. The mountain dwelling Utes did not collide with Colorado

settlers until 1879. When they did, the whites defeated them and removed them to an arid reservation in the southwestern corner of the territory. For an account see Brown, pp. 349-67.

25. Ubbelohde, A Colorado History, pp. 135-53.

26. Silver veins uncovered at Georgetown in 1863-64 created a flurry of boom town activity but did not create a rush or stimulate much emigration from eastern and midwestern states. Miners made small discoveries in South Park and along the continental divide throughout the decade. The next bonanza was at Leadville in 1878-79. The last gold rush in Colorado was to Cripple Creek in the 1890's.

27. Hafen, Colorado and Its People, Vol. II, pp. 691-93, indicates that miners produced over $2, 500, 000 yearly. In 1868, 1869, and 1870 gold sales totalled $2, 010, 000, $3, 000, 000 and $3, 100, 000 respectively.

28. United States Census, 1860, p. 549; 1870, p. 723. Between 1858 and 1867, miners extracted and marketed over $25, 000, 000 worth of gold, as we have seen above. Other metals also contributed to Colorado's growth. Before 1867, Coloradans mined only $406, 139 worth of silver. In 1868, they sold over $266, 000 worth of silver, $630, 000 in 1869, and $660, 000 in 1870. Other useful metals yielded less but furnished the basis for future growth. Copper and lead were mined in small quantities. In 1870, copper sales reached $44, 140 and lead gained about $15, 000. Coloradans also dug coal, producing 25, 100 tons between 1858 and 1867. The worth of this coal was $50, 200. Receipts for coal production for the years between 1868 and 1870 averaged about $21, 000 per year. A great increase of production of these useful but unglamourous minerals came in the 1870's. Hafen, Colorado and Its People, Vol. II, pp. 691-93.

29. Richardson, Beyond the Mississippi, p. 333.

30. Ibid.; U. S. Census, 1860, p. 549; 1870, Vol. I, p. 723.

31. U. S. Department of the Interior, Bureau of the Census, Tenth Census of the U. S., 1880, p. 3; Twelfth Census of the U. S., 1900, pp. 32-33, 100.

32. See R. A. Lemassena, Colorado's Mountain Railroads, 5 Vols. (Golden, Colo.: Smoking Stack Press, 1963-68).

33. Ubbelohde, p. 119.

34. Rocky Mountain News, September-December, 1861; September-December, 1866.

35. Bayard Taylor, Colorado: A Summer Trip, pp. 36, 131.

36. Young, Echoes from Arcadia, pp. 87-88.

37. U. S. Census, 1860, p. 605; 1870, p. 8, 328. Census marshals did not include Indians in aggregate population figures nor in the tables of race, age, sex, native origin, or occupation, except for the few assimilated into white society. Percentages cited in the following do not include the Indians, since they were not an integral part of the mining town society, except when they left their tribal connections.

38. U. S. Department of the Interior, Bureau of the Census, Seventh Census of the U. S., 1850, p. 102; U. S. Census, 1860, pp. 33, 599, 606; U. S. Census, 1870, Vol. I, p. 299.

39. U. S. Census, 1860, p. 548; 1870, p. 95.

40. Ibid., 1860, pp. 546-47; 1870, p. 723.

41. Ibid., 1860, p. 549; 1870, pp. 347, 723.

42. Ibid., 1860, p. 549; 1870, pp. 328-35.

43. Ibid., 1860, p. 549; 1870, p. 723.

44. Ibid.

45. The number probably did fall off considerably, but changes in nomenclature preclude exact comparison. The total was probably far above the seventeen noted in the census. The census takers may have included "saloon keeper" in the category of "hotel and restaurant keeper," which appeared on the 1870 list but

not on the 1860 tabulation. In 1860, saloons functioned as restaurants and make-shift hotels. In 1870, most hotels and restaurants had bars and functioned in part, as saloons. The change in terminology may be indicative of a change of social attitudes. While keeping in mind that an 1860 saloon was not the same as an 1870 hotel or restaurant, we can conclude that in 1860, 207 people ran saloons and hotels, and in 1870, 298 men and women engaged in roughly the same business. United States Census, 1860, p. 549; 1870, Vol. I, p. 723.

46. *Ibid.*, 1860, p. 549; 1870, Vol. I, p. 723.

CHAPTER 4

ECCLESIASTICAL DEVELOPMENT IN THE AFTERMATH OF THE GOLD RUSH: 1861-1870

Part I

The missionaries in Denver and the mining camps faced serious obstacles: materialism, secularism,[1] occasional violence, poverty, shortage of workers, inadequate buildings, and transience. By dogged persistence, they overcame some of these.

For even if the gold rush had ended in 1861,[2] the rapacity it had spawned remained. A faintly supercilious observer, Bayard Taylor, amused by the gold mania, remarked:

> Every man you meet has his pocket full of specimens. When you are introduced to a stranger he produces a piece of "blossom rock," a "sulpheret," or a "chloride." The landlord of the hotel where you stop confidentially informs you that he owns 25,000 feet--"the richest lode in the country--assays $1,300 to the cord, sir!" The clerk is the happy possessor of 10,000 feet; the porter (where there is any) has at least 5,000; while the chambermaid boasts of her own "Susanna Lode" or "Bridget Lode." The baker has specimens beside his bread; the dispenser of lager beer looks important and mysterious; the druggist is apt to give you "chlorides" instead of aperients; and the lawyer, who takes his fees in "feet" (money being scarce) dreams of realizing millions after the Pacific Railroad reaches Denver.[3]

This ludicrous picture was only slightly overdrawn; the inhabitants of the gold regions still held high hopes for future fortunes from the mines. William Phipps, Congregational missionary in Boulder, saw gold fever as a challenge. Greedy people in mining regions needed the gospel badly, he thought.

> It seems to me, if there is any part of our country where good earnest, active ministers are needed more than at any other, it is in the region of gold and silver mines. "The love of money is the root of all evil;" if there is any place where the roots grow luxuriantly, it is in a gold lode. It seems the rocky soil of which Christ spoke in the parable, and in which religion finds little nourishment. It dies immediately, in many cases; and therefore the necessity of continually throwing in the seed, and keeping it well watered.[4]

Many missionaries, like Phipps, confidently expected that they could transform Coloradans' values, replacing the love of gold with love of God.

Hand in hand with materialism went secularism. The missionaries found the lack of "Sabbath observance" to be the most visible manifestation of secularism in the mining communities. Storekeepers and saloon owners rarely closed on Sunday, because Sunday was market day for miners and farmers. Sabbath observance improved as ministers established regular worship, and Sunday closing increased steadily throughout the sixties. Still ministers continued to complain. For example, Episcopal Bishop George Randall wrote,

> Every intelligent Christian can readily imagine, what in this age must be the terrible condition of a community, who are destitute of sanctuary privileges, --how the Lord's day will be desecrated, --how vice and immorality will prevail. I had a fearful illustration of this as I rode into Nevada [City]. A large crowd had gathered in the street, and when they stood aside to allow my carriage to pass through, we saw the body of a man, who, but a few minutes before, had been shot dead in front of a saloon. There lay his lifeless body, weltering in its blood, just where it fell. What a scene in a Christian land, in the charming sunlight of a beautiful Sunday afternoon![5]

Francis Byrne, an Episcopal minister in Nevadaville, commented,

> The miners, I found, had limited advantages of a religious character; the sacredness of the Sabbath was hardly recognized. Sunday traffic and worldly

> amusements with painful profanity and intemperance prevailed to a sad extent, at the time.[6]

The missionaries believed that Sabbath observance could be more effectively encouraged by resident ministers. In many instances they were right. Byrne reported that within a few weeks of his arrival "a vital change took place. Sabbath desecration was, to a great extent, discontinued."[7]

As churchmen dealt with Sabbath neglect, they hoped to stem religious indifference and erosion of their value system. They did not have to face other possible manifestations of secularism such as avowed atheism or deism.

Widespread criminal violence declined sharply after the lawless gold rush, but occasional violent episodes posed threats to peaceful evangelizing. Further, itinerant ministers feared Indian raids. Consequently, preachers almost always carried pistols in their saddle bags or rifles under wagon seats.[8] O. A. Willard, Denver's Methodist presiding elder, shot and wounded a man in self-defense.[9] A bishop traveled with a small arsenal of arms.[10] Those who did not carry arms often wished they did. Episcopal priest William A. Fuller was in a wagon train when Indians attacked and killed the driver. The horses bolted; Fuller trying to control the runaways fell off the coach and barely escaped being crushed by the wheels. The pursuing Indians followed the coach and horses. Fuller ran to a nearby river, tore off his clothes, and swam to an island in the middle. Seeing two men running toward him, he discovered them to be soldiers from a nearby fort. He swam to them, and they all rode quickly to the fort. His escape was regarded as little short of a miracle, and Bishop Daniel Tuttle felt that "God's loving Providence saved him for His work."[11]

All of the missionary pioneers needed more money than congregations could pay them, and some suffered from actual poverty. St. John's in Denver, one of the few self-supporting churches, kept afloat financially because the rector accepted land instead of cash, as we have already seen.[12] Presbyterian and Congregational voluntary societies sent quarterly payments to their missionaries to supplement their inadequate stipends.[13] Methodist itinerants likewise found conference salaries too meager. Some ministers turned to secular work to earn money for food. Methodist John Dyer, for example, contracted to carry mail over the continental divide while riding his circuit. He also worked as subscription agent for the Rocky Mountain News.[14] Others deprived themselves of common comforts; for instance, Joseph Machebeuf and Jean Raverdy owned only one overcoat; each wore it on alternate days throughout the winter of 1862-1863. Their rectory was no more than a set of closets. Machebeuf slept on the floor for six years before he could afford to buy a bed.[15]

Dangers and hardships made the missionary field unattractive to many settled ministers and seminary graduates, especially during the war years. In all of the denominations the need for preachers was greater than the supply of eager candidates. Methodists had larger circuits than they could manage easily. Denominations favoring settled pastors (Roman Catholic, Episcopal, Congregational, and Presbyterian) had to leave some areas unstaffed. Nevertheless, nearly every mining town had either a resident minister or a regularly scheduled circuit rider by 1863. If the denominations had been willing to form union congregations, the clerical staff would almost have sufficed. But denominations competed, each wanting its own congregation in every town. William Crawford sent almost weekly pleas for more ministers to the American Home Missionary Society. Once he wrote,

> I have been sorely disappointed by your letter informing me that no one has been secured to labor with me in Colorado.... Can you not find some man who, by dint of constant persuasion and argument, will be made to feel that it is his duty to come? Cannot Mr. ________ work with someone else, as he did with *me*?

Bishop George Randall scolded eastern Episcopalians for not sending more men,

> Of what avail [is it] to send me across the plains to see the spiritual desolation of the land, with nobody to help me sow that seed, by which the wilderness shall be made to blossom as the rose, and the solitary place shall become glad, and the mountains shall break forth with singing?

Both men wondered why young ministers thought of coming west as a sacrifice whereas doctors, lawyers, merchants, mechanics, and farmers regarded migration as an opportunity for betterment. "Shall not the children of light be as self-denyingly wise as the children of the world?" asked Randall.[16]

Poverty and the meagerness of the clerical force remained problems for some time. Further, churchmen could not find enough places for worship. In 1862, though all of the church organizations in Denver had some sort of hall, only the Episcopalians and the Roman Catholics owned brick buildings. The others rented the Masonic Hall, the court house, or the Apollo Theater. The proprietor of the People's Theater usually loaned his. The Apollo, early situated over a saloon, seated about 300 on rough wooden benches. The stage illuminated by candles served as an altar and the pulpit place. In winter, it had no heat and was extremely cold. The room above the saloon was a poor theater; it made an even worse church. At first, churchmen held services above while regular business went on below in the saloon; in the summer of 1862, however, the Methodists found the saloon dealer willing to suspend business during church hours. This was desirable because the floor had large gaps which admitted the sounds of conviviality from below. Alexander Rankin commented on this: "I could hear them slamming the cards on the table and rattling chips while I preached. It was used week nights for a theatre, not a pleasant place to worship." Albert Richardson remarked that worshippers could hear the clinking of glasses, the rattle of poker chips, and the raucous attempts of boozy revelers at singing.[17]

Langrishe's theaters, which he loaned rent free, although serving much better, were, after all, theaters. Those Protestants who thought the theater sinful doubtless had to readjust their thinking, and even those who approved of the theater found the procedure novel. Maurice Morris tells of attending church at Langrishe's Central City theater.

> I was invited to hear the Bishop of the diocese (I think) preach in the theater, and administer the rite of confirmation to the candidates who might present themselves. And so at three o'clock it came to pass that the parson told the sexton, and the sexton tolled the bell outside the theatre, and at half-past the service began--the curtain being raised. There, sitting in the conventional sofa of the stage, was my Lord Bishop, magnificent in his robes, and with him, of course, an assistant priest. A table placed on the stage, close to the footlights, represented the altar, while near the orchestral seats, a harmonium was placed for the choir, who sat round it, and rendered the musical portion of the service--a large one too--extremely well.[18]

Though many of the congregations did not need to hold services above saloons or in theaters, they often found their assembly halls close to saloons. This constant reminder made the uneasy coexistence of order and disorder even more uneasy. Once Rankin recalled that while preaching in a building near a saloon, "Just as I announced my text I heard a pistol shot, at close of meeting was told a man was killed in the saloon."[19] This problem of finding decent quarters illustrates the juxtaposition of order and chaos, the coexistence of the pious and impious.

Presbyterian Amos Billingsley triumphed over the demon rum when he converted a saloon into a church building. His glee at having "foiled Satan" at the town of Buckskin Joe carried him over some very difficult times in a mountain tour. So elated was he that the following day he spontaneously burst into song and climbed a tree to do his daily devotions, an uncommon performance for a normally solemn man.[20]

The denominations managed to build churches slowly. They had more trouble during the war years than they were to have later. Other problems continued, however.

Though transience declined sharply after 1861, frontiersmen continued to move around a great deal. Some ministers abandoned the field disillusioned or exhausted by the rugged life. Some retired to secular livings. Others felt called elsewhere. Over the decade, more came than went, and Colorado's clergy grew from eleven in 1860, to fifty-four in 1870.[21] Though some congregations withered when clergymen left, most churches managed to secure replacements.

In 1862, Jacob Adriance, worn out and bitter, left Colorado for an assignment in the East. John Chivington chided him, as a soldier deserting the battlefield,[22] even though Chivington himself had left the ministry for the military and politics. But even with Adriance and Chivington departed, Sylvester Lloyd, J. W. Caughlin, William A. Kenney, John Dyer, William H. Fisher, Oliver A. Willard, D. H. Petefish, Charles King, and Baxter C. Dennis all began work in Colorado in 1861 and 1862. Lloyd, Caughlin, Fisher, Petefish, King and Dennis spent just one year in the mountains. Kenney died from diphtheria.[23] Willard, brother of feminist Frances A. Willard, served four years as circuit rider and presiding elder. A frail young man, he seemed unsuited at first for rugged frontier life, but he demonstrated his energy and abilities quickly. Though not so dashing a leader as

Chivington, he proved temperamentally akin to the pioneers. Chivington remarked, "Mr. Willard could preach equal to any young man I ever heard." His education and quick wit made him a good preacher. His early training, influenced by the revivalism and social reformism of Charles Grandison Finney at Oberlin, served him well in Colorado.[24] John Dyer, of whom we shall hear more, came to Colorado on a vacation, fell in love with the country, and spent the rest of his life there.

Methodist policy required frequent circuit changes (often every year) and thus took transience for granted, but many other ministers also moved often. As we have seen, Alexander Rankin left in 1860. Amos Billingsley replaced Rankin the following year. Billingsley's reactions to his new field were not uncommon among new-comers. Billingsley arrived in Denver from his post in Nebraska on April 26, 1861. He registered at a hotel, which, he remarked dyspeptically, stood "in the midst of business and stirring music in the gambling saloons hard by." Denver Presbyterians welcomed him, and about fifty came to the city hall to hear him preach. In three weeks, his congregations had grown to 230, "the largest seen west of the Missouri River," he boasted. Though his earlier anxieties dwindled as he attracted so many eager listeners, he still found the society curiously mixed. Though he liked his congregations and became almost ecstatic about encounters with a few earnest inquirers, the rowdies disgusted him. He worried:

> Strange! Strange that I can live in the midst of so many sinners whose pulse are beating the march to hell--promenading the road to ruin--piling the fagots for their own eternal burning (Lord God of hosts have mercy on me), and feel so little for their salvation.[25]

Billingsley did not stay long, though he truly loved going to the mountain mining camps. He simply could not make a living there. In 1862, he left Colorado first to serve as army chaplain in Ohio and later to work with southern freedmen.

Others came and went in a regular pattern. Thomas A. Smith served the Roman Catholic parish in Central City for almost three years; then, angry about something, he abruptly left the Territory. Presbyterian Lewis Hamilton retired, as did Methodist William Howbert. Replacements arrived from the States or from other areas of Colorado. Alanson R. Day replaced Billingsley; Jean Raverdy left Denver to cover for Smith; George Warner came to shepherd Hamilton's flock.[26] In spite of all this, regular mission work proceeded with a fair degree of continuity and stability.

Not all of the new-comers replaced departing ministers. Some established new missions and others, new denominations. William Crawford brought Congregationalism; William Whitehead established the first regular Baptist assembly; and a Reverend Mr. Magee organized an African Methodist Episcopal church.

Crawford came to Colorado from Massachusetts at the request of Colorado Congregationalists who did not (as some of their number did) want to worship with the Presbyterians. Layman Amos Bixby acted as a representative of partisan Congregationalists when he wrote to the secretary of the American Home Missionary Society that he and his friends felt like "sheep without a shepherd" with "no temple toward which they can turn their faces and pray." Bixby warned, "In a short period of time these mountains and valleys will contain a population of millions; and laggard Congregationalism may not recover its lost ground in the present or any future age of the religious history of Colorado." Other denominations, he continued, were busily spreading the gospel in every mountain camp; "but by-and-by drowsy Congregationalism will come to the realization that a nation was born in a day and it took no note of it." This plea, accompanied by assurance of Colorado's relative social stability, worked. The society drafted Crawford, who regretfully left Massachusetts, abandoned plans for a vacation, and arrived in Central City in June of 1863.[27]

Twenty-five Congregationalists greeted him, and together they organized a church. Crawford surveyed the territory and reported his finding to the A. H. M. S. He judged his late start a great handicap but thought that with additional clergy, he could establish Congregationalism firmly in Colorado. The society officials were neither so eager nor so optimistic as Crawford and refused to send more ministers until Crawford demonstrated the permanence of his Central City assembly.

Despite his enthusiasm, Crawford proceeded cautiously. He decided to enroll "only living, working Christians" as members and to exclude "those calling themselves Congregational but not living as Christians." Even so, his mission proved a success, with the membership remaining stable and service attendance averaging seventy-five each Sunday.[28] Congregationalist growth and expansion before the end of the war was, however, slight. Hampered by lack of clergy and his late start, Crawford concentrated on ministering to those already professed as members of his denomination.

The Baptists established the next new churches in Colorado. Baptists in Golden, a farming village near Denver, organized a church in August, 1863. With William Whitehead in charge, this enterprising group achieved stability. Whitehead left within a year, but his replacement, Thomas Potter of the American Baptist Home Mission Society, came immediately and insured continuity. In December of the same year, Walter McDonald Potter, another agent of the mission society, gathered a small congregation in Denver. Walter Potter came to Colorado partly because the climate was said to be healthy. Probably a tubercular, he failed to recover and died two years after his arrival. But while he lived, he served the Baptists and preached with "culture, refinement, and promise." The congregation remained small throughout his pastorate and for several years thereafter. Early in 1864, the Baptist mission society sent Almond Barelle to revive the congregation established in Central City during the gold rush. Barelle made a hopeful start and did quite well until he fell ill during 1865. Without his leadership, the assembly failed.[29]

Sometime in the mid-sixties, a Reverend Mr. Magee established an African Methodist Episcopal church in Denver. Almost all of the small black community joined and participated. The congregation continued under Magee's leadership for several years. Apparently the church served as a social, economic, and political community as well as a religious assembly. Unfortunately, we know very little about this interesting group.[30]

Though transience seems to have been the norm, a few ministers long-resident in Colorado seem to have had the largest influence on religious and social development. Their work shows how the churches grew and how ministers influenced the social development. An outstanding example was frontier hero John Dyer. His career illustrates how a Methodist minister carried the gospel and his denomination's traditions to frontier towns in Colorado. A revivalist in the tradition of Peter Cartwright and James B. Finley, Dyer's work epitomizes Methodist rural evangelism. Convinced that sinners needed to be frightened into faith, he preached vigorously of hell and damnation as background to his proclamation of God's promises of grace and mercy. He loved preaching and thrived on "protracted meetings." He did his best work in the small mining camps which sprang up around each new discovery. He was happiest walking, sometimes on snow shoes from camp to camp, visiting in every cabin along the way.

Born in Ohio in 1812, when Ohio was frontier, Dyer followed the line of sparse settlement into Illinois, then to Wisconsin. After ordination in 1855, he moved west again to Minnesota. In 1860, his son Elias joined gold rushers to Colorado. The father fell ill in 1861, and he decided to go visit Elias in Denver to recuperate from his illness. He packed his carpet bag and rode to Denver on horseback. Father and son met briefly in the city, but Dyer became restless and decided to venture into the mountains. He pawned his watch, bought supplies, borrowed a buffalo robe from Elias, and set out for Buckskin Joe, fifty miles away in South Park. As soon as he arrived, he began street preaching, held a protracted meeting, and organized a class of twenty men--a real busman's holiday.

Dyer spent the rest of the summer of 1861 in South Park preaching at the camps which flowered around promising strikes. In September, he climbed to California Gulch (later Leadville) and found a Methodist supply preacher about to leave in disgrace. At his request, Dyer agreed to assume the charge of a hundred mile circuit straddling the continental divide. He found only six or seven resident Methodist members in his circuit. Here was the kind of challenge that Dyer liked to meet. For the rest of the mining season, he visited such places as Kent's Gulch, Georgia Bar, Gunnison, and, of course, California Gulch preaching to crowds of over one hundred. When the mines closed because of heavy December snows, Dyer headed for the miners' winter quarters and held "protracted meetings," often lasting ten nights or more.

Dyer was an evangelist at heart, but he was a pastor as well. He cared deeply about the souls of his people and tried to establish classes, as had been his custom elsewhere. But regular meetings did not fit into the transient lives of Colorado mining pioneers, though they might have been managed in Denver. Unable to sustain a group long enough to get a really good class going in the camps, Dyer abandoned this program. Instead, he resorted to cabin by cabin visitation. In the course of these visits, he made hundreds of friends and won the love and respect of almost all. He also developed considerable influence, which he exerted in the interest of both religious faith and good citizenship. For instance, there was a tax assessor in a mountain region who was afraid to enforce the law. Miners had rendered the local government impotent by their refusal to pay taxes. The assessor feared failure and possible violence at the hands of resentful miners. Dyer, known and respected by all, accompanied the assessor on his round, and the official had no trouble. This little vignette, probably repeated often in other circumstances, illustrates the quiet leadership of the pioneer clergy in secular affairs.

Dyer also worked hard to improve miner's morality. His particular targets became dancing and drinking. He bellowed with rage and indignation once when parishioners asked to use the church organ for a dance. He objected to dancing because he felt that it often led to broken marriages. His advocacy of temperance was typical of Methodist ministers in that day. Unlike other pastors, however, he did not object strenuously to card playing--often simply asking gamblers to take a break from their game to attend his sermon. Nor did he oppose gold hunting; in fact, he prospected extensively himself.[31]

Dyer's work brought many seekers, probationers, and members into the Methodist churches over the two and a half decades of his mountain ministry. His specialty seems to have been preaching the gospel in sparsely settled, newly opened territories. Between 1861 and 1872, most of his assignments were to new circuits in South Park, San Luis Park, and New Mexico.[32]

Rural evangelical Protestantism, as practiced by Dyer, was but one (though probably the most distinctive or unique) part of the richly diverse religious scene in nineteenth century America. Though Christianity in frontier Colorado was not remarkably pluralistic, neither was it monolithic. In the six denominations active among Colorado pioneers, one finds several styles of missionizing. Most of these modes, as in Dyer's case, sprang from roots planted in earlier years. Even within Methodism, one finds more than a single style.

Methodists in such towns as Denver and Central City abandoned the camp meeting of rural evangelism for close attention to Christian nurture and education. Even so, Denver and Central City Methodist ministers clung to the hope that large scale revivals would occur, but this seldom happened in the towns even while revivalism continued in rural areas.

During the war years, Methodist church expansion proceeded but very slowly. In 1863, the creation of a Colorado conference separate from the Kansas Conference and the construction of a large Gothic church in Denver gave Colorado Methodists a sense of permanence.[33] But conference records show small increases in the numbers of ministers and circuits.[34] Growth in membership was correspondingly small. Sunday school membership, however, grew steadily.[35] Christian nurture received heavy emphasis among town ministers.

From 1864-1869, Bethuel T. Vincent served as presiding elder of the Denver District, which included all towns of any size. He led the Sunday School movement, and his leadership paid off in a lively concern for religious education among Colorado's clergy and laity. Born in Alabama in 1834, Vincent grew up in Pennsylvania, where his family crusaded for schools and adult education. He studied at the new Garrett Biblical Institute in Evanston, Illinois, and served as minister in that state until he came to Colorado in 1863. There he found Sunday school classes operating with pitifully inadequate study materials. Vincent decided to establish a local periodical for student reading. He edited and wrote much of the paper, which he called the Sunday School Casket.[36] Colorado Methodists also entered the field of general education, as we shall see shortly.

Though the Methodists played a central role, other denominations also expanded and were active in social development. The most visible during the war years were the Roman Catholics and Episcopalians. With their highly structured, sacerdotal, more nearly churchly style, they stand in contrast to the more informal Methodists.

The Roman Catholics quietly flourished under the leadership of Joseph P. Machebeuf, later vicar apostolic and bishop. Since he could not obtain many priests to serve the mining-town parishes, he itinerated about as freely as any Methodist circuit rider, traversing the length and breadth of the mining districts many times during the sixties. He preached and administered the sacraments to many whose only contacts with their church were his periodic visits. His followers loved and revered him, though they probably dozed and yawned through his rambling but gentle sermons.[37]

By his efforts, he drew many into the fold. Machebeuf declared that by 1864 his church in Denver was the strongest of any in the area. A none-too-sympathetic observer, Episcopal Bishop George Randall, commented that in 1866 the Roman Catholic church commanded great strength in Colorado Territory.[38]

As long as the Colorado area fell under the jurisdiction of the Bishop of New Mexico, Machebeuf had no authority to recruit secular or religious clergy. He simply had to take whomever the Bishop could send; but the New Mexican prelate did not have anyone extra to help. Machebeuf did have an able lieutenant in Jean Raverdy, who also itinerated, helped with the Denver parish, and served the church in Central City for several years. Machebeuf enjoyed the services of Thomas A. Smith for three years, and since he spoke English, his presence was a real boon. Machebeuf was quite fortunate in having almost continuous help in the parishes around Conejos in southern Colorado, since this district was so far from Denver that he could not travel there with any regularity.

Despite their small clerical force, Colorado Roman Catholics built three schools before 1870 and acquired land for many more. Most Protestants viewed these schools as a most potent force for winning converts.[39] Catholics saw schools as a means to keep the flock intact and pressed their educational program forward in spite of discouraging obstacles.[40]

The Episcopalians were by no means so numerous as the Methodists and Roman Catholics, but so many key civic leaders adhered to this tradition that the denomination proved to be more important in community projects than size might indicate.

The key figure in Episcopal missions was the missionary bishop. Without him, little mission expansion could take place. In 1859, Episcopal bishops elected Joseph C. Talbot as missionary bishop for the huge diocese, as we have seen. After Talbot's first visitation, he did not return to Colorado until 1862, when John Kehler resigned to become an army chaplain. Then Talbot journeyed to Denver to oversee matters, traveling with his assistant, Isaac Hagar. Denver residents greeted him heartily and turned out in droves to hear him preach. The bishop confirmed several people, bought the chapel built by the Southern Methodists, and set the people to refurbishing and enlarging the building. He guided St. John's vestry to call Horace Hitchings as rector and installed Hagar as temporary rector until Hitchings could arrive from Massachusetts. He then toured the mining camps and towns. A small but lively group of Episcopalians in Central City greeted him with a request to form a parish. Talbot complied and created St. Paul's. He instructed Hagar to visit there regularly until he could find a rector. His tour complete, Talbot returned to his home in Nebraska City.[41]

Affairs in the western territories required the bishop's attention again in the summer of 1863. He took Francis Granger with him to fill the rectorship of St. Paul's in Central City. William O. Jarvis also took up work in nearby mining towns, but neither man stayed long on the Colorado frontier. Talbot consecrated an addition to St. John's, confirmed a class prepared by Hagar, and solicited funds in all established settlements.[42]

Hitchings found life in Colorado very pleasant indeed, but he felt the need of an episcopal visit and sent repeated pleas to Talbot in both 1864 and 1865. Talbot, however, had far more than he could possibly do and had to demur. He did send Alvin B. Jennings to Central City in 1864, when Granger left. Feeling that he could not do his job properly, Talbot begged the delegates to the General Convention of 1865 to redraw diocesan lines and give Colorado a resident bishop. He argued persuasively:

> Every part of this vast field must be traversed, if at all, by horsepower. Between the great centers of population, the country is an unbroken wilderness. The Missionary Bishop must ride 600 miles from Nebraska, over the wilderness, to reach the populated portions of Colorado; 1,000 more to get to Montana; and thence another 1,000 from Montana, through Utah, into Nevada; and in every one of these, even in Utah, now open to missionary labor, his personal labor, his personal presence is required, if the Church is to be established, and the souls to which he is sent are to have the ministrations of the gospel. It surely cannot be that the Protestant Episcopal Church in this country will think her duty done to these portions of her missionary field by leaving them, as they now are, under the care of a single Bishop, resident 2,000 miles from the western limit of his jurisdiction. It would be as reasonable to expect efficient Episcopal over-

> sight and administration of the Diocese of Massachusetts or New York from a Bishop resident in London.[43]

His arguments won the day; the convention created a missionary diocese (including Colorado and Parts Adjacent) and elected George Maxwell Randall as its bishop.[44] Thus, as the Civil War ended Colorado Episcopalians headed by a resident bishop could begin a significant work of church extension, just as the population of the territory began to expand once more.

Presbyterian growth and influence in society bear some resemblance to those of the Episcopalians. Though relatively few in number, the Presbyterians counted some key civic leaders among their members. Presbyterian socials and fund-raising events drew many of Denver's elite and served as models of upright behavior.[45]

As we have seen, the Presbyterians could not expand as they wished without centralized leadership and changes in denominational polity which, in requiring permanence, was better suited to the eastern seaboard than to an advancing and fluctuating frontier. Furthermore, the Presbyterian clergy tended to search out and minister to already professed Presbyterians (as did the Congregationalists), making little effort to widen the circle of their hearers. Curiously, the Presbyterians made no moves to establish schools in the Territory, though they had established many in other semi-frontier regions.

Though church extension during the war years was more restricted than any of the missionaries wanted, they had planted the seed which would sprout and grow in the following years.

Part II

In April, 1865, when the Civil War ended, Colorado clergy and laymen greeted the news with joy. Though no fighting had taken place in the Territory, war had slowed migration and retarded frontier development. During the war, amazing industrial expansion began in northern states. After the war, the expansion became a boom. Many economic benefits of this growth spilled over onto the Colorado frontier. Between 1865 and 1870, Colorado churchmen could deal better with poverty, shortage of ministers, and inadequate buildings.

After the Civil War, migration to Colorado picked up again. The trains of migrants contained more farmers, merchants, and laborers than gold miners.[46] The former groups settled more often than not. Farmers interested in tilling the land and merchants intent on increasing their store supported churches more readily than did transient miners. Though none of the obstacles facing Colorado's pioneer clergy disappeared, all of them diminished between 1865 and 1870.

As Colorado's society stabilized, the field became more attractive to missionaries and seminary graduates. Strong denominational leaders found recruiting much easier after the war. They also raised funds more easily in Colorado and on begging expeditions back East. Buildings went up, and congregations grew.

Congregationalist William Crawford finally managed to secure some aid. A group of Congregationalists in Denver requested a missionary and got ebullient Norman McLeod in late 1864. McLeod, however, soon went on leave to try to convert Mormons in Utah. Crawford, tired of writing letters to the missionary society with no result, went east to recruit for himself and found three Andover men eager to spread the gospel in Colorado. The Andover Band--George Goodrich, Harvey Mellis, and Nathan Thompson--returned with Crawford. The Indian wars were at their height just then, and the ministers rode with shotguns in hand. They did not need them but found the journey very exciting anyway. The young men took up missions in Denver, Empire, and the Boulder Valley when they arrived.[47] They, in turn, urged friends to join them. Goodrich wrote,

> One cannot fully estimate the privilege of laboring in the "regions beyond" until he has heard some of these brethren, in prayer thanking the Lord, with grieving view and tearful eyes, that He has at length heard their prayer and sent them again the Gospel.[48]

Goodrich enjoyed his stay in Denver, where he shepherded McLeod's flock. When McLeod returned, Goodrich left for the East. In 1866, Harvey Mellis died suddenly of heart disease, and William Phipps was sent to replace him. A year later, William Crawford received a call from a

Massachusetts congregation and, feeling he had established Congregationalism on a solid base in Colorado, left. E. P. Tenney, outstanding educator, replaced him.[49]

When Crawford left, the Congregational ministers missed his strong leadership, since Crawford had acted as a de facto missions superintendent. Norman McLeod seemed a likely successor. The missionaries decided to try to change their polity. They held a conference and suggested that the society allow McLeod de jure status as superintendent.[50] As we have seen, eastern authorities blocked the plan. The Congregationalist's effort was significant because it indicates how useful centralized organization was in frontier regions. The Colorado Congregationalists thought that the lack of strong, central leadership hampered their expansion in Colorado.

Even so, the Congregationalists established stable organizations in Denver, Central City, Empire, Georgetown, and Boulder. Four of the groups had small buildings by 1870.[51] Total Congregationalist membership, however, was smaller than the ministers had hoped. Several factors explain the small numbers. First, a small proportion of Colorado's residents in 1870 came from New England, the stronghold of Congregationalism. Second, Crawford and his colleagues maintained stricter discipline than was common among Colorado Christians. Third, the Congregationalists started their program of evangelization late. Frontier missionaries thought that being "first on the ground" was a big advantage, and Congregational missionaries never were. In Colorado they moved into communities with established churches and had to compete for members.

Even though Congregational groups were tiny, the ministers congratulated themselves on the quality of their membership. A high percentage were college educated, and almost all were deeply committed Christians. Furthermore, attendance at Sunday services far exceeded membership. Coloradans were hearing the gospel.[52]

Strong centralized leadership and early possession of the field seem, indeed, to have benefitted Methodists and Roman Catholics. Congregationalists cast envious eyes on their large, active memberships.[53] The Methodists had, even before war's end, established a strong base in Colorado. With a workable polity, support from key civic leaders, and a new sense of stability, Colorado Methodism expanded in the post-war years. As we have seen above, the clerical force grew larger and more nearly permanent. In 1866, only six circuits remained without clerical supervision. There were two church buildings and eleven organized Sunday schools. Members and probationers numbered 331. In the following year, membership increased to 425. In 1868, the number rose to 561. Members built substantial buildings in Central City and Georgetown during 1869, and their numbers rose again to 645. In 1870, 770 people declared themselves as members and probationers. Congregations owned sixteen church buildings, whose combined worth totalled $85,000.[54] These increases indicate a steady growth in Coloradans' interest in religious matters. B. T. Vincent, presiding elder of the Denver District for much of this period, made annual reports that speak of a healthy revival spirit in all of the charges.[55]

Though Methodist circuits were projected over the whole territory at all times, not all were manned at all times and not all were fully organized. By 1870, most of the circuits had achieved some measure of stability. Substantial structures and strong congregations were to be found in Denver, Central City, and Georgetown. Buildings of less permanence were at Black Hawk, Golden, Boulder, Empire, Colorado City, Canon City, Pueblo, and Fairplay.[56]

By and large, the Methodist church operated as an efficient machine with a heart. Slow and steady expansion into new areas, periodic quiet revivals, regular meetings of laity and clergy, vigorous programs in Sunday school education, and a sturdy building program marked its progress throughout the closing years of the pioneer period.

This expansion allowed Methodists to retain their dominance among Protestants. But Roman Catholic growth exceeded even that of the Methodists. Between war's end and summer, 1870, several new priests came. Coloradans established a number of new parishes, and members built many places of worship. Roman Catholicism flourished among the Mexican-American population. A number of "Anglos" also adhered to that tradition. Machebeuf's constant (and none too successful) search for English-speaking, American-trained priests suggests that not all Colorado Roman Catholics were Mexican-American, though most probably were.[57]

Nor was all of the growth due to an expanded clerical force. Indeed, lay people in Golden gathered a congregation and built a chapel months before Machebeuf could send them a priest. In the interim, Machebeuf himself made regular visits to hold services.[58]

Machebeuf's leadership was, without doubt, one of the key factors in Roman Catholic expansion. As we have seen, during the war, he persisted quietly in the face of poverty, transience, and violence that plagued all frontier missionaries. After the war, his program took an aggressive turn. In 1866, he applied to the Baltimore Plenary Council, which in turn petitioned the Congregation of the Propaganda in Rome for the separation of Colorado from New Mexico and the establishment of a new diocesan jurisdiction. Rome moved slowly but finally agreed to the proposal and made Colorado a vicariate apostolic early in 1868. Officials in Rome appointed Machebeuf as vicar apostolic, and he assumed the title of bishop.

Pressed for funds to pay for land and in need of priests, Machebeuf journeyed east before his consecration as bishop. He visited seminaries, where he spoke glowingly of Colorado as a field for service. He preached vigorously in the churches of Baltimore, Washington, Philadelphia, New York, Albany, Buffalo, Cleveland, and Sandusky. There he told of the present needs and future hopes of his territory. He ended his tour in Cincinnati, where he received consecration as bishop on August 16, 1868.

Shortly, he returned to Denver with no new priests and very little money to show for his months of work. But proud Denver citizens welcomed him nonetheless with a parade and reception. The Catholics were proud of their bishop, and the Protestants took pride in Rome's tacit recognition of their performance. Machebeuf returned to his many duties. He toured the territory to confirm the nearly 150 children prepared during his absence. He traveled to Utah, met with Brigham Young, and assessed the possibilities of missions in Utah. Then he once more turned to the personnel problem.[59]

Between 1866 and 1868, the bishop of New Mexico, now Jean B. Salpointe, lent several priests to Machebeuf.[60] Salpointe himself spent some months ministering to Roman Catholics in southern Colorado settlements. None of those from New Mexico mastered English well enough to work effectively in Denver or the mining camps; they all returned to New Mexico.

Since Machebeuf had found no American-trained clergy

on his 1868 tour, he decided to recruit in Europe in 1869. He also needed more money. He toured continental seminaries, made a plea for men and money before the Society for the Propagation of the Faith, and tried to justify his debts to the Pope. Late in 1869, he returned to Denver with five priests and a large loan. Only one of his new clerics spoke English. Machebeuf gave him charge of the Denver parish and sent the others to the Mexican-American parishes in southern Colorado.[61]

Between 1860 and 1870, in spite of all the problems, the Roman Catholic population increased greatly during the sixties. By 1870, Catholics constituted fourteen parishes with buildings capable of seating 8,575 people. Even if the pews were only partly filled each Sunday, the Roman Catholics were by far the most numerous of the Christian groups. This enormous increase almost certainly occurred as a result of migration from New Mexico. Over eight thousand persons born in New Mexico moved to Colorado between 1860 and 1870. All of them may not have been Roman Catholic, but most of them probably were. In this decade, over 90 per cent of the New Mexican population was Roman Catholic.[62]

In his first decade in Colorado, Bishop Machebeuf laid plans for an extensive benevolent network. But most of his projects had to wait until the 1870's and 1880's. However, in the sixties, Catholic societies held fund raising festivals for the projected benevolencies, confident that they could soon build them.[63] Non-Catholic Coloradans generally conceded the worth of such projects and contributed to the funds.

Bishop Machebeuf, ever in need of more men and more money, calculated that he could reach his goals most effectively if he could convince orders of religious clergy to serve under him. Pleas made in the sixties were finally answered in 1871, when Jesuits took over the work in southern Colorado parishes.[64] Their coming freed Machebeuf's men to work in the towns and camps around Denver. This meant that Catholics, like all the other Christians, enjoyed their greatest expansion after the pioneer era was over.

As strong leadership seems to have helped Methodist and Roman Catholic missions, the appointment of a resident bishop seems to have given Colorado's Episcopalians a needed lift. George Randall spent some months after his election drumming up eastern support for his missionary diocese. In

June, 1866, he finally arrived in Denver, bringing with him newly ordained William A. Fuller. The bishop immediately visited all settled outposts in the territory. He decided to recruit priests writing that Colorado "is a field abounding in labor but full of promise, and with God's blessing upon the ministration of the missionary, there is every prospect of success."[65]

Randall set Fuller to work in Nevadaville and left for the East again. He delivered more than two hundred fund raising speeches during his eight month tour. Randall then persuaded four young ministers to accept charges in Colorado. Cortlandt Whitehead, Frank Winslow, William J. Lynd, and Francis Byrne accordingly took up mission work in Black Hawk, Empire, Golden, and Nevadaville.[66]

By 1870, Randall had charge of nine established parishes, which had eight buildings.[67] Though he did not have enough priests for all of them, he assigned care of Idaho Springs and Georgetown to the priest at Empire.

Randall, though a New England brahmin, acquired a folksy frontier manner during his years in Colorado. He learned to joke with cowboys, laborers, and miners and even took an occasional drink with them when invited. He worked effectively with local Masons, too. He proved an efficient administrator even though he allowed near parochial autonomy. His assumption of democratic manners and his desire to allow local authority made him a very popular figure in Colorado.[68]

While the denominations with episcopal polity actively sought to extend their memberships by proselytism, the Presbyterians and Baptists did not. Their leaders worked only to care for those already declared as members. Baptist missions remained small in Colorado throughout the pioneer era. The Baptist pastors often stayed no more than a year. Most Baptist congregations spent months with no clerical leadership at all. The Denver church lost its pastor, Walter Potter when he died in 1865. Eight months passed before Ira D. Clark came to replace him. Clark stayed a year, and during his tenure, he began construction of a church building. But the project was overambitious and work had to be stopped when only the basement had been completed. The Baptists worshipped there and called it the "Church of the Holy Dug-Out."[69] Baptist minister Winfield Scott, arriving in Denver in 1871, described it as "the meanest place for a decent city I ever saw." He declared that the basement was "sufficiently dismal to drive all but the most faithful to other congregations." In fact, it was shunned by "all except those who have good health, Baptist backbone, sufficient nerve and faith to face, enter, and carry on in this pit."[70]

In 1866, Clark presided over the first meeting of the Rocky Mountain Baptist Association, which consisted of six churches claiming an aggregate membership of 159. Clark left Denver in June, 1867. Almost a year later, A. M. Averill became Baptist pastor. He, too, stayed only a year, leaving in May of 1869. Again Denver Baptists had no leader for a full year. In May, 1870, Lewis Raymond came for a year's ministry. During his tenure, Baptists staged their first season of revival. Discontinuity of leadership kept Baptist membership small, but church expansion did occur.[71]

Baptist congregations in the mining camps fared even worse than the one in Denver. Churches established in Canon City by B. M. Adams in 1865 and in Colorado City in 1866 struggled to remain viable but failed. Walter Potter organized a six-member black congregation, Zion Baptist Church in Denver, but the active congregation under Magee attracted the largest portion of Denver's black citizens, leaving the Baptist group very small.[72]

Presbyterian missions in the post-war era concentrated on establishing congregations for Presbyterians rather than proselytizing. However, Sheldon Jackson shook up the Presbyterians when he assumed the position of missions superintendent in 1869 and began an aggressive campaign to win more members. Between war's end and Jackson's arrival, Presbyterian expansion proceeded rather slowly. With a comparatively large clerical force,[73] Presbyterians continued work in Denver, Central City, and Black Hawk, and established churches at Idaho Springs and Boulder Valley. New School-Old School division retarded the expansion, as did a policy requiring evidence of stability before organization. Furthermore, Presbyterians had no centralized leadership, so important on moving frontiers.

Sheldon Jackson, an aggressive and impatient missionary in Iowa, felt fettered by Presbyterian policy. Predicting correctly that railroad extension into the Far West would create a population boom and observing that centralized leadership aided church extension in frontier regions, he lobbied vigorously for the creation of a superintendency of missions. The Board of Missions refused him from 1865 to 1869.

Jackson said of this opposition, "When first such an office was proposed it was looked upon by many as a step toward papacy--or at least toward prelacy."[74] But they capitulated in 1869, as negotiations to reunite the Old and New Schools were drawing to a close. Though officials gave Jackson his superintendency, they granted him no money, perhaps reasoning that a centralized authority without funds could do little to change congregational autonomy. Jackson, however, plunged forward and assumed charge of Iowa, Nebraska, Wyoming, Colorado, Utah, and Montana. He proved to be such a good fund-raiser that he and his lieutenants did not need much support from the Board of Missions.[75]

Jackson's methods included assignment of missionaries to railroad lines and temporary railroad towns, quick organization without proof of community permanence, and centralized leadership of all missions. He roamed the Rocky Mountains for a decade, establishing congregations in all settlements, no matter how small or how transient their population. He effectively changed Rocky Mountain Presbyterian missions from traditional Presbyterian patterns to an almost Methodist model.[76]

Though most of his achievements belong to the 1870's, he began his work in Colorado in 1869. In 1869-70, he traveled 29,000 miles and organized twenty-three churches (seven of them in Colorado). All were small (four to ten members) and of doubtful permanence. Jackson believed that the West might soon become the most important part of the country, but he did not think this would happen without promotion. He, therefore, launched a publicity campaign for Colorado and the Rocky Mountain West that any railroad company would have envied.[77] Jackson does not belong to Colorado's era of frontier isolation; he belongs to the railroad boom era. His work in the months before the trains came was, then, a foreshadowing.

When the new age began, Colorado was no longer a gold rush society. Over the 1860's, civilizers had created communities almost like those in the Midwest.[78] Further, they had laid down social patterns that persisted even as rails brought on industrial boom. A measure of progress of the process of civilizing may be seen in analysis of ecclesiastical growth between 1860 and 1870.

In June, 1860, eleven ministers lived in Colorado. Church people had organized at least six and, perhaps, as many as ten small congregations by the end of the year. Few had the resources, materials, or permanence to erect church buildings, and almost all held meetings and services in log cabins, saloons, theaters, court rooms, and lodge halls. However, in 1860, Southern Methodists built a chapel in Denver, and Roman Catholics managed to build a small church, which they consecrated on Christmas Eve, 1860.[79]

Throughout the sixties, missionaries successfully established many more congregations, membership increased, several missions became self-supporting, and most congregations managed to build places of worship. By 1870, census takers found that church congregations and parishes numbered fifty-six and resident clergymen, fifty-four.[80] Though the population had increased by less than five thousand or 16.2 percent since 1860, the number of ministers had quintupled, and the number of church organizations had mushroomed similarly. Though there is no completely reliable measure of the increase in church membership and participation, denominational statistics give us an approximate and partial view.

We have already seen how the Methodists grew steadily over the decade under study.[81] Not only did the churches grow, but the character of the churches and communities changed. Membership and attendance increased at the same time that families began to make up a large part of the population. Methodist Sunday School statistics confirm this finding. Throughout the years under consideration, the numbers of Sunday School children expanded steadily. In 1860, there were none. In 1861, clergy reported 212; in 1862, 233; in 1863, 409; in 1865, 556; in 1866, 676; in 1867, 885; in 1868, 754; in 1869, 1,290; and in 1870, 1,555.[82]

Membership statistics tell only a part of the story of churchly participation in the nineteenth century. Though churches often had few members, flourishing congregations appeared each Sunday; attendance often exceeded membership. Congregationalists and Presbyterians regularly reported attendance figures which amounted to more than three times the number enrolled.[83] Other denominations requiring some form of declaration of membership or a marked conversion experience recorded similar disparities in membership and attendance. On former frontiers, church communities had required strict discipline and barred from communion or fellowship those who did not live up to some standard of moral behavior. Such people felt the need to go to church but would not join. Often, only one member of a family joined even though all attended. In 1870, Methodist churches could hold 3,815 people, but Methodist society members and probationers totalled only 770.[84] Since building materials and church funds were scarce, the pioneers did not erect buildings larger than they needed. New buildings usually were full at the first services and inadequate soon after, much as today's city freeways.

Despite shortages, town dwellers built churches as soon as they could. In early days, they competed for the few buildings available. Sometimes they had to cancel services for lack of a meeting place. Most agreed with Henry Kendall, general secretary of the New School Presbyterian mission society, when he wrote, "An edifice is an indispensable necessity to every congregation before it can become self-sustaining, or give the community the impression of permanency and success."[85] Therefore, congregations zealously erected structures to convince their neighbors and prospective settlers of the stability and permanence of their organizations. Boosterism, both civic and denominational, accounts in part for energetic building programs. By 1870, Colorado church people had erected many edifices, forty-seven of which were standing and in use; only eight groups had to rent. These buildings could seat about 44 percent of the people in the territory; the seating capacity totalled 17,495.[86] In ten years, they had built all but two of these, many several times because the wooden structures often burned. Since almost every congregation held two services and Sunday School each Sabbath and since many had week night meetings, it is possible that half or more of the population attended worship on a regular basis. This rather startling hypothesis contrasts sharply with the legendary picture of the frontier as a godless wilderness.

As civilization advanced and the people consolidated their institutions, more and more people joined churches and attended church services and social events. They also supported benevolencies with enthusiasm. Between 1860 and 1870, the number of church organizations increased dramatically as we have seen, to fifty-five.[87] The rise in church attendance and other religious activity demonstrates the extent to which the Colorado frontier had changed from a society of adventuresome and lonely miners known to be violent, profane, wordly, and intemperate to a group of communities conforming to standards judged to be civilized and moral.

NOTES

1. Materialism, in this context, means belief that the most important values are to be found in the furtherance of material progress and well-being. It includes but is more than simple greed. Secularism is a habit of mind which emphasizes the worldly and temporal over against the religious and ecclesiastical.

2. Though mining continued after 1861, the rush of amateur miners diminished when the war began. Gold hunters, in small numbers, migrated to Colorado after 1861. But most mining was done by experienced laborers in the hire of large absentee owners. The bulk of the migrants after 1861 were farmers, merchants, craftsmen, laborers, and their families. They naturally thought the gold hunting interesting and many staked claims to dig on the weekends or during their spare time. Few of them actually hit pay dirt, and none of them could extract the gold from the heavy, refractory quartz in which most precious metals are enclosed.

3. Bayard Taylor, p. 59.

4. William Phipps to Dr. Badger, January 15, 1867, Letter, A. H. M. S. correspondence.

5. Randall, First Report, p. 9.

6. Francis Byrne, Memoir, ms., Colorado State Historical Society, Denver, p. 49.

7. Ibid.

8. Daniel S. Tuttle, Reminiscences of a Missionary Bishop (New York: T. Whittaker, 1906), pp. 70-72.

9. Rocky Mountain News, August 28, 1865.

10. Tuttle, pp. 70-72.

11. Tuttle, p. 70.

12. Kehler, Diary, January 30, 1861, June 3, 1862.

13. A. H. M. S., Correspondence, Colorado File, 1863-70,

passim; Andrew Murray, Skyline Synod (Denver: Golden Bell Press, 1971), pp. 11-12.

14. Dyer, Snow Shoe Itinerant, pp. 163-78.

15. Howlett, Life of Machebeuf, pp. 334, 362.

16. Crawford to Badger, September 18, 1863, Letter, A. H. M. S. Correspondence; Randall, pp. 19-21.

17. Rankin, quoted in E. P. Wells, "Historical Sketch of Central Presbyterian Church" (Denver: Published privately, 1891), p. 5; Richardson, p. 306.

18. Morris, p. 131.

19. Rankin, in Wells, p. 5.

20. Billingsley, Journal, July 14-19, 1862.

21. U. S. Census, 1860, p. 549; U. S. Dept. of the Interior, Census Bureau, Ninth Census of the United States, 1870, Vol. I, p. 723.

22. Chivington, "Footprints. . .," Rocky Mountain Christian Advocate (October 31, 1889), p. 2.

23. Annual Conference Minutes of the Methodist Episcopal Church, 1863, pp. 22, 130-31.

24. Chivington, "Footprints. . .," Rocky Mountain Christian Advocate, November 7, 1889, p. 2; Frances Willard, Glimpses of Fifty Years (Chicago: H. J. Smith & Co., 1889), pp. 60-61, 85.

25. Billingsley, Journal, April 26, 27, 28, May 5, 12, 14, June 7, 11, 1861.

26. Howlett, Life of Machebeuf, p. 325; Murray, Skyline Synod, p. 45; Annual Conference Minutes, 1861-1870; Breck, The Episcopal Church in Colorado, pp. 1-104; A. H. M. S. Correspondence, Colorado File, 1863-1870; Walter Hopkins et al., The Bible and the Gold Rush (Denver: Big Mountain Press, 1963), pp. 11-46.

27. Amos Bixby to Mr. Reed, April 25, 1863, Letter, A. H. M. S. Correspondence; Hopkins, pp. 17-19.

28. William Crawford to Mr. Badger, July 13, 1863, Letter; Report to the Society, March, 1864, A. H. M. S. Correspondence.

29. Olsen, pp. 146-58; quotation in Eugene Parsons, "Mother of Churches," ms., Colorado State Historical Society, Denver, pp. 3, 7; Rocky Mountain News, January 4, February 18, 1865; April 11, 1866.

30. Rocky Mountain News, April 11, 1865.

31. Dyer, pp. 14-261.

32. Annual Conference Minutes of the Methodist Episcopal Church, 1861-1872.

33. Ibid., 1863, pp. 130-31.

34. Between 1861 and 1865, the Methodist ministerial force grew from 7 to 10. By 1870, the total reached 18. Though such increases are not staggering, an interesting trend toward permanence appears as one examines the record:

Year	New Ministers	Ministers Resident For One Year or More	Total
1861-62	5	2	7
1862-63	5	2	7
1863-64	3	3	6
1864-65	4	4	8
1865-66	3	7	10
1866-67	1	7	8
1867-68	2	7	9
1868-69	2	7	9
1869-70	9	9	18

35. See Table II, Appendix C, p. 229.

36. Bethuel T. Vincent, Papers, ms., Colorado State Historical Society, Denver.

37. Howlett, pp. 291-96, 325-27, 341, 369, 413; William H. Jones, The History of Catholic Education in the State of Colorado (Washington: Catholic University of America Press, 1955), p. 72.

38. Howlett, p. 314; Randall, pp. 15-17, 23. Though no

membership statistics are available to document these observations, one may conclude from religious censi of 1870 and later that growth proceeded rather steadily throughout the sixties.

39. See for example, Randall, pp. 16-17.

40. See pp. 125-27.

41. Joseph C. Talbot, Diary, May-August, 1862; Rocky Mountain News, June 22, 30, July 5, 14, 19, 21, 24, 26, 1862.

42. Talbot, Journal, 1863.

43. General Convention Journal of the Protestant Episcopal Church, U. S. A., 1865, p. 321.

44. Breck, pp. 29-30.

45. See p. 136.

46. U. S. Census, 1870, Vol. I. p. 723.

47. Norman McLeod to Dr. Badger, August 8, 1864; Jonathan Blanchard to Dr. Badger, October 3, 1864; McLeod to Badger, November 15, 1864; McLeod to Badger, January 5, 1865; William Crawford to Badger, March 8, 1865; Nathan Thompson to Badger, January 22, 1866; G. D. Goodrich to Badger, February 21, 1866, Letters, A. H. M. S. Correspondence.

48. Goodrich to Badger, February 21, 1866, Letter, A. H. M. S. Correspondence.

49. McLeod to Badger, December 8, 1867; Crawford to Badger, June 1, 1866; William Phipps to Badger, January 15, 1867; E. P. Tenney to ________, October 12, 1868, Letters, A. H. M. S. Correspondence.

50. E. P. Tenney to ________, October 12, 1868; E. P. Tenney, to the Secretaries of the American Home Missionary Society, October 27, 1868, Letters, A. H. M. S. Correspondence.

51. A. H. M. S. Correspondence, 1864-1870; U. S. Census, 1870, Vol. II, p. 531. The A. H. M. S. records and the census do not agree on the number of organizations. In this instance, I accept the society's testimony as more reliable, since the missionaries were in a better position to report accurately.

52. For example, see Nathan Thompson to Badger, January 22, 1866; Thompson to Badger, March Report, 1867; Phipps to Badger, April 15, 1867; Thompson to Badger, May 15, 1867; G. D. Goodrich to Badger, June Report, 1867; Thompson to Badger, July 16, 1867; Crawford to Badger, July 26, 1867; Phipps to Badger, July 30, 1867; *et passim* A. H. M. S. Correspondence, 1868-70.

53. Crawford to Badger, July 13, August 7, 31, November 12, 1863; November 16, 1864, *et passim*, Letters, A. H. M. S. Correspondence.

54. *Annual Conference Minutes of the Methodist Episcopal Church*, 1866, pp. 121-22; 1867, p. 141; 1868, pp. 165-66; 1869, pp. 148-49; 1870, pp. 156-57.

55. B. T. Vincent, Report of the Denver District, 1869-70, ms., State Historical Society of Colorado, Denver, p. 1.

56. *Annual Conference Minutes of the Methodist Episcopal Church*, 1870, pp. 156-57.

57. Howlett, pp. 340-46, 354-60.

58. *Ibid.*, p. 328.

59. *Ibid.*, p. 345.

60. They were Frs. Faure, DeBliecke, and Matthonet.

61. Howlett, pp. 353-63.

62. U. S. Census, 1870, Vol. I, pp. 335, 531, 548, 328-42; Ralph E. Twitchell, *The Leading Facts of New Mexican History*, Vol. II (Cedar Rapids, Iowa: The Torch Press, 1912), pp. 349-55, 395, 426, 482-88.

63. Howlett, p. 341.

64. Manuel Espinosa (ed.), "The Opening of the First Jesuit Mission in Colorado," Mid-America, Vol. XVIII (1936), pp. 272-75.

65. Randall, p. 9.

66. Breck, pp. 35-40.

67. U. S. Census, 1870, Vol. I, p. 531. Episcopal parishes were situated in Denver, Central City, Black Hawk, Empire, Golden, Nevadaville, Pueblo, Idaho Springs, and Georgetown.

68. See Owen Wister, The Virginian (New York: Grosset & Dunlap, 1902). One of the minor characters in this novel of the West is said to have been modelled on Bishop Randall. The Bishop is portrayed as a genial man, popular with the cowboys, in contrast to a rigid, censorious circuit rider.

69. Parsons, "Mother of Churches," pp. 2-6.

70. Quoted in Olsen, pp. 197-98.

71. Parsons, "Mother of Churches," pp. 2-6; Baptist membership in Denver grew from nine in 1864 to forty-three in 1870. Totals for the years include nine in 1864, seventeen in 1865, eighteen in 1866, thirty-one in 1867, thirty-two in 1868, thirty-three in 1869, and forty-three in 1870.

72. Olsen, pp. 152-63.

73. Presbyterians at work in Colorado between 1865 and 1870 included Alanson R. Day (Denver), Lewis Hamilton (retired), George W. Warner (Central City), Theodore Marsh (Central City and Black Hawk), George Rice (Idaho Springs), C. M. Campbell (Boulder Valley), J. B. McClure (Denver), Albert F. Lyle (Black Hawk), George S. Adams (Black Hawk and Pueblo), Ambrose Y. Moore (Denver), Edward P. Wells (Denver), H. E. Hamilton (Black Hawk), Sheldon Jackson (Supt.), and W. Y. Brown (Denver).

74. Quoted by Andrew Murray, "A History of Presbyterianism in Colorado," Th. D. dissertation, Princeton Theological Seminary, 1947, p. 33.

75. Robert Stewart, Sheldon Jackson: Pathfinder and Prospector of the Missionary Vanguard in the Rocky Mountains and Alaska (New York: Fleming H. Revell Co., 1908), pp. 93-135.

76. Ibid.

77. Ibid.; see also two dissertations based on Jackson's correspondence and clippings: Alvin K. Bailey, "The Strategy of Sheldon Jackson in Opening the West for National Missions, 1860-1880," unpublished Ph. D. dissertation, Yale University, 1948, and Thomas S. Goslin, "Henry Kendall and the Evangelization of a Continent," unpublished Ph. D. dissertation, University of Pennsylvania, 1948.

78. See pp. 58-64.

79. See Chapter 2, pp. 36, 40.

80. U. S. Census, 1870, Vol. I, pp. 723, 531.

81. See pp. 80, 86.

82. Annual Conference Minutes of the Methodist Episcopal Church, 1860-70; All of the scholars may not have been children. Some adults attended Sunday school as well. However, the bulk of the enrollment was probably children.

83. See, for example, Rankin, Diary, 1860; Billingsley, Journal, 1861-62; Crawford, March Report to A. H. M. S., 1863.

84. U. S. Census, 1870, Vol. I, p. 531; Annual Conference Minutes of the Methodist Episcopal Church, 1870, p. 157.

85. Quoted by Thomas S. Goslin, "Henry Kendall and the Evangelization of a Continent," unpublished Ph. D. dissertation, University of Pennsylvania, 1948, p. 90.

86. U. S. Census, 1870, Vol. I, p. 531.

87. U. S. Census, 1870, Vol. I, p. 531. The denominational

distribution was as follows:

Denomination	No. of Buildings	Congregations	Sittings
Roman Catholic	14	14	8, 575
Methodist	14	14	3, 815
Episcopal	8	9	2, 000
Presbyterian	5	6	1, 200
Congregational	4	4	1, 050
Baptist	4	5	855
Disciples	-	2	---
A. M. E. (?)	-	1	---

No information is available on the two Disciples' congregations.

CHAPTER 5

THE MISSIONARIES AT WORK: PREACHING, REVIVALS, AND SOCIAL REFORMS

Imbedded in the culture, religion constituted a powerful formative force in the developing communities of Colorado. In the late 1850's and in the 1860's, ministers had enormous influence. As Timothy Smith puts it:

> There is abundant factual witness to the immense power of the clergy.... Clergymen inspired the dominant social movement of the period, the crusade for humanitarian reform, at every stage. They were the principal arbiters of manners and morals and the most venerated citizens of every community.[1]

Frontiersmen, eager to build replicas of established American towns, had little interest in stripping the clergy of its importance. On the contrary, they looked to the missionaries to lead their civilizing enterprises. Many laymen wanted the ministers to create order and morality, while the laity worked in the economic and political realms.

But the clergy did more than oversee order and morality. First, ministers provided the uprooted people with a link to tradition. The churches furnished a tie to the living past. Second, the ministers and churches supplied a sense of group identity. In migration, group identity got lost. Without it, there was chaos; with it, order became possible. The pioneer churches, established and nurtured by the missionaries, became a social matrix out of which community order grew. The traditional tasks of clergy and churches issued from this matrix, too.

The missionary task was partly unique and partly traditional. The new function was to serve as an ordering force; the old included preaching the gospel, administering the sacraments, caring for the poor, the sick, and the helpless, comforting the spiritually afflicted, guiding seekers, and encouraging holy living or Christian perfection. The ministers saw the traditional roles as the most important ones. But in order to do these tasks, they needed to establish some kind of order. Their major job was to Christianize the people, but their prior task was to civilize them. Since most of the pioneers and miners came from civilized communities and wanted to create similar ones in the mountain wilderness, the missionaries had to help in creating ordered society rather than imposing the American brand of civilization on another life style, as missionaries to the Pacific Islands did, for example.

Success came quickly--much more rapidly than most of the missionaries dreamed possible. They had little trouble forming small, intimate groups which gave lonely pioneers a sense of group identity. The groups grew every year, as we have seen above.[2] From the first, even while transients came and went, missionaries found ready hearers for their preaching of the holy Word. Preaching and urging holy living were the most important societal functions of the Protestant pioneer clergy after congregations had been formed. The Roman Catholics concentrated less on preaching and more on sacramental piety and education. Through these the missionaries helped shape the lives of those in their congregations and the larger community, for the church members then carried something of their religion into other aspects of communal living.

What did the pioneer church-goers hear from the pulpit? We cannot examine the contents of early sermons, for almost all of the missionaries spoke extemporaneously. Even those accustomed to written sermons threw them away.[3] The tale of a visiting dignitary illustrates why. An archdeacon from the East, visiting the frontier dropped his bag into a stream while fording it. He and his assistant carefully hung their belongings, including the sermons, up to dry. But a sudden thunderstorm drenched them again. Thereafter the archdeacon preached extemporaneously. His host remarked that the experience had been a blessing, for the man's sermons were never dry again.[4] Though this is probably a tall tale, the point is valid. Written sermons had little place in the lives of traveling preachers, and western congregations came to see this as a positive virtue.

Even though the lack of manuscripts for study limits us, clues appear in other sources. Diary notations of sermon texts are helpful, as are recordings of titles. Newspaper reporters and observers left some descriptions of sermon styles and contents.

Two main themes appear to have dominated Protestant preaching on this frontier: human sinfulness and divine redemption of repentent sinners. Most of the preachers chose texts from the New Testament to deal with these themes. A few selected occasional Old Testament passages, usually from the promissory sections of Isaiah. The ministers often chided the miners for caring too much about riches. They emphasized the transitoriness of earthly delights and exhorted them to turn their attention to Christ the redeemer. As a means to salvation, they urged repentance, followed by orderly behavior.

Jacob Adriance is characteristic in his selection of themes. He told "the story of the Lamb of God that taketh away the sins of the world and who giveth the true riches that fade not away," Peter Winne recalled.[5] Accordingly, his favorite text was John 3.16: "For God so loved the world, that he gave his only begotten Son, that whosoever believeth in him should not perish, but have everlasting life." He encouraged the miners to hear the Word as the necessary means to salvation. He spoke several times on Matthew's verse, "And what was sown in good ground means the man who listens to the message and understands it," and, he added, does not worry about being rich. Concern for riches chokes out the gospel message, the preacher concluded. Adriance spent considerable time chiding the greedy miners about their materialism, because he believed that people seeking gold forget God and thereby forfeit salvation.

In another sermon about money, he reminded the congregation of the story in Matthew about the slave who insisted that his friend repay a small debt just after the master had forgiven him an enormous debt. When Christ forgives us our huge sins, it is wrong to insist that mere monetary debts be paid. Again, greed for gold makes people forget charity. He quoted from Luke in another discourse on rapaciousness. His text was, "Take heed, and beware of covetousness, for a man's life consisteth not in the abundance of the things which he possesseth." Adriance sought to turn the men toward the spiritual values even in the gold fields. He did not try to deflect the miners from their search but tried to help them put wealth in a proper perspective.

Adriance not only tried to dissuade the miners from undue acquisitiveness but also wanted to persuade them to live by all of God's commands, including doing good, living soberly and seriously, and obeying the laws. He hoped to make an impression on rowdy adventurers in sermons based on Acts 8.22-23: "So repent of this wickedness of yours, and pray to the Lord, to see if you may not be forgiven for thinking of such a thing. For I see that you are a bitter poison and a bundle of iniquity!" His exhortations to put aside sin and beg for salvation rested on the premise that people can and should avoid temptations and that such abstinence would bring forgiveness. He probably told his hearers of the rewards for seeking Christian perfection when he preached from James 1.12: "Blessed is the man that endureth temptation; for when he is tried, he shall receive the crown of life, which the Lord hath promised to them that love him."

The kind of life he wanted for the miners and for himself appears in his choice of sermon texts on righteousness. A description of an orderly, godly community which Adriance hoped to see established in this "strange land" may be found in Romans 5.1: "So as we have been made upright by faith, let us live in peace with God, through Lord Jesus Christ, by whom we have been introduced through faith to the favor of God." Another text from which Adriance probably began exhortation to improved morality was Deuteronomy 10.12-13: "And now, O Israel, what does the Lord your God require of you but to fear the Lord your God, walk in all his ways, love him, serve the Lord your God with all your mind and heart, by keeping the commands of the Lord and his statutes that I am commanding you today for your good?"

But another theme upon which the young man preached often indicates that he probably did not succeed too well in improving miners' morals or values. He frequently read verses of lament about those who do not hear the message. For instance, in his farewell sermon he chose Isaiah 48.18: "If only you had hearkened to my commands, then would your welfare have been like a river, and your righteousness like the waves of the sea." Adriance spoke of his discouragement and exhaustion as he left the territory. Though he had been able to gather hearers, he felt that too few had truly heard, understood, and done what the gospel commanded.[6]

John M. Chivington is said to have preached direct, simple exhortations with little attention to doctrine and much to personal uprightness in the community context. His sermon texts, as recorded by Jacob Adriance, center on the theme of Christ's suffering for the redemption of the holy. That this ebullient man should concentrate on Christ's suffering and the afterlife of the blessed seems contradictory. However, this very emphasis may have given depth to his otherwise pragmatic approach.

Chivington's first sermon in Colorado was based on the verse, "It must needs be that Christ should suffer." Shortly, he began a sermon with a similar passage. He read from Luke 24.46-47: "And Jesus said unto them, Thus is it written, and thus it behoved Christ to suffer, and to rise from the dead the third day; And that repentance and remission of sins should be preached in his name among all nations, beginning at Jerusalem." As he began his ministry in the mountain camps, he thus reminded his hearers that his mission came from God for the purpose of leading sinners to redemption.

On a later occasion, he told his listeners that human affliction of the moment is slight when it is in the service of Christ. His text was II Corinthians 4.17: "For our light affliction, which is but for a moment, worketh for us a far more exceeding and eternal weight of glory." Since this sermon was delivered shortly after the beginning of the Civil War, it is possible that he was speaking to the current issue of the day and reminding the people that their difficulties would lead to the abolition of slavery and the preservation of the Union. If he did not talk of these things that day, he certainly did on other occasions, as we shall see.

On the afterlife, he often referred to Isaiah. Early in his ministry in Colorado, he preached on Isaiah 35.8-9: "And an highway shall be there, and a way, and it shall be called the way of holiness; the unclean shall not pass over it; but it shall be for those: the wayfaring men, though fools, shall not err therein." For those who followed the holy way, in this life, the next shall be glorious. "No lion shall be there, nor any ravenous beast shall go up thereon, it shall not be found there; but the redeemed shall walk there." Thus, shall the redeemed escape the afflictions of this world when they shall go into the kingdom which is to be.

Another sermon based on the hereafter began with a reading from Psalm 27.4: "One thing have I desired of the Lord, that will I seek after; that I may dwell in the house of the Lord all the days of my life, to behold the beauty of the Lord, and to enquire in his temple." Again he spoke of either the hereafter or the presence of God in the church when he began a sermon based on Psalm 122. 1: "I was glad when they said unto me, Let us go into the house of the Lord."

Chivington dwelt sometimes on the Old Testament prophecies. One favorite sermon text that follows a prophecy of the coming of the savior and the subjection of nature's wilderness was Isaiah 11. 9: "They shall not hurt nor destroy in all my holy mountain; for the earth shall be full of the knowledge (glory) of the Lord, as the waters cover the sea."

Perhaps most nearly characteristic of Chivington's sermon content was a passage from John 1. 36: "Behold the Lamb of God!" Chivington's flamboyance and dramatic flair seem to be solidly based in a devotion to the prophetic promises of both covenants,[7] though advocacy of social reform also engaged his attention, as we shall see later.

John Kehler, whose most active preaching years coincided with those of Adriance, seems to have been far less discouraged by his hearers' reception of the Word, even though the crowds he gathered were considerably smaller. Kehler, characterized as an effective but not especially powerful preacher, chose different themes and texts. His primary emphasis was upon the saving power of Christ. He seems to have made no particular effort in sermons to chide the miners for their rapaciousness. His favorite text came from I Corinthians 1. 23: "But we preach Christ crucified, unto the Jews a stumbling-block, and unto the Greeks foolishness." Almost all of his texts dealt with Christ's redeeming incarnation.

When Kehler preached in the mountain mining camps, he chose texts from the sections of Isaiah promising redemption through a messiah. In both camp and town, he spoke from other New Testament texts which promised God's blessings. He quoted Jesus' words recorded in John 16. 33: "These things I have spoken unto you, that in me ye might have peace. In the world ye shall have tribulations: but be of good cheer; I have overcome the world." These final words in Jesus' farewell to his disciples follow a long passage of promises about the coming of the spirit and comforter. Kehler's texts dealt with Christ's victory over worldly things and death.

Though he seldom chided the miners or the townsmen for remiss behavior, he did remind his hearers that Christ saved people in order that they might do good. He preached from Paul's letter in which Paul tells Titus to exhort the people to act soberly and devoutly because Jesus Christ "gave himself for us, that he might redeem us from all iniquity and purify unto himself a peculiar people, zealous of good works." The choice of this particular verse (2.14) seems especially apt among a group of people, many of whom regarded themselves as a peculiar or chosen people sent to make the wilderness blossom.[8]

While Kehler emphasized redemption, his bishop Joseph C. Talbot preached often on Christ's love. His favorite source for texts was I Corinthians 13. Two frequently used texts were: "And though I bestow all my goods to feed the poor, and though I give my body to be burned, and have not charity, it profiteth me nothing" and "Now abideth faith, hope, charity, these three; but the greatest of these is charity."

He firmly believed that love of God and love of man could be practiced best through the sacraments of the Episcopal church. He spent many sermon hours explaining the usages and practices of his denomination. To introduce his discourse on the eucharist, he chose I Corinthians 11.26: "For as often as ye eat this bread, and drink this cup, ye do show the Lord's death till he come." At baptisms and confirmations, he preached from Mark 16.16: "He that believeth and is baptized shall be saved; but he that believeth not shall be damned." Another text on baptism was Acts 8.36: "And as they went on their way, they came unto a certain water; and the eunuch said, See, here is water; what doth hinder me to be baptized."

Talbot's lectures on Anglicanism and its sacraments usually drew large crowds in the towns and villages. Most of those attending came from other traditions but seemed curious about Talbot and interested in his discourses. A visitor to the country heard Talbot in Central City and exclaimed,

> I do not think I ever heard a more temperate and charitable defence of the formulas of the Church... than I heard in the sermon preached by Bishop Talbot, from the text, "What mean ye by this service?"[9]

On another occasion, hundreds of Denver citizens appeared to hear the bishop launch out against the heretical teachings of the Socians and the Unitarians. A reporter from the Rocky Mountain News pronounced it to be "a clear, logical, and lively discourse." The writer continued:

> His style is calculated to interest a congregation and chain their attention to the close. While not what critics might call truly eloquent or soul-stirring as a speaker, his Reverence is a good orator and rhetorician, and seems like just the man who is needed at this time to successfully build up the interests of the Church in this town and Territory.... The sermon yesterday morning was rather on the doctrinal and didactic order. Unitarianism and Socianism each received a volley of argument that seemed to silence their batteries of error and unbelief.[10]

Talbot chose a number of texts which might have been the starting place for sermons on good works. A discourse on upright behavior could very well have followed his reading from Jeremiah 6.16: "Thus saith the Lord, Stand ye in the ways, and see, and ask for the old paths, where is the good way, and walk therein, and ye shall find rest for your souls." He probably urged miners and townsmen to live pious lives when he spoke on I Timothy 4.8: "Godliness is profitable unto all things, having promise of the life that now is and of that which is to come."

Salvation and how to attain it seem to have been themes of importance to Talbot. He began several talks with a quotation from Acts 16.30: "And [Paul] brought them out, and said, Sirs, what must I do to be saved?" The answer given in the next verse is to believe in Christ Jesus. Another text with the same theme served as a frequent choice: "This is a faithful saying, and worthy of all acceptation, that Christ Jesus came into the world to save sinners" (I Timothy 1.15). In return for salvation, the bishop probably told his hearers, one must give himself to God, as Paul urged his Roman correspondents: "I beseech you therefore, brethren, by the mercies of God, that ye present your bodies a living sacrifice, holy, acceptable unto God, which is your reasonable service." Talbot appears to have urged Coloradans to concern themselves with grace, salvation, godly living, and love.

On the occasion of the consecration of St. John in the Wilderness' new chapel, the bishop chose a particularly interesting text from I Kings:

> I have surely built thee an house to dwell in,
> a settled place for thee to abide in for ever....
> But will God indeed dwell on the earth?
> behold, the heaven and heaven of heavens cannot
> contain thee;
> how much less this house that I have builded?

To frontiersmen bursting with pride at their new brick building rising above the almost barren prairie, a sermon based on such a text probably reminded them that God is great, man is small, human efforts no matter how grand are nothing compared with God's creative and sustaining activities.[11]

Talbot's successor, George M. Randall, preached on a variety of texts reiterating many of the same themes. One rather obscure choice appeared several times in his list of texts: "As your example in wholesome instruction, keep before you what you learned from me, in the faith and love that come through union with Christ Jesus." This passage from II Timothy 1.13 weaves together an injunction to godly behavior and a reminder of Christ's redemption of those who are faithful and loving.[12]

Cortlandt Whitehead, later bishop in Pennsylvania, began his preaching career in Black Hawk as one of Randall's lieutenants. More than any other preacher in his denomination in Colorado, he deplored the avid search for wealth in the gold mines and real estate. He exhorted ambitious men to remember the transience of material things. Not surprisingly, he often chose as text Luke's admonition: "[Foolish] is he that layeth up treasure for himself and is not rich toward God." Transience and the shortness of earthly life appeared again when the young priest spoke from Isaiah 40.8: "The grass withereth, the flower fadeth; but the word of our God shall stand for ever."

Though an able churchman and a fiery preacher, young Whitehead's congregation at Black Hawk did not flourish. He probably felt very discouraged when he preached to a dwindling congregation on Acts 20.27: "For I have not shunned to declare unto you all the counsel of God." Again, he may have become angered at community response or its lack, when he discoursed on Matthew 23.34: "Wherefore, behold, I send unto you prophets and wise men and scribes; and some of them ye shall kill and crucify; and some of them shall ye scourge in your synagogues, and persecute them from city to city."[13]

Amos Billingsley took an other-worldly approach. Though as eager as any to improve community morals, he preached often on the afterlife. In a sermon on heaven, he quoted John 14. 2: "In my Father's house are many mansions; if it were not so, I would have told you. I go to prepare a place for you." Of most importance to Billingsley was finding and knowing God. His strenuous personal piety seems to have been aimed at knowing God. He recommended such piety as his to his followers and preached from Job 23. 3: "Oh that I knew where I might find him! that I might come even to his seat!" He did not despair of finding God but did not seem too sure of achieving it in this life, in this world. Several of his favorite texts dealt with the parousia and its new creation. Revelations 5. 9-12 is but one example:

> And they sung a new song, saying, Thou art worthy to take the book, and to open the seals thereof; for thou wast slain, and hast redeemed us to God by thy blood out of every kindred, and tongue, and people, and nation; Saying with a loud voice, Worthy is the Lamb that was slain to receive power, and riches, and wisdom, and strength, and honour, and glory, and blessing.

Another vision of the new creation used as a text was Isaiah 60. 20: "The sun shall no more go down; neither shall the moon withdraw itself; for the Lord shall be thine everlasting light, and the days of thy mourning shall be ended." On the theme on everlasting bliss, he spoke from Psalm 16: "Thou wilt shew me the path of life; in thy presence is the fullness of joy; at thy right hand there are pleasures for evermore."

Billingsley frequently reminded his congregation that this life is short and the afterlife without end. At funerals, he preached from Proverbs 27. 1: "Boast not thyself of tomorrow; for thou knowest not what a day may bring forth." At other times, he told his hearers following Amos, "To die is to gain."

Even though Billingsley seemed more concerned with life after death than with this world, he did preach from texts which directed present behavior. He recommended a better life when he spoke from I Peter 2. 17: "Honour all men.

Love the brotherhood. Fear God. Honour the King." He urged Denver citizens to abide by the decrees of the new territorial government when he addressed them from Exodus 18. 25: "And Moses chose able men out of all Israel and made them heads over the people, rulers of thousands, rulers of hundreds, rulers of fifties, and rulers of tens." He probably told the audience that God ordains civil government so that his people might do his work and prosper.[14]

Congregationalist William Phipps preached learned and slightly didactic sermons. When he dedicated a church building in Central City, the local newspaper summarized his sermon and praised his oratory profusely. Phipps discoursed on the New Jerusalem, "a scene of perfect blessedness, [where] all is life, splendor, and happiness." But the chosen scripture text read, "I saw no temple therein." He explained how scripture could describe the new city without a temple, when the temple had been the chief glory of the old. The preacher is reported to have approached the problem this way:

> It would assist us in the outset to inquire what it was that gave the chief distinction and highest sacredness to the ancient temple. It was not the immense shining stones, the beams of cedar, the embroidery, the carving, or the gold, but it was the presence of the Lord. In its interior recesses, above the mercy seat, and between the cherubims, was his visible symbol, the concentrated brightness or the "glory of the Lord." This it was that gave the ancient temple its highest glory and distinction.... It was dear to them because in it they could hold communion with God. But ... the temple at the best afforded but a partial satisfaction. Everything about it said that while Jehovah was locally near, he was morally afar off. A human priesthood and an elaborate ritual were interposed between the Israelite and his God. He knew that he could approach God to a certain point but no farther. There was a wall of separation which could not be broken down.... In heaven all mediations and obstacles will be done away, and there will be direct access to God.[15]

Phipps then quoted scripture and saints on the presence of the throne of God near which the Lamb sat in heaven. These two rather than a temple made the New Jerusalem. The preacher concluded with a two-fold application. First, the worshippers must inquire about "what kind of a preparation is required for the employments and joys of another world." Second, they must test their hopes against the revealed realities of the New Jerusalem. The new sanctuary must then be used for the true worship of God and His Son, without the interposition of human rituals between God and man.[16]

Phipps wrote an article for the Home Missionary which he probably used as a sermon or lecture as well. In any case, the piece reveals something of his homiletic style. He drew an analogy between prospecting and missionizing. The miner absorbed in the search for gold "reminds one of Bunyan's representation of the man with the muckrake, who could not look upward to the crown held over his head but occupied himself raking together the sticks and straw upon the ground." But the analogy may be taken further,

> The search for the treasure hid in these mountains illustrates the search for the treasure there is in Christ. The prospector picks up a piece of quartz, and it tells him "go up above it for the lode." We open the Bible and read, "Seek those things which are above." The Bible is the blossom rock which has been sent down from Heaven. Every passage which Christ uttered is a separate piece. Learning from them all, we follow on in the direction whither they lead, till we come to the Rock, Christ Jesus, and become possessed of an inheritance in that city whose gates are pearls and whose streets are paved with gold.
>
> I have spoken of the many holes which have been dug in some of these mountains. Thousands of them reveal no valuable property. The men had hope when they commenced digging but their hope failed. The mountains are sad pictures of disappointed hope. So there are many whose hopes of heavenly treasure will fail because they are not upon the true Rock of Christ. Leaving the blossom rock, which came down from Heaven they imagine the true riches exist in a worthless piece which somewhat resembles the true. They trace it out only to be disappointed at the Last.
>
> In Christ alone, there is a mine containing infinite eternal riches. It must be sought by those who would obtain it. We cannot buy it of another. We can never purchase it for we

> have nothing wherewith to pay the infinite price demanded for it. Yet it is free to those who find it, and the words sent down from above are, "Seek and ye shall find."[17]

In both samples of Phipps' thought, we see him clearly suggesting that the materialism and earthly pride of the Coloradans disturbed him far more than occasional violence or sins of the flesh. He exhorted the miners to raise their sights from earthly matters to divine wisdom as revealed in scripture. In this way, he hoped to elevate community morals.

None of the available sources indicates the sermon themes or texts chosen by Roman Catholic priests for their homilies. In fact, the only reference to any sermons preached by Roman Catholics is that cited earlier--Machebeuf delivered long and rambling sermons.[18] Many of the Roman Catholic clergy in Colorado spoke little or no English. French and Italian were the native tongues of a large number. It seems likely that most of them did not preach until they had learned English, which was often a rather long time after immigration.[19]

This analysis of preaching indicates that most of the ministers made no radical departures from the usual homiletic practices of the day. The ministers in Colorado emphasized biblical motifs. The texts concentrated on righteousness and holy living, divine love, Jesus as redeemer, the transience of earthly life, and the joys of heaven. Most of the texts and themes came from the New Testament and Old Testament passages promising future atonement and restoration.

A few differences appear among the denominations. Methodists tended to focus on holy living and righteousness more than did Episcopalians, Presbyterians, and Congregationalists. The Episcopalians spent more sermon hours on the role of Christ as redeemer, though preachers of all denominations used this theme. The bishop defended and explained Episcopal practices in an effort to overcome some settlers' dislike of ritual liturgy. In this, they were unique among the pioneer ministers. Presbyterian Amos Billingsley spoke much of heaven and its promised joys, but this seems to have been more a personal preference than a denominational trait. The Congregationalists delivered learned and didactic sermons in which they carefully explained biblical passages. Only the Congregationalists seem to have used written sermons; other denominations adopted the frontier custom of extemporaneous discourse. Whatever their differences though, all seemed to preach the gospel of Christ as redeemer and guide in ways totally commensurate with standard practice of the day.

Such preaching, exhorting, and instructing at regular services in towns, villages, and mining camps proved a most effective device for explaining the Christian gospel and pressing for holy living. But revivals allowed ministers to reach hearers not on their regular circuits or in settled congregations. Colorado Methodist missionaries held rural camp meetings and urban protracted meetings to reach these people and to increase membership in churches and classes.

Revivalism is such an important part of American Protestant Christianity that it requires close attention here, even though other historians have told the story well.[20] The form which revivalism took in frontier Colorado differed slightly from the more familiar forms of the First and Second Great Awakenings. During these spontaneous visitations of the Spirit, many American Christians experienced increased spirituality and renewal of vitality, while churches increased in membership. After the first waves of enthusiasm passed, revivalism lived on in two forms: institutionalized revivals and social reforms. Both appeared on the Colorado frontier.

The Methodists brought institutionalized revivalism to this frontier. Stamped indelibly by the Second Awakening, preachers such as Adriance, Chivington, Dyer, Willard, and Vincent hoped to continue to receive the benefits of the visitations of the Spirit by which they themselves had become convicted, converted, and blessed. They hoped to create churches in which the joy of revivals was the continuing pattern rather than a rare high point in religious experience. For them revivalism was Christianity. When they received a call to preach the gospel, they learned to preach the revivalists' gospel from frontier mentors. Since almost all of them received their education "on the job" they had little or no chance to see any other style of worship or evangelism.

Methodist polity made their task relatively easy. Even though Methodist officials never drew up rules for revivals and never incorporated revival techniques in the Books of Discipline, they devised the quarterly meeting, which served as a vehicle for camp and protracted meetings.[21] Within each district, the presiding elder set dates every quarter on which members from several circuit points gathered for holy communion, preaching, lay witness, and general community fellowship. On the Colorado frontier, revivals frequently happened at these gatherings.

The Methodists employed their own brand of Charles G. Finney's "new measures" with great success.[22] Carefully planned quarterly meetings made it possible for the Spirit to descend and to invigorate and nourish many souls regularly.

Jacob Adriance and George Fisher held the first revival recorded in Colorado. They had spent the summer and fall of 1859, organizing classes and congregations. Neither was an ordained elder; so they could not call a quarterly conference. But they felt the need of revival in their infant societies as miners settled into winter quarters. The two scheduled preaching and experience meetings in Denver, Auraria, Boulder, and Arapahoe. Two local preachers volunteered their services. For more than three weeks, the four men rotated from point to point, preaching every night in crowded log cabins. Adriance rejoiced over the "deep feeling" that many displayed, even though he was disappointed when no one came forward to the mourners' bench.[23] Probably most of those attending had already experienced conversion and simply renewed covenant vows.

When presiding elder, John Chivington, reached Colorado in the summer of 1860, he quickly established quarterly meetings. Chivington, a compelling preacher, drew enormous crowds and sometimes led large-scale revivals. He described one at Mountain City as "the most extraordinary [meeting] ever held in this or any other country." He continued:

> There were present thousands upon thousands of people from every State and Territory in the Union, and from almost every country of Europe, declaring the wonderful works of God. Nearly a thousand communed at the Lord's Supper. 24

He probably exaggerated the number present and communing. But Landon Taylor, a visiting preacher, agreed that the gathering was extraordinary.

Elder Chivington preached to a large multitude near

> Mountain City, seated on the hill-side. Oh, what a scope was here for the exercise of all the powers of the mind! Poetry, philosophy, eloquence, and song might have gathered inspiration to unfold their richness upon the one hand, and to have sung their music on the other. We were not bordering upon Mount Sinae where the glory surrounded Moses, but we were standing on Mount Zion--if not with harps in our hands, with the presence of our Savior in our midst, and the accents of praise upon our lips; and from this distant standpoint, I fancy that I yet see the towering cliffs, the stately pines, the clear atmosphere, and hear the stirring songs, all uniting together and saying, "All thy works shall praise thee, O Lord, and thy saints shall bless thee."[25]

Other meetings brought less exciting responses.[26] But in the long run, the regular observance of the rites probably counted for more.

A reporter for the Denver News (probably O. J. Goldrick) described a camp meeting at Buckskin Joe shortly after the mines opened. The preacher roared out against men who drank and became "wedded to their euchre decks." Miners sitting on pine stumps ringed around a bon-fire heard the speaker "lay down the law and prophets," as he made "persuasive petitions for the restoration of virtue and morality among the sin stricken and God forsaken prospectors after the gold that perisheth." Though the sermon was long and much of the theology too complicated for the audience (in the reporter's judgment), the miners listened raptly and many wept. When the exhorter finished, they sang hymns loud and long. A penitent rose and exhorted the rest to repent of their sins and change their ways of living. Fervent prayers and more hymns closed the meeting.[27]

Similar meetings at regular intervals led Denver preachers William Kenney and B. T. Vincent to speak of the "revival spirit" that animated most of the congregations in their charge. They noted that quarterly meetings increased both membership rolls and church attendance. Vincent reported that frequent "serial meetings" in Denver promoted "spiritual health."[28]

John Dyer, of all the Methodist evangelists, gave the most energy and thought to revivals. He believed that salvation depended on an act of demonstrable conversion. No person would make a true conversion unless he first realized the terrible dangers of his sinfulness. Fear was almost necessarily prior to conviction and conversion. Therefore, Dyer censured those preachers who did not preach about eternal punishment and the "horrors of hell."

When he took up his mission in Colorado, Dyer resolved that his charges "should have a full gospel." They must hear, he declared that those "determined to enjoy the sinful pleasures of the world" are "unforgiven sinners." Redemption came from Christ through grace but only on the condition of human repentance. Preachers who "smooth the word for fear of mortal men" do not preach the gospel. He wrote, "When the terrors of the Book are kept out of sight, convictions are slight and conversions not ... clear. The New Testament has both heaven and hell described. The Gospel is both. To preach only one is to fail in one's call." He described his way: "I told them, in an exhortation, that they were hair-hung and breath-shaken over the gulf of eternal despair.... O, may God send men after his own heart, who can thunder his wrath as well as display the glories of his great salvation!"[29]

Dyer defended not only the content of revival preaching but also the enthusiasm and excitement, which so disturbed critics of revivalism. They seemed as necessary to conversion as did fear.

> A man or woman must be excited enough to start them in any cause. Men must believe there is danger, or they will not start. This is the reason that our Savior gave the awful doctrine of damnation without repentance, as well as all the invitations to the gospel. Both the threatenings and persuasions must be presented. Hence, convictions are slight and conversions are not so clear as they ought to be, when our preachers, instead of showing a sinner his danger, "snugly keep damnation out of sight."[30]

Dyer's beliefs led him to pursue souls tirelessly. He literally preached whenever and wherever he got a chance. He saw his day as an era of "small things" and discoursed "wherever a few gathered." Once, when the snow stood six feet deep at Gold Run, he gathered the entire population of the camp, totalling twenty-five. Four were Methodists, but seventeen of the others converted before the ten day meeting ended. Another time, a handful gathered for several days around two wagons and three tents. Of this assemblage and its revival Dyer wrote, "Few know how we appreciated these seasons, after our long exile among people taken with sin of every grade, none even to sympathize with us and cheer us along our way."[31]

Despite all this activity, no general awakening came to Colorado's frontier Christians. Congregationalists, Baptists, and Presbyterians who had grown up during the Second Great Awakening waited and hoped for the descent of the Spirit but scorned the techniques of the Methodists and valued congregational autonomy too much to combine in planning anything like quarterly meetings. On rare occasions, Baptists in newly settled areas held camp meetings. But when regular congregations gathered, camp meetings disappeared. Denver Baptists experienced a small but cheering revival in 1870 and doubled their membership.[32] But immigration in 1870 could as easily account for the increase.

Congregationalist William Phipps described the feelings of one waiting for the Spirit's descent:

> Millions of treasure lie buried all about us, in vaults so secure that as yet they defy the art of man to pick the lock, and they laugh at the man, who with a pick and shovel, goes moping about among the rocks, casting wistful, sorrowful glances at the spots on the mountains where the rock containing a fortune peeps out to the light of day. The work of the Home Missionary may be likened to that of the moping miner. He carries gospel and picks and digs away at this and that stony heart but when he "pans out," scarce a "color" can be obtained. Shall we wait for a new process by which to save souls? Aye! We must wait on God by faith and prayer. Such waiting is not in vain.[33]

His waiting paid off. In 1868, he wrote home, "A great tidal wave of revival has reached even across the broad plains." The "spirit is moving here upon the hearts of a few, and two have recently given evidence of renewed hearts." He hoped that it would be the beginning of a "great work."[34] But it was not. It was, as Dyer knew, an era of "small things."

Small meetings held regularly and persistently, however,

did help the Methodists to establish the largest and most vigorous Protestant churches in the territory. Revivalism practiced in institutional form was not the exclusive invention of Colorado pioneers. It flourished all over the country but proved especially effective in sparsely settled areas such as Colorado. Frontier evangelists did not produce a new theory or a new technique.

In some ways, the use of revivalism was a conservative reaction to changed social circumstances. Some view revivalism and its companion social reform as a conservative reaction or response to social dislocation brought on by westward movement and the industrial revolution.[35] Revivalism in Colorado represents an attempt to establish practices and values learned in the East or Midwest during the Second Great Awakening. The revivalists, especially Dyer, insisted that their teachings represented the true gospel and refused to abandon ideas and forms learned in another time and another place. Thus, the revivalism of the Colorado frontier may be regarded as a conservative reaction insofar as its proponents sought to carry traditions from their old homes to their new homes.

The social reform that accompanied revivalism on the Colorado frontier was also a practical and useful movement. Perhaps even more than revivalism, social reform performed a highly practical and conservative function in the emerging communities. The missionaries' main goal (and that of many lay leaders) was to create orderly and godly communities in which they might get on with the business of saving souls without the distraction of drunken brawls, rowdy gambling halls, and gun battles in the streets.

Social reform in frontier Colorado differed somewhat from that of eastern evangelists. Timothy Smith reminds us that the city revivalists of the late 1850's participated in the liberal tradition of that day.[36] The evangelists fought for abolition of slavery, prison reform, women's suffrage, child labor laws, and other measures to free the oppressed members of American society. In another mode, they supported efforts to spread the gospel at home and abroad, to encourage temperance, to urge Sabbath observance and Bible study, to support Sunday Schools, and so on. The former constituted an attempt to change American society. The latter was an effort to improve on the existing society. Coloradans carrying useful eastern traditions to the West concentrated almost entirely on the reforms that would make society better. They had no particular desire to engage in radical regroupings of social patterns and made no efforts to improve the lot of oppressed minorities. Colorado's evangelistic social reformers did not belong to the liberal group described by Timothy Smith. They urged temperance, Sabbath observance, and education so that they could survive in the wilderness and build orderly, stable, and productive communities. One apparent exception was the widespread evangelistic support of antislavery and abolition movements. But since Colorado lay outside the area where slavery was likely to exist, abolition of the "peculiar institution" made little difference. Furthermore, by the time of the Colorado gold rush, abolition had become a political issue on which people aligned by section, rather than a moral issue. Colorado antislavery advocates, as so many of their compatriots elsewhere, had lost sight of granting civil and social rights to Negroes and saw slavery as a crime against the Union rather than a crime against black men and women. For Coloradans, the antislavery crusade was a pragmatic concern. Coloradans knew that secession and war endangered the survival of the nation and the stability of their newly formed society. Though several of Colorado's missionaries took stands against slavery, they preached against the war rather than bondage. John Dyer, John Chivington, and Amos Billingsley delivered fiery sermons urging support of the Union and calling for the defeat of the Confederacy.

Chivington, in his usual all or nothing style, declared (quoting Stephen A. Douglas) that as long as the war lasted, there were two classes: patriots and traitors. A few southerners in the congregation jumped up to protest. But the rest cheered Chivington and shouted down the protestors. Chivington recalled:

> During the sermon I told the excited multitude that I was God's free man and did not intend to speak any doubtful words on the great question at issue, nor yet hold my peace. That I was a man of lawful age and full size (six feet four and a half inches and well-proportioned), and an American citizen before I became a minister, and if the Church had required me to renounce any of my rights of manhood or American citizenship before I could become her minister, I should have very respectfully declined.

After Chivington resigned his ministry to join the army, he

continued to "preach up" the war from pulpits all over the mining region.[37]

Dyer likened the Confederacy to a sinner at the anxious bench.

> In speaking of the full surrender of a sinner to God in order to his being taken back into favor, I declared that it must be unconditional; and as I had just heard of our war being a reality, I illustrated by what terms would be granted the rebels--they never could be received back except on unconditional surrender--and added, that though it might be through fire and blood, it would come.

The congregation then "jumped to their feet in approval" and cheered the preacher's "patriotic sentiment."[38]

Billingsley left only a passing reference to his war sermons. His feelings toward slavery may have been less politically inclined than those of Dyer and Chivington. After the war, he took up the cause of the freedman. Believing that full citizenship depended upon proper education, he moved to the South and spent the rest of his life teaching in schools for freedmen.[39]

George Phillips, principal of Colorado Seminary, deplored slavery in a lecture series, published in book form as The American Republic and Human Liberty Foreshadowed in Scripture. Though he delivered the lectures in Ohio, he probably spoke on the subject in Colorado, too. Phillips' main theme is the identification of the United States as the new or restored Israel; but he referred often to slavery as "our national apostasy." The slave system retards American progress, he argued. It "rolls back the civilization of two thousand years, blots out the central idea of Christianity, and re-establishes a worse than pagan barbarism."[40]

Phillips expressed greater concern for the bad effects of the peculiar institution on the nation as a whole than for the injustices done the slaves.

> The enormity of this scheme did not consist so much in the outrage perpetrated against the liberties of the enslaved ... as [in] an irretrievable offence ... against ... the root idea of our nationality and civilization, as well as against God's redemptive plans for lifting up the world out of its fallen condition.[41]

Furthermore, he asserted that slavery caused Americans to fall into irreverence for God, Sabbath desecration, political demagogery, "intemperance, profanity, and licentiousness."[42] Like so many reformers of his day, Phillips supposed that one evil produced all the other wrongs visible to the human eye and that prohibition of that evil would perfect society.

According to him, slavery stood as the only obstacle in America's path to world dominion as God's chosen people. Lincoln's Emancipation Proclamation had made the Civil War a holy battle to end slavery. Its outcome would surely be the return of the nation to its rightful destiny as the state chosen by God to lead the world to freedom.

> The present war is a terrible remedy for a terrible disease, and God, who maketh the wrath of man to praise him is bringing out of it much good to the nation and the world.... We shall do away with that national impiety which has been growing upon us as a people, and over which the true patriot has so long mourned.[43]

Colorado frontiersmen heartily supported the Union cause, endorsed their preachers' statements opposing slavery and favoring war, and rejoiced in Union victories. In spite of all this, their main reforming concerns lay elsewhere. No slaves lived in the Rocky Mountains. But profane and intemperate people did live among the devout civilizers. Those building an orderly society put their greatest energies into efforts to improve the wayward among them. Therefore, Coloradans crusaded for temperance, Sabbath observance, and education. In these campaigns, missionaries received much aid from lay people. Temperance, Sabbath observance, and benevolencies (especially schools) seemed most salutary to civilizers. Methodists engaged in all of these reform activities. The Presbyterians worked mainly for temperance and Sunday closings. The Episcopalians, Roman Catholics, and Congregationalists focussed their energies on schools and other benevolencies. Temperance insured alertness, necessary for survival during the rough frontier period or so long as Indian attack seemed likely. Further, once towns had been established, temperance seemed essential if citizens were to enjoy any peace and quiet. Frontiersmen in Colorado believed that drunkenness caused the vast majority of violent episodes. Rightly or wrongly, they blamed alcohol for almost all of the shootings, duels, fights, and brawls. As Alexander Rankin said, "The disturbances and outbreaks are to be traced to the drinking and gambling houses."[44] Thus, their temperance crusade aimed to produce an alert and orderly citizenry.

Rankin and John Chivington launched Denver's first crusade for temperance. The sensational murder trial and execution of James Gordon was the catalyst. Gordon, a promising young engineer, had killed a man during a drunken brawl. The court sentenced Gordon to death. While awaiting execution, Gordon passionately urged all who would listen to avoid drink; he blamed his rage and subsequent violence on alcohol. Rankin and Chivington took up there and urged their followers to abstinence, and they excoriated the saloon keepers and liquor dealers as agents of the devil. The Rocky Mountain News applauded their crusade; but the competing Herald, though sympathetic with the preachers' cause, criticized their zeal as excessive. Rankin declared, early on in his ministry in Colorado, "The only remedy for the abominations of liquor, gambling, swearing, and Sabbath profanation is the gospel. When churches are established these things will be measurably cured."[45]

Chivington's temperance crusade bore the marks of pragmatism. Chivington worked closely with the Masons in efforts to "clean up" the saloon district. This meant pressuring the proprietors of especially rowdy saloons and those containing brothels to leave town. Chivington usually tacitly distinguished between good saloons and bad ones; he made no great effort to close those that functioned as working men's clubs. Instead, he enlisted (or extorted) the proprietors' aid; Denver's leading saloon keepers donated generously to church building funds.[46]

Other preachers, including John Dyer, Alanson R. Day, and George Warner, warned their congregations of the dangers of drink. Day conducted a series of lectures urging prohibition. He rented the Denver Theater and attracted crowds from all denominations for several nights. The News reported that audience reaction was good and his speeches "powerful, practical and independent, and interesting."[47]

Sober living, however desirable, was only the beginning. Christian missionaries naturally favored Sabbath observance, since they considered it essential in bringing traditional influences to bear on society. They encouraged one and all to attend church and to cease all work on Sundays. In the early years of Colorado's settlement, shops, saloons, dance halls, and offices stayed open on Sundays to serve the miners. Though most men did not dig in the mines on Sundays, many of them did their trading that day. Churchmen and laymen alike worked hard to encourage Sunday closings. The crusade had little effect at first. When some businessmen agreed to close, they found that they lost business to their less pious competitors. Clerical persuasion alone failed. But the influential laymen who composed the vestries and boards of the churches ultimately convinced the vast majority to observe Sunday closing. By 1863, the Denver paper reported, "Most of our business houses were closed on last Sabbath. The general agreement on the part of our leading businessmen to keep closed on Sundays would have none other than a most beneficial tendency, commercially, and socially."[48]

Even Alexander Rankin had to admit that improvements came very early. He wrote to his wife in November, 1860, "Our efforts to propagate the gospel in this city have exerted a very apparent effect on public morals. The Sabbath is better observed, more people attend public worship, and there is less open wickedness."[49]

The missionaries knew that God commands his people not only to live soberly and worship Him but also to love and help one another, especially the young and weak. Though Colorado Christians saw no need to work for greater social and political rights for minorities, they did recognize the need for schools, orphan asylums, poor houses, and hospitals. All of these benevolencies cost a great deal and required trained persons to run them. Before 1870, Colorado missionaries built schools and one hospital.

Roman Catholics built the first schools, but other denominations with episcopal polity were not far behind. The first church-related school in the territory was St. Mary's Academy in Denver. The academy opened for classes in 1863. The school proved an instant success, drawing the best daughters of the territory to its doors. The Protestants looked on with horror, as the Roman Catholics began teaching their tradition to good Protestant girls as well as young Catholics. The Methodists, who did not generally establish schools, approached the key Protestants of Denver and solicited funds for the erection of the largest, most elegant buildings in town. They created Colorado Seminary for young ladies and opened for instruction shortly after the Catholics began St. Mary's.[50]

The Episcopalians, eager to equal or outdo the efforts of their competitors, began raising funds in the East for a girls' school. The boys were not forgotten, but because girls were expected to be the future guardians of community morals, their right education seemed to come first. The Episcopal academy for girls opened in 1868. Wolfe Hall, as the school was called for its principle benefactor, immediately ran into financial difficulties that finally forced its closing. But the school functioned throughout the pioneer period and beyond.[51]

While the competition for the Territory's daughters went on in Denver, the Episcopalians and Catholics launched a quiet but more lasting program of education. In Central City, Episcopalian Francis Granger and his wife opened a high school and a night school for adults. They could not secure the services of teachers, so the two did all the teaching themselves. When the Grangers left, Alvin B. Jennings and his wife took over the work. Roman Catholics established a high school for boys in Denver early in the decade. Both of these ventures survived the hard times.[52]

Congregationalists, for decades the founders of frontier colleges, also began planning schools. When Norman McLeod arrived in Denver, he immediately began soliciting funds and land donations for a college. He secured a large donation of land in Boulder and bullied the legislature into chartering a university. Despite many obstacles, the school opened in 1872 and later became the University of Colorado. In a like manner, Colorado Seminary later became the University of Denver.[53] A boys' school in Denver, Jarvis Hall, was to be Episcopalians' collegiate institution. However, financial troubles led to the school's closing.[54]

Bishop Machebeuf naturally planned to build an elementary school in every parish, as was the practice among Roman Catholics who felt that the public schools were dominated by the Protestants. He bought tracts of land for every parish school but was not able to build up the network until the railroad boom. However, during the pioneer era, he managed to build a school in Denver and one in Trinidad, a new cattle town in southern Colorado. The latter school was staffed by a remarkable group of nuns headed by Sister Blandina Segale, who almost single-handedly built the school building. The venture flourished and served not only as a parochial school but also as a public school for many years. In another southern Colorado town, the nuns served as public school teachers until the school board asked them not to wear their habits while in the classroom. The sisters then withdrew to form a parish school where the Protestants would not try to impose restrictions.[55]

The educational ventures of the church people filled a crucial need in the new society. The public schools suffered even graver financial disabilities than did the church schools. Though the public schools opened in 1863, they did not really serve the public needs until several years later. In the meantime, the church schools did the job.

Hospitals were a pressing need in all of the communities. A small private hospital met the basic needs of Denver's sick. The Catholics began early to build a hospital in Central City. Residents of all shades of belief joined in to help raise money for the badly needed facility. Fairs, festivals, and donation parties drew all. Such activities in Central City and Denver led a Denver journalist to admit, "Much as opposing denominations may denounce the Roman Catholic church, all must admit that in the work for general good our Catholic church of this city has by no means been a laggard, but on the contrary [has] led the advance."[56]

Though the Roman Catholics and Episcopalians had plans for a wide network of benevolencies, they could not pursue them in the pioneer era for lack of funds. After the railroad boom began, the churches could and did begin their benevolent work in earnest.[57]

Preaching, revivalism, and social reforms in frontier Colorado were practical instruments in the civilizing process. The missionaries concentrated on winning souls and convincing the disorderly to behave better. They concentrated their reforming efforts on temperance and Sabbath observance because many drank too much and disrupted the holy day with commerce and pleasure-seeking. Practical men addressed the present problems and ignored the reforms aimed at greater equality for all. Again, when faced with limited funds, they concentrated their benevolent efforts on education, as the surest way to produce a new generation of godly and orderly people to carry on in their stead.

The reforming and reviving work of the missionaries depended in large measure on active participation among the laity. Church and society interacted in the cooperative endeavors centering on reform principles, as we shall see in the next chapter. The social functions of the missionaries overlapped with the functions of the lay and civic leaders. Both groups believed that stable society was ultimately grounded in a moral, disciplined, hard-working body of individuals bound together by common devotion to a creative and providential deity. Religion, which required piety, good behavior, and regular worship, was the bed-rock of society. The pioneer missionaries, as revivalists, reformers, moral leaders, and religious teachers, served as the agents of civilization. The churches were the institutions in which all could participate in order to create the sustaining principle of order. Schools, benevolencies, reform societies, and fraternal lodges were in functional terms auxiliaries of the churches, almost extensions of them.

NOTES

1. Timothy Smith, Revivalism and Social Reform: American Protestantism on the Eve of the Civil War (New York: Harper Torchbooks, 1957), p. 36. Smith draws his evidence from eastern and midwestern sources. However, Coloradans also fit into this pattern. None of the lay sources says anything but good about the clergymen.

2. See Chapters 2 and 4.

3. See Rankin, p. 30.

4. Claude A. Beesley, The Episcopal Church in North Texas (Wichita Falls: Privately published, 1952), pp. 38-39.

5. Winne, "Historical Gleanings," The Trail, Vol. VIII (September, 1915), p. 8.

6. Adriance, Diary, July 3, August 14, 21, 28, September 7, 10, 27, October 2, 16, 17, 23, 30, November 6, 7, December 4, 18, 19, 1859; February 10, June 24, July 1, 22, August 12, October 21, 1860; January 13, 21, March 10, May 19, 26, 1861; February 16, 1862.

7. Ibid., June 17, July 15, September 2, November 4, 1860; June 8, 1861.

8. Kehler, Diary, 1860-62 passim and especially February 5, 12, 19, July 29, 1860; March 3, 1861.

9. Morris, p. 132.

10. Rocky Mountain News, July 22, 1862.

11. Talbot, Diary, June 22, 29, July 6, 7, 20, 21, 22, 24, 25, 26, 27, August 1, 1862; June 14, August 9, November 22, 1863.

12. Records of St. Mark's Parish, Black Hawk, Colo., November, 1867-June, 1870, pp. 1-46, passim.

13. Ibid.

14. Billingsley, Journal, June 2, 13, 16, August 18, September 2, December 15, 1861; January 2, February 10, March 16, 1862.

15. (Central City) Miner's Register, February 19, 1867.

16. Ibid.

17. Manuscript sent by William Phipps to Dr. Badger, July 30, 1867, A. H. M. S. Correspondence.

18. Jones, p. 72.

19. Howlett, Life of Machebeuf, pp. 288, 326, 337, 368, 371; Howlett, "Recollections of My Life and Reflections on Times and Events During It," ms., Chancery Office, Denver, pp. 40-41, 63.

20. See William W. Sweet, Revivalism in America (New York: Abingdon Press, 1944); Bernard A. Weisberger, They Gathered at the River (Chicago: Quadrangle Paperbacks, 1958); Whitney R. Cross, The Burned-Over District (Ithaca: Cornell University Press, 1950); William G. McLoughlin, Modern Revivalism (New York: Ronald Press, 1957).

21. Miyakawa, Protestants and Pioneers, pp. 159-73.

22. New measures included use of the "anxious" or "mourners' bench," where penitents sat while the congregation prayed for them, planned seasons of protracted or serial meetings, intensive small group inquiry, and a style of preaching characterized by a kind of advocacy. For description see Charles G. Finney,

Lectures on Revivals of Religon (London: Simplin, Marshall & Co., 1840).

23. Adriance, Diary, January 21-February 11, 1860.

24. Chivington, "Footprints...," Rocky Mountain Christian Advocate, September 26, 1889, p. 2.

25. Landon Taylor, The Battlefield Reviewed (Chicago: Published privately, 1881), pp. 231-32.

26. Adriance, Diary, July 14-15, September 1-2, November 3-4, 1860; January 5, May 12, June 8-9, 1861.

27. Rocky Mountain News, August 29, 1861.

28. Rocky Mountain News, January 7, 1862; B. T. Vincent, 1868-69 Report, Denver District, ms., Colorado State Historical Society, Denver, pp. 9-11.

29. Dyer, Snow Shoe Itinerant, pp. 201-202, 328, 345.

30. Ibid., p. 328.

31. Ibid., pp. 208-209.

32. Eugene Parsons, "Mother of Churches," p. 6.

33. William Phipps to Dr. Badger, April 14, 1868, Letters, A. H. M. S. Correspondence.

34. Ibid.

35. See, for example, Rowland Berthoff, Social Order and Disorder in America (New York: Harper & Row, 1971), pp. 254-56, 273-74.

36. Smith, pp. 8, 46-47, 60.

37. Chivington, "Footprints...," Rocky Mountain Christian Advocate, October 24, 1889, p. 2.

38. Dyer, pp. 122-23.

39. Billingsley, Journal, October 1, 1862; Editor's note, Colorado Magazine, Vol. XL (October, 1963), pp. 241-42.

40. George S. Phillips, *The American Republic and Human Liberty Foreshadowed in Scripture* (Cincinnati: Poe & Hitchcock, 1864), pp. 12, 177.

41. *Ibid.*, p. 177.

42. *Ibid.*

43. *Ibid.*, pp. 12-13.

44. Rankin, p. 90.

45. *Ibid.*, pp. 110-17, for a description of the trial and temperance sermons; quotation on p. 92.

46. Craig, *The Fighting Parson*, pp. 30-31, 36, 44-46, 49, 51.

47. *Rocky Mountain News*, June 27, 1864.

48. *Ibid.*, June 9, 1863.

49. Rankin, p. 132.

50. Jones, *History of Catholic Education in the State of Colorado*, pp. 80-195; Howlett, *Life of Machebeuf*, pp. 341, 363-64, 368, 371-72, 376 ff., 419.

51. Breck, *The Episcopal Church in Colorado*, pp. 43, 47, 61, 64, 71, 76, 78, 104.

52. *Ibid.*, p. 42; Jones, pp. 80-195.

53. McLeod to Badger, 1865-66, *passim*, Letters, A. H. M. S. Correspondence.

54. Breck, pp. 57-60, 76-78.

55. Jones, pp. 80-84; see also Sr. Blandina Segale, *At the End of the Santa Fe Trail* (Milwaukee: Bruce Pub. Co., 1948) and segment of her narrative in John Tracy Ellis, *Documents of American Catholic History* (Milwaukee: Bruce Pub. Co., 1942), p. 405.

56. *Rocky Mountain News*, April 16, 1867.

57. Howlett, pp. 368-419; Breck, pp. 113-191.

CHAPTER 6

THE ROLES OF COLORADO CHRISTIANS IN THE PIONEER SOCIETY

Churchmen's action in society in frontier Colorado, as in the rest of America, was limited by the separation of church and state. However much Colorado's pioneers approved of the principle, they did not want the separation of religion and society. Nor had those who instituted the revolutionary separation of church and state early in the national period. Thomas Jefferson and other rationalists, in curious alliance with left-wing Protestant pietists, furnished the rationale for separation. Jefferson thought that all religious groups possessed common essential principles which when held by the populace produced "order in government and obedience to the laws."[1] By 1859, most Americans had internalized Jefferson's ideas of the necessity of religion as a stabilizing factor in society. Colorado's frontiersmen simply assumed that religious presence aided in the establishment of order and seldom remarked on the influence of religion on social order.

The clergymen's very presence was reassuring to Colorado's civilizers. Sometimes the clerics took direct action. They often cooperated with lay leaders. For example, clergy and lay people worked together in the crusade for Sunday closings. In other matters, ecclesiastical and lay leaders pursued the same goals but without joint action. For instance, religious leaders established denominational schools, while legislators provided for public schools. On another level, they shared certain presuppositions about how society ought to work. Here religious and social thought overlapped. Our first task is to examine the roles of clerics and lay people in society. The second task, pursued in the next chapter, is to look at some of Colorado's leaders' socio-religious thought.

Church and society acted together when clergy and laity set out to build orderly communities, shape morality, and alleviate human misery. Many, if not most, of the Colorado frontiersmen brought with them the convictions that religion is the cement of society,[2] and that God through Christ and His church is bringing His kingdom closer and closer to erring but hoping persons. Such convictions dictated that religion, carried by the churches, should inform all human activities, even those clearly lodged in the secular realm. Since ministers, by mutual agreement, did not hold public office or serve often in public institutions, they acted in civic affairs as private citizens. Because of this limitation, some religious functions passed to men and women in secular employment--journalists, educators, and elected officials.

We shall look first at the actions of clergy in civic affairs and second at the religious activities of lay leaders. The clergy had little to do with political, military, and economic matters; in social concerns, they cut a wider swath. Ministers who had military or political ambitions generally gave up their ministerial vocations. For example, John Chivington resigned his commission as a Methodist elder when he joined the army and launched his abortive political career. He continued to preach, but he did so as a lay preacher.[3]

Ministers served as legislative and military chaplains. Every constitutional convention session, legislative meeting, or council gathering opened with a prayer delivered by a local or visiting minister. William Goode, Jacob Adriance, Amos Billingsley, and several other missionaries prayed regularly over the law-makers.[4] John Kehler ministered to the First Regiment of Colorado Volunteers for almost four years.[5]

The legislative chaplains took no part in policy making. Though it is impossible to know how much they influenced the delegates, we may be sure that their presence had some effect. Beyond their symbolic and ceremonial importance, it is likely that each day the ministers reminded the lawmakers that God, not man, is the ruling sovereign, that grace and human effort make good possible, and that God, not man, ordains some kind of civil government even while God confers considerable responsibility on people to seek justice and truth. Perhaps legislators absorbed a part of these messages.

Army chaplains acted less as ceremonial leaders and more as pastors for the volunteers. Kehler preached, celebrated the eucharist, comforted the sick, wounded, and troubled, and buried the dead. As chaplain, his work had some symbolic importance. He prayed for union victories and gave his clerical stamp of approval to the cause.[6]

Clergymen participated in the economic sector even less than they did in the political and military. The ministers preached against covetousness, as we have seen in the previous chapter. Further, they constantly asked men and women to pledge money for their salaries, building funds, and benevolencies. Many of the denominational leaders spent much energy and time in such activities. One bishop remarked ruefully, "On Saturday and Sunday I am priest and bishop to confess, preach, officiate, etc.; on Monday and the rest of the week banker, contractor, architect, mason, collector, in a word, a little of everything."[7] Even so, these activities were intended to finance the church rather than influence society in its development.

In times of disaster or civil disorder, citizens looked to their clergy for leadership. When the Platte River flooded Denver in 1864, Joseph Machebeuf and John Kehler organized relief measures.[8] When, in the same year, Denver and Central City residents armed against possible Indian attack, Norman McLeod and William Crawford took command. McLeod mustered a brigade of young men whom he led in military drills. Crawford joined other leaders to form an adult militia company.[9] Clergymen sometimes tried to moderate the mob passions that sometimes ruled people's courts or vigilante meetings but with little or no success. William Howbert and H. H. Johnson desperately and unsuccessfully tried to stop a lynching in Colorado City.[10] John Dyer had as little influence with a mob in Fairplay.[11]

Ministers as citizens, had their greatest influence in social matters. Protestant ministers often joined lay voluntary societies. Fraternal lodges, such as the Masons and Good Templars whose members tried to promote sobriety, order, and education, attracted Protestant clergy as arenas of participation in civic affairs beyond their church doors. John Chivington, Horace Hitchings, W. A. Kenney, George Randall, and others poured energy and devotion into Masonic work. Chivington, as we have seen, acted as Grand Master of the Denver group. Hitchings and Randall held offices in the same organization.[12] Clergymen supported the temperance efforts of the Good Templars, who operated in Central City.[13]

Clerics acted in the civic sector when they established benevolencies. Hospitals and schools (and later poor houses, orphan asylums, homes for wayward girls, old people's homes) built and run by the denominations served the populace. Church-related schools provided an especially potent instrument for clerical action in and upon society. In the early years, Colorado clergymen even worked directly in the public schools. Walter Potter ran unsuccessfully for territorial superintendent of schools. Despite his defeat, he continued to work with public school officials and to encourage his congregation to send their children to the public schools. Nathan Thompson was chosen to be superintendent of Boulder's public schools. He and other Congregationalist ministers founded a college in Boulder that later became the state university. Roman Catholic nuns taught in public schools in Trinidad.[14] But these men and women proved the exception rather than the rule. Public schools were the province of lay men and women. However, religious influence was very strong, as we shall see later.[15]

We cannot measure the extent of churchly and social interaction by looking only at clerical involvement in community affairs. The clergy exercised their influence in and through churches, where they preached the gospel and administered the sacraments. But churches are composed of lay people. The laity who absorb the gospel (however imperfectly) act in the secular community and try to shape it according to principles of love and justice. It was the devout laity that achieved the visible interaction of church and society in Colorado. The missionary played the roles of inceptor and carrier of tradition; the churches formed the link between the people and the living spirit of Christ. The laity received a sense of identity within the Christian tradition, participated in the communal workings of the Spirit, and carried the fruits of the Spirit into their work in the world.

The hope of pious laymen and ministers working in the world was to transform the world so that the kingdom of Christ would be finally created on earth. Despite their incomplete realization of this goal, they continued to expect progress toward the desired end. The fabled optimism of frontier life sprang in part from this vision and in part from the seemingly limitless opportunities of open land.[16] Few Colorado Christians held a coherent, fully conscious belief in the coming kingdom. But they had inherited the colonial vision of the New World as the New Israel and the site of

God's coming kingdom. The complicated notions of kingdom need not be detailed here,[17] but we must note that lay persons carried out much of the social action that they understood to be gospel command and they did so because God intends to create his kingdom on earth.

There is an interesting correlation between lay leadership in church affairs and civic affairs. Often the most prominent advocates of order belonged to churches and served as vestry members or trustees. Judges, governors, railroad entrepreneurs, lawyers, doctors, newspaper editors, and real estate magnets formed an interlocking directorate of churches, schools, lodges, government, and business. Important civic leaders who also acted as energetic church persons included John Evans (Methodist; physician, territorial governor, railroad entrepreneur, philanthropist), William Gilpin (Presbyterian; territorial governor, geopolitician, and rancher), William Larimer (Presbyterian; town builder), Amos Steck (Episcopalian; miner, mayor of Denver), Richard E. Whitsett (Episcopalian; merchant, land dealer), Henry Wildman (Episcopalian; merchant), Thomas Bayaud (Episcopalian; merchant and land holder), Richard Sopris (Presbyterian-Congregationalist; merchant, soldier), David Collier (Episcopalian; territorial judge), and Charles Armour (Episcopalian; territorial judge).[18]

These men and others like them wielded considerable power in both church and society. They managed the temporal affairs of the churches; they donated land and money for church buildings; in some denominations, they called the clergy; and they influenced their fellow citizens by example in ethical affairs. That they were often rapacious financially did not seem too great a contradiction to a people convinced that progress would produce plenty for all. The lay leaders believed that orderly, productive communities composed of temperate, churchgoing, industrious, and loyal individuals would, first, make earthly life better, second, help usher in the kingdom of God, and third, insure the spread of Christianity and republican government abroad by the strength of example.

We may assume that many of the lay leaders tried to live faithful lives grounded in Christian spirituality. Some, perhaps many of them, failed to understand the gospel message warning against undue devotion to wealth. And this created a problem for church and society. Rapacious in business and pious in other areas of their lives, many of the merchants joined the ministers in a mutually rewarding but morally ambiguous relationship. Order was the first article in their social creed. Hard work and productivity was the second. The merchants adhered to both. Furthermore, the ministers found themselves dependent on lay leadership for employment, livelihood, and community support. So long as the open frontier allowed opportunity and modest prosperity for all and so long as the industrialists did not have a large enough labor supply to exact long hours for low pay, no social sin seemed to arise from their accumulation of wealth. When the wealthy contributed large sums to churches and charities the ministers could scarcely chastise them for greed. John Evans, the richest man in the territory, gave enormous sums not only to each and every Methodist church in the area but also to new churches established by other Protestant denominations.[19]

Trouble came in the 1880's and 1890's when the industrial system matured a bit. Foreign labor willing to work for pennies arrived, and the industrialists exploited men, women, and children in amassing their fortunes. The ministers, having no doctrine of social sin and social salvation, found themselves unable to censure men who worked hard, made large profits, and gave generously to institutions of order such as churches, schools, and benevolencies. Clergy also faced the practical difficulty of being dependent on vestries and boards of trustees composed of these same rich men. Without them, their institutions would flounder; with them, they accommodated to an economic ethic that denied equality to an increasingly large and relatively powerless segment of the people. Patterns cut out during the pioneer period carried over into the post-frontier industrial era when they no longer accorded with the commands of the gospel.

But if lay leaders in some sense abdicated responsibility in business ethics and forced the clergymen into a moral dilemma (of which, though, most of them did not seem to be aware), they did not relinquish their duties to teach traditional moral behavior to the populace. They supported not only the churches but also those auxiliary social institutions that instructed the public on temperance, Sabbath observance, and other principles of social order--newspapers, theaters, schools, and public lectures.

Denver's Rocky Mountain News and Central City's Register constantly lectured their readers on the merits of Sabbath observance, temperance, education, and orderly living.[20]

News editor William Byers entered the battle for Sabbath observance early. In his first edition, he ran a long article extolling the value of the Sabbath for labor, family, church, state, and soul. The author asserted that every human blessing flows from Sabbath keeping. For example, it allows free government.

> A state without a Sabbath must be without liberty. To a free state the Sabbath brings the support of some of the most powerful elements of self-government. It inspires respect for law, divine and human. It fosters the sense of omnipotent deity and of man's dependence and accountability. It engenders a lively conscience, more potent to restrain from crime than all legislative or judicial guards. Its educational force ... quickens the intellect and moulds the heart of a nation. It gives ... occasion for illustrating the equality of man before God and inculcating the great lesson of brotherhood. It is the foe of despotism and the ally of freedom.

The argument assumes that God-fearing individuals make responsible citizens. Responsible citizens create and sustain order, peace, and virtue. These elements make up a free state. There is no need for repression when men behave according to Christian principles. As reformers are wont to do, this author claimed almost magical powers for his favorite crusade. Sabbath observance can do away with the need for standing armies and tax collectors, he claimed.[21]

Problems of state and society turned out to be less simple of solution than reformers thought. The significance of the ideology behind this piece is its bed-rock belief in divine ordering of human society. The writer who lauded the Sabbath as a panacea had a deep faith that God creates, directs, and provides for viable social organization. God's creation of the Sabbath and his command to observe it are but a sign of divine sovereignty. Frontier civilizers almost never articulated their forebears' belief that God rules all men, that governments are God's creations, that people are dependent on divine initiative, and that God is bringing the kingdom to those who own their dependence. But their notions of proper social order were grounded in these articles of faith. Their conviction that Sabbath observance guaranteed liberty is best understood in light of this faith.

In accordance with his belief that Sabbath observances would advance the cause of social order, Byers urged church attendance in almost every Saturday evening edition. (He issued no Sunday paper.) Furthermore, he cajoled business people to close on Sundays. He declared that no one would lose business by Sunday closings, even though miners habitually shopped that day. He argued that the practice would help the city's "image" and that it would pay in the long run; it would have, he wrote "a most beneficial tendency, commercially and socially. The influence of such a movement would not only be creditable to our city, in the eyes of Christendom, but would operate beneficially in every respect, and in the end it would surely pay."[22] Other notices were less utilitarian and more straightforward. One columnist asserted, "It is the province of propriety, policy and duty to obey the Sabbath--in letter and in spirit."[23] Another defined the Sabbath as "that desirable day of rest, which like the blessed sunshine and the genial rain, comes with benefit for those who belong to the Christian church and those who do not."[24]

The editors displayed pragmatic morality on the temperance issue. None of them advocated tee-total abstinence, but they deplored public drunkenness as leading to disorder and violence. They campaigned against the sale of alcohol to soldiers, because drunken volunteers damaged property and sometimes "shot up the town." They applauded churchmen's temperance sermons and included some temperance articles in items copied from eastern newspapers.[25] In 1864, Byers declared, "A temperance reformation here is one of the chief things needful. Let us have less whiskey shops, jails and provo's [probably an archaic version of "provost", which in this context would mean a "keeper of a prison,"] and more school houses."[26]

The News linked not only temperance and education but also religion and education. The editors regarded them as cornerstones of civilization. The church and the school house "work always and ever for the public good."[27] This linking is instructive, for it reveals the conviction that both preacher and teacher function as molders of public behavior. Churches instruct and discipline adults; schools do the same for children. Citizens of all ages learn to work hard, live moderately, and honor divine commands. When people internalize these precepts, they behave decently without external restraints. Thus, a truly free society is possible. According to this reasoning, institutions of moral instruction are essential for social liberty. Once all learn the rules of moral behavior, a free, orderly, productive society will be ready for God to bring his kingdom fully.

Though important theological presuppositions underlay the journalists' support of churches and schools, civic boosterism played a part. Byers and his co-workers told their readers that communities with sound religious and educational institutions received a "good press" elsewhere. Prospective emigrants would move to such towns more readily. Population expansion would create greater prosperity. Civic boosters no doubt cheered when Byers wrote, "Good church advantages are one of the greatest recommendations to a city or a community of American citizens."[28] To interpret such boosterism as the primary opinion of the social function of religion in society is to overlook the more nearly fundamental view of the churches as agencies of moral education in self-government.

While Byers and his colleagues supported churches in print, Jack and Jeannette Langrishe, Denver's foremost pioneer actors, buttressed ethical teachings in comedy, tragedy and melodrama. The preachers' job was to preach the gospel, the journalists' task was to report the news, and the actors' goal was to entertain. But all felt a responsibility to help in the job of civilizing. They believed that sound civilization arises when individuals practice temperance, eschew violence, work hard, and so on. Pulpit, press, and stage influenced public behavior. Pioneer Coloradans felt as strongly about the influence of these as we do about the influence of mass media. Pulpit and press were accepted means of molding actions and encouraging sound community life. The moral influence of the stage, however, was something unique in the American frontier experience. Frontier companies such as Langrishe's successfully overcame the stigma that actors had borne for two centures in America. They challenged the stereotyped image of thespians as unstable, immoral, unreliable rascals. They did so by living exemplary lives, participating in civic affairs, and by presenting dramas with moral messages.

The Langrishes adhered to the code of orderly behavior and made sure that the members of their troupe did likewise. The <u>News</u> reported, "Contrary to common public notions respecting theatrical people, Mr. and Mrs. Langrishe are esteemed as highly socially as any in Denver."[29] Byers wrote that Jack's "affable, unaffected and gentlemanly manners and mode of driving business ... have procured for him a peculiarly popular reputation."[30] Another journalist praised the actor's "gentlemanly deportment" in private life.[31] A contemporary historian recorded that Langrishe's troupe was "always of the better caste for, aside from his own and Mr. Dougherty's (his partner) natural choice of such associates on the boards, their estimable wives could never descend to be associated there in any way with actors of low reputation."[32]

Langrishe and his co-workers made their homes in Denver and Central City, even though they took extensive tours to every mining camp and town in the Rocky Mountains. In their home towns, and in other places which they played regularly, they became active participants in community affairs. Langrishe and Dougherty belonged to St. Paul's Episcopal Church in Central City and attended St. John's when in Denver. Before these churches erected buildings, Langrishe lent his theater rent-free to the congregations, as we have seen above. When St. Paul's and St. John's built churches, he did the same for churches of other denominations. He became a lay reader and read Morning Prayer, buried the dead, and baptized babies when no priest was available. After his retirement from the stage, he gave elocution lessons to several priests.[33]

By his energetic attempts in community betterment, he endeared "himself to all Denver--even those ... diametrically opposed to his peculiar profession according him honor."[34] In Denver, Central City, Georgetown, Virginia City, Montana and everywhere that he owned a theater, he readily lent the buildings for public meetings and community celebrations. He subscribed to local attempts to help the poor and unfortunate. He staged benefit performances for the Denver poor fund, the Central City hospital drive, the Virginia City widows and orphans home, and other charitable enterprises. He belonged to the Masons and the Fenians and played benefit performances for both.[35]

Even more important, his plays served not only to entertain but also to instruct in morality. A Denver man wrote that "wholesome lessons, both in religion and morality, may be taught on the stage as well as in the pulpit or academy."[36] The News declared, "The drama is always worthy of patronage and support, for it ranks among the arts, and when legitimate, has a wide influence for good."[37] Colorado's journalists agreed repeatedly that Langrishe's productions were above reproach, aloof "from all ... evil influences," and "acceptable to all classes, the best society finding there a place of pleasant recreation."[38] Another writer assured his readers that all persons "of critical observation and refinement appear to take it as guaranteed that nothing will be done on this stage or off it, to displease or disgust them in the least."[39]

The company's repertoire indicates its stringent sense of propriety. The most popular plays were Shakespeare's tragedies and history plays. Langrishe repeated Othello, Macbeth, and Richard III most often. So conscious of maintaining high standards of taste was Langrishe that he censored even these, excising bawdy or suggestive passages. Next to Shakespearean drama, the most popular selections were melodramas and adaptations of Charles Dickens' and Walter Scott's works. A Central City man wrote that he loved melodrama because it guaranteed a "certain final triumph of virtue."[40] Three spectacularly successful plays in which virtue triumphed unequivocally appeared constantly among Langrishe's playbills: Uncle Tom's Cabin, Ten Nights in a Bar Room, and The Drunkard. Harriet B. Stowe's abolitionist tract and the two temperance pieces enjoyed enduring popularity among Colorado's play-goers.[41]

While religion and culture overlapped in such an unlikely place as the theater, they naturally did so in the usual places, including the school house. Church and school taught many of the same lessons. Colorado's civilizers learned much of their theology and ethics as school children. The school readers give us as clear and simple a picture of the civilizers' thought as can be found anywhere.

William H. McGuffey's famous readers enjoyed wide circulation during the middle years of the nineteenth century. Other readers copied his style and content, hoping to equal his success.[42] The selections influenced character growth and thought enormously, for the young scholars not only read but also memorized long passages. The ideas imprinted themselves on plastic young minds in such a way that long after the lessons had been forgotten, the style and content remained as part of the scholars' mental furniture.

The lessons are less stern and more pragmatic than the older books that began the alphabet with A, "In Adam's fall, we sinned all." But the editors meant to preach. Henry H. Vail, McGuffey's close associate, wrote, "The readers are the only texts used in all schools affording opportunity for distinct ethical teaching." He continued, "The reader should cover the whole field of morals and manners and in language that will impress their teaching indelibly upon the mind of every pupil.... No other texts used in the school room bear directly and positively upon the formation of character in the pupils." He boasted that the books taught "true patriotism, integrity, honesty, industry, temperance, courage, politeness, and all other moral and intellectual virtues." The aim of education ought to be the forming of "high moral principles which are at the foundation of character." These McGuffey guaranteed to supply.[43]

McGuffey and Vail believed that religion formed the foundation of society. A passage titled, "Religion the Only Basis of Society," taught that "religion is a social concern; for it operates powerfully on society, contributing in various ways to its stability and prosperity." Since God creates social forms, "the recognition of him must enforce all social duty, and enlightened piety must give its whole strength to public order." Religious instruction undergirds society, for it reminds man of God's sustaining activities and forces him to put his high regard of human law in its proper perspective. To believe that human laws sustain society is as foolish as believing "that were the sun quenched in the heavens, our torches would illuminate, and our fires quicken and fertilize the creation." Without religion, people would behave according to their nature, as sinful barbarians. The author summed up,

> Erase all thought and fear of God from a community, and selfishness and sensuality would absorb the whole man. Appetite, knowing no restraint, and suffering, having no solace or hope, would trample in scorn on the restraints of human laws. Virtue, duty, principle, would be mocked and suborned as unmenacing sounds. A sordid self-interest would supplant every feeling; and man would become, in fact, what the theory in atheism declares him to be--a companion for brutes.[44]

As religion is essential to social order, so the Bible is essential for religious understanding. Several readings show how and why so many Americans regarded the Bible as their moral constitution. One, from Jean J. Rousseau, lauds revelation in Scripture as superior to the philosopy of the Greek sages. Philosophers "with all their pomp" are "contemptible" when compared to the "simple and sublime" scripture. "The majesty of the Scriptures strikes me with astonishment, and the sanctity of the Gospel addresses itself to my heart."[45] One of the Grimke sisters, famous American reformers, praised the Bible as "the noblest [classic] that has ever honored and dignified the language of mortals." The holy book inspires high ideals in all. "Humility and resignation, purity, order and peace, faith, hope, and charity" flow from Scripture.

> If, raising our eyes from time to eternity, from the world of mortals to the world of just men made perfect, from the visible creation, marvelous, beautiful, and glorious as it is, to the invisible creation of angels and seraphs, from thw foot-stool of God to the throne of God himself, we ask, what are the blessings that flow from the single volume, let the question be answered by the pen of the evangelist, the harp of the prophet, and the records of the book of life.
> Such is the best of classics the world has ever admired; such, the noblest that man has ever adopted as a guide.[46]

The readers contain many passages from the Bible itself. All of them celebrate the joyousness of biblical religion. The joyful songs contrast sharply with many of the stories told of proud men cast down and small children dying. The selection is by no means accidental. The editors meant to teach that life is short while God is eternal and merciful to those who have faith. A sampling of the biblical material includes psalms and passages beginning, "Bless the Lord, Oh my soul! Oh Lord, my God; thou art very great; thou art clothed with honor and majesty;" "The heavens declare the glory of God and the firmament showeth his handiwork;" "Oh give thanks unto the Lord; call upon his name;" "Oh Lord, our Lord, how excellent is thy name in all the earth!;" "I will say of the Lord, he is my refuge and my fortress, my God in him will I trust;" "Oh come, let us sing unto the Lord;" "The Lord is my shepherd, I shall not want." Clearly, McGuffey wished to impress upon children the majesty, power, and graciousness of God.[47]

He included several stories from the Old and New Testaments, all focussed on the beauty of people's right relation with God. The editor sometimes quoted verbatim and sometimes paraphrased according to the difficulty of language and content.[48]

Works of the great English poets, especially Shakespeare and Milton, wielded almost as great an influence as the Bible. McGuffey and his associates carefully chose passages from the poets with religious or moral content. An example is John Milton's "Battle in Heaven" from Paradise Lost. Another comes from Shakespeare's Othello. "The Folly of Intoxication" is an exchange between Cassio and Iago. Cassio laments the loss of reputation after a bout of drunkenness. He cries, "I will rather sue to be despised. Drunk! and squabble! swagger! swear! and discourse fustian with one's own shadow! Oh, thou invincible spirit of wine! If thou hast no name to be known by, let us call thee devil."[49]

American reformers on temperance and other issues also found ample space in McGuffey's pages. Henry Ward Beecher, influential preacher, wrote several selections on temperance. He begins one such article with an Old Testament composite,

> Wine is a mocker, and strong drink is raging. (Proverbs 20:1) Who hath woe? who hath sorrow? who hath contentions? who hath babbling? who hath wounds without a cause? who hath redness of eyes? They that tarry long at the wine. (Proverbs 23:29-30)

Drink robs men of the proper uses of intellect, leads to violence, and ruins the hopes of the young, Beecher contends.

> Could I call around me, in one vast assembly, the young men of this nation, I would say: Hopes of my country blessed be ye of the Lord, now in the dew of your youth. But look well to your footsteps; for vipers, and scorpions, and adders surround your way. Look at the generation who have just preceded you. The morning of their life was cloudless, and it dawned as brightly as your own. But behold, now, the smitten, enfeebled, inflamed debauched idle, poor, irreligious, and vicious, with halting step, dragging onward to meet an early grave. Their bright prospects are clouded, and their sun is set, never to rise.

Worse, he declared, drunkenness impoverishes families and deprives innocent women and children. He pleaded, "This is your noon and your night, unless you shun those habits of intemperance which have thus early made theirs a day of clouds and of thick darkness." Beecher believed that the temperance movement would wipe out alcohol within the next generation. His vision looked like this:

> Alms-houses and jails and penitentiaries and state-prisons will then stand only as so many monuments of the vices of an age gone by; and the evils consequent upon the use of ardent spirits shall exist only upon the historian's page, as so many records of former degenerancy and errors of mankind.[50]

Beecher expected temperance to cure all social ills and usher in an era of unimpeded progress toward the kingdom.

Another temperance piece (unsigned) likens the still to a poisonous worm.

> There is a species of worm, found in various parts of this State, which conveys a poison of a nature so deadly, that compared with it, even the venom of the rattlesnake is harmless. To guard our readers against this foe of human kind, is the object of this lesson.... Youths of America, would you know the name of this reptile? It is called the Worm of the Still.[51]

Many Americans regarded gambling as imprudent. Some of the evangelists labeled it a sin akin to drink. Revivalist Timothy Flint warned the young that at first gambling might seem a harmless game, but "the love of gambling steals, perhaps, more often than any other sin, with an imperceptible influence on its victim." Worse, it was "the prolific stem, the fruitful parent, of all other vices. Blasphemy, falsehood, cheating, drunkenness, quarreling, and murder, are all naturally connected with gambling."[52]

McGuffey's authors lauded the social and personal benefits of Sabbath observance. Dr. Spring's discourse is typical and deserves quotation.

> The Sabbath lies at the foundation of all true morality. Morality flows from principle. Let the principles of moral obligation become relaxed, and the practice of morality will not long survive the overthrow. No man can long preserve the morals of his children, without the impressions of religious obligation....

> In the fearful struggle between virtue and vice, notwithstanding the powerful auxiliaries which wickedness finds in the bosoms of men, and in the seduction and influence of popular example, wherever the Sabbath has been suffered to live, the trembling interests of moral virtue have always been revered and sustained.

Sabbath breaking causes crime, Spring asserts, because it undermines the social structure. He believed that Sabbath observance, not laws, makes an orderly society.

The prisons in our own land could probably tell us, that

> they have scarcely a solitary tenant, who had not broken over the restraints of the Sabbath, before he was abandoned to crime.... The Sabbath is the keystone of the arch which sustains the temple of virtue.

Not only does Sunday observance promote virtue but it also creates prosperity. Spring continued, "The God of Heaven has said, "Them that honor me, will I honor." You will not often find a notorious Sabbath-breaker a permanently prosperous man; and a Sabbath-breaking community is never a happy and prosperous community.[53]

A short story points out the benefits of Sabbath observance. It is a simple tale of two men. One worked on Sundays and lost all of his wealth; the other rested and worshipped on Sundays and earned prosperity and happiness.[54] The injunction to obey the moral code in order to get rich in both Spring's discourse and this story stands in odd juxtaposition to the selections exalting the joys of the other world and degrading the pleasures of this one. But the articles do not, any more than the world view which they represent, sort out all the doctrines to construct a coherent system.

On wealth, the editors walked a thin line. Riches, if gained by virtue, could be God's blessing. But the search for wealth may be soul-destroying and wealth once achieved can corrupt man. A poem called "The Miser" spells out the details.

> Gold, many hunted, sweat and bled for gold;
> Waked all the night and labored all the day;

And what was this allurement, dost thou ask?
A dust dug from the bowels of the earth,
Which being cast into the fire, came out
A shining thing that fools admired, and called
A god; and in devout and humble plight
Before it kneeled, the greater to the less.

The gold hunter is

Most fallen, most prone, most earthly, most debased
Of all that sold Eternity for Time.
None bargained on so easy terms with Death.

The miser is the "most inhuman wretch ... the sorest of evils."[55]

Greed is a sin; but hard work, prosperity, and generosity are virtues. William Wirt lauded work. He declared that each man shapes his destiny by work or loses all by laziness. He concluded, "Of this be assured, I speak from observation a certain truth: There is no excellence without great labor."[56]

Henry W. Longfellow, popular poet, also celebrated the dignity of labor.

Life is real! Life is earnest!
And the grave is not its goal...

Let us, then be up and doing,
With a heart for any fate;
Still achieving, still pursuing,
Learn to labor and to wait.

His perennial favorite, "The Village Blacksmith," personifies the virtue of work.

His brow is wet with honest sweat;
He earns whate'er he can,
And looks the whole world in the face,
For he owes not any man.

The blacksmith was also pious, loyal, and loving.

He goes, on Sunday to the church,
And sits among his boys;
He hears the parson pray and preach,

> He hears his daughter's voice,
> Singing in the village choir,
> And it makes his heart rejoice.[57]

Many reformers of this era thought that universal education would make everyone temperant, charitable, pious, diligent, and thrifty.

McGuffey reprinted passages from Beecher's "Plea for the West," in which the preacher cried:

> We must educate! We must educate! or we must perish by our own prosperity. If we do not, short will be our race from the cradle to grave. If, in our haste to be rich and mighty, we outrun our literary and religious institutions, they will never overtake us; or only come up after the battle of liberty is fought and lost.[58]

Though encouraged to work, learn, and prosper, the young readers found many passages rehearsing the transitoriness of life, temperal existence as a proving ground, and the blessings of the life to come. Implied throughout is the idea that one earns his salvation by good deeds on earth. One essayist declared, "The Bible everywhere conveys the idea that this life is not our home, but a state of probation, that is, of trial and discipline, which is intended to prepare us for another."[59] Another depicted the day of judgment, as the great assize.

> Before that assembly every man's good deeds will be declared, and his most secret sins disclosed. As no elevation of rank will then give a title to respect, no obscurity of condition shall exclude the just from public honor, or screen the guilty from public shame.[60]

Many of the essays, stories, and poems about the transitory quality of earthly life have a curious morbid quality. Stories about innocent, beautiful, and loving children who die young are indicative of the maudlin sentimentality of much 19th century popular culture. It stands in marked contrast to the bright optimism of the reformers.

Patriotic themes with semi-religious content appear repeatedly in the readers. The authors echo the idea that America has a special role in God's creation of the kingdom on earth. One example describes the New England Puritans who spawned the American Revolution as men on a holy mission to resist oppression. They serve as example for all; they were destined "for the high and special purpose of showing to the world that the civil and religious rights of man, the rights of self-government, of conscience, and independent thought, are not merely things to be talked of." Their notions of revolution came from biblical principles. They acted upon their faith. "As deeply seated as was the principle of liberty and resistance to arbitrary power, in the breast of the Puritans, it was not more so than their piety and sense of religious obligation. They were emphatically a people whose God was the Lord." They governed according to a religious pattern; "whenever a few of them settled a town, they immediately gathered themselves into a church, and their elders were magistrates, and their code of laws was the Pentateuch."[61] This rather simple stereotyping of our country's early merchant, farmer, and adventurer settlers has held sway in most school books ever since, despite Perry Miller's[62] and others' valiant efforts to portray our Puritan ancestors more realistically. The real significance of the essay is its implicit understanding of America as the God-designated model for the world to copy.

Several of the selections implicitly style America as the New Israel--a land and people particularly favored by God. McGuffey reprinted a speech, in which Patrick Henry implies the theme.

> Three millions of people, armed in the holy cause of liberty, and in such a country as that which we possess, are invincible by any force which our enemy can send against us. Besides, we shall not fight our battles--alone. There is a just God who presides over the destinies of nations; and who will raise up friends to fight our battles for us.[63]

Even though separation of church and state limited direct clerical participation in civic affairs, church leaders did take part in the formation of orderly communities. Perhaps even more important, key lay people took up the churchly message, especially in matters of morality, and instructed the populace through such media as the newspapers, theaters, and schools. As lay persons assumed semi-clerical functions, social and religious ideas, which often dovetail, began to merge in some areas.

NOTES

1. Quoted by Sidney Mead, The Lively Experiment, p. 63.

2. Cf. Emile Durkheim, The Elementary Forms of Religious Life (New York: The Free Press, 1965; first U. S. edition, 1915).

3. Minutes of Annual Conferences of the Methodist Episcopal Church, 1862, p. 23.

4. Jacob Adriance, Diary, August 2, 3, November 13, 1859; Goode, Outposts of Zion, pp. 445-46; Billingsley, Journal, p. 252, Sept. 8, 1861.

5. Kehler, Diary, November 1, 1861.

6. Ibid.

7. Howlett, Life of Machebeuf, p. 377.

8. Ibid., pp. 317-18; William O'Ryan and Thomas Malone, History of the Catholic Church in Colorado (Denver: C. J. Kelley, 1889), pp. 59-61.

9. Norman McLeod to Dr. Badger, Aug. 25, 1864; William Crawford to Badger, Sept. 25, 1864, Letters, A. H. M. S. Correspondence.

10. Howbert, Memories of a Long Life, pp. 46-47.

11. Dyer, Snow Shoe Itinerant, pp. 152-55.

12. Rocky Mountain News, August 26, 30, December 13, 30, 1861; June 27, 1864.

13. Perrigo, "A Social History of Central City, Colorado, 1859-1900," pp. 237-249.

14. Rocky Mountain News, September 8, 1865; Hopkins, The Bible and the Gold Rush, p. 125; Jones, History of Catholic Education in the State of Colorado, pp. 80-84.

15. See pp. 142-50.

16. See Walter P. Webb's Great Frontier (Austin: University

of Texas Press, 1951), pp. 103-179, for his analysis of individualism and optimism produced by material abundance and "free" land. I agree with Webb's analysis but would like to add to the list of causal factors the impact of the idea of the kingdom.

17. See H. Richard Niebuhr, The Kingdom of God in America (New York: Harper Torchbooks, 1959; first edition, 1939).

18. John Alton Templin, "A History of Methodism in Denver, 1876-1912," Th. D. dissertation, Iliff, 1956, pp. 32-33, 98-99; Breck, The Episcopal Church in Colorado, pp. 8-9, 277-78; Cooper, Our Presbytery of Denver, p. 9.

19. Rocky Mountain News, September 7, 1865; McMechen, Life of Governor John Evans.

20. I have chosen examples from the News because it was established earlier in the pioneer period and more nearly reflects the struggle to impose order in the crucial years, 1859-61. However, Lynn Perrigo assures us that the Register, under David Collier, in "A Social History of Central City," pp. 230-37, was a powerful moral force.

21. Rocky Mountain News, April 25, 1859.

22. Ibid., April 22, 1859.

23. Ibid., December 3, 1864.

24. Ibid., August 18, 1863.

25. Ibid., October, 1860.

26. Ibid., June 27, 1864.

27. Ibid., August 27, 1859.

28. Ibid., July 19, 1862.

29. Ibid., Feb. 24, 1869.

30. Ibid., April 8, 1861.

31. *Montana Post*, Nov. 16, 1867.

32. *History of Clear Creek and Boulder Valleys, Colorado* (Chicago: O. L. Baskin, 1880), p. 253.

33. Parish Record Book, St. Paul's, Central City, pp. 12-13; Ethelbert Talbot, *My People of the Plains* (New York: Harper & Bros., 1906), p. 96; Tuttle, *Reminiscences of a Missionary Bishop*, p. 415.

34. *Rocky Mountain News*, April 6, 1867.

35. (Denver) *Weekly Commonwealth and Republican*, December 16, 1863.

36. *Rocky Mountain News*, October 20, 1870.

37. *Ibid.*, October 24, 1870.

38. *Ibid.*, December 10, 1861.

39. (Central City) *Daily Miners Register*, October 3, 1865.

40. Young, *Echoes from Arcadia*, pp. 32-33.

41. David Grimsted, *Melodrama Unveiled*, 1800-1850 (Chicago: University of Chicago Press, 1968); see also Cochran, "Jack Langrishe ..."

42. Lewis E. Atherton, *Main Street on the Middle Border* (Bloomington: Indiana University Press, 1954), p. 65; Atherton reports that over 100,000,000 copies of McGuffey's readers sold between 1800 and 1900. They were well-received all over the country but especially so in the Midwest. Since most of Colorado's civilizers came from the Midwest, analysis of readers popular in that region is appropriate.

43. Henry H. Vail, *A History of the McGuffey Readers* (Cleveland: Burrow Bros. Co., 1911), p. 2.

44. William H. McGuffey (ed.), *New Fifth Eclectic Reader* (Cincinnati: Winthrop B. Smith & Co., 1857), pp. 306-307.

45. *Ibid.*, pp. 280-82.

46. *Ibid.*, pp. 288-89.

47. *Ibid.*, pp. 108-12, 127-30.

48. *Ibid.*; even the Bible had to be censored on occasion. That is, they never included stories which emphasized the human weaknesses of Old Testament heroes or the New Testament apostles. For example, we do not find the stories of David and Bathsheba, Abraham and Sarah in Egypt, or Peter's denial of his relationship with Jesus.

49. McGuffey (ed.), *New Sixth Eclectic Reader* (Cincinnati: Sargent, Wilson & Hinkle, 1857), pp. 132-33, 240-41.

50. *Fifth Reader*, pp. 83-85.

51. *Ibid.*, pp. 192-93.

52. *Ibid.*, pp. 204-208.

53. *Sixth Reader*, pp. 421-23.

54. *Fifth Reader*, pp. 105-107.

55. *Ibid.*, pp. 209-210.

56. *Ibid.*, pp. 148-49.

57. *Sixth Reader*, pp. 212, 86-87.

58. *Fifth Reader*, pp. 150-53.

59. *Ibid.*, p. 178.

60. *Sixth Reader*, p. 105.

61. *Fifth Reader*, pp. 249-52.

62. See Perry Miller, *The New England Mind* (New York: Macmillan, 1939), *The Puritans* (New York: American Book Co., 1938).

63. *Sixth Reader*, p. 120.

CHAPTER 7

CIVILIZATION AND DESTINY IN COLORADO PIONEERS' THOUGHT

Many Colorado pioneers held a system of belief in which national and Christian values and aspirations dovetailed--a religion of the republic or a kind of religious nationalism.[1] American Christians who migrated to open frontiers often regarded themselves as part of a divine plan to people the world with folk, Christian in religion and republican in government. Since religious language permeated the speech of the Colorado frontiersmen, constant references to divine purpose are to be expected. But religious thought also permeated their social ideas. Their notions of destiny, mission, civilization, and kingdom are examples of the ways in which religion and culture interrelated in the pioneer era. Previous interpretations[2] of the American intellectual heritage are helpful, but exploration of some pioneers' thought is necessary.

Colorado pioneers, even those who thought little about such matters, generally agreed on some version of the following: God rules His earthly realm and delegates many responsibilities to His elected or chosen people. The kingdom is to come, and it seems likely to begin or to have already begun in America.

Most of the preachers and lay leaders in Colorado held a post-millenial view of the kingdom. Christ's reign on earth had already begun. The postmillenialists expected earthly life to become progressively (and rapidly) more nearly just, brotherly, joyful, and prosperous. They grounded their hopes in social order and progress directed by enlightened, converted, and redeemed persons. Though the postmillenialist tradition later produced many social critics,[3] those of our period trusted republican government, voluntary religion, and the free enterprise system. With these tools, they confidently expected to improve the world under the providence of God. Some expected the system to work with almost no changes. Others lobbied for wider suffrage, prison reform, abolition of slavery, limitations on child labor, broader education, increased church membership, temperance, and Bible reading. They expected these reforms to produce orderly and prosperous communities, as we have seen.[4]

Many Coloradans had a vague expectation while others held an articulated theory of the coming kingdom. Almost all, no matter what their religious convictions, expected progressive social improvement with little or no change of basic social structures. Even though Colorado's mining towns carried the seeds of urban industrial problems, the pioneers did not (and probably could not) see them. Instead, they recognized the visible signs of progress toward orderly, self-sustaining, and prosperous towns, villages, and farms. Their society was, they believed, an extension of America's work in building up God's kingdom. By their labor, they had advanced the moving frontier line; they had pushed civilization across the prairies and into the Rocky Mountains.

Civilization, broadly conceived, means a relatively high level of cultural and technological development. For the frontier folk it meant, more particularly, a social organism characterized by productive labor in field, farm, and town, organized republican government, regular religious observance, common schools for children of all social classes, and easily accessible channels of trade. This kind of civilization seemed suited to God's work in bringing his kingdom. They felt themselves to be akin to Israelites in the pre-monarchical period and thus to be God's chosen people. God commands them, they thought, 1) to carry their kind of civilization to the rest of the world or 2) to provide a shining example which other peoples would recognize as superior and copy. America's political expansionists had argued that God intended the United States to stretch from ocean to ocean. To reach these boundaries was the nation's manifest destiny, a goal, easily perceived, for persons directed by God for a special purpose. The more zealous expansionists favored United States' acquisition of all of North America. A few looked covetously at Central and South America, too. The expansionists used much religious language in their arguments. Mission was their most constantly used metaphor. The spread of civilization was the religious and social counterpart of political manifest destiny.

The Colorado pioneers had no stake in the political expansionists' dreams. The victors of the Mexican War achieved manifest destiny. (Only the most zealous thought much about further political expansion at mid-century.) But they acted and thought as the agents of civilization. They conceived of themselves as civilizers--destined to settle and build civilized society in all parts of the mid-section of North America. They had a mission. Few lay persons thought of themselves as actually sent by God. The laity assumed that they migrated voluntarily and freely. But a notion (usually half-realized) of national calling underlay many of their actions and thoughts. God intended the previously untilled earth to flower by the labor of American pioneers. The wilderness was to be made to blossom. The miners supplemented this pastoral imagery with the idea that God intended them to take the golden treasure from the mountains and to turn it to good commercial use in the building of orderly and prosperous towns and villages.

Precise analysis of socio-religious thought in frontier Colorado is difficult because many mid-nineteenth century Americans clothed political, economic, and social doctrines in religious garb. Manifest destiny, mission, and civilization (as these terms were generally understood by Colorado's pioneers) are prime examples of the secularization of formerly religious ideas. Few deliberately tried to delude their hearers by attaching religious significance (by linguistic association) to political expansionism, displacement of native peoples, or economic aggrandizement. Most sprinkled their rhetoric with biblical phrases and references to the divine because they were accustomed to do so and, more importantly, because they believed that the remarkable movement westward, the increasing economic prosperity of the nation, the rise of technology, the amazing productivity of American farms, and the increasing freedom of much of the populace were signs of God's special favor on the American nation. The progress was simply too rapid, too unprecedented, too magnificent to be other than the work of God's chosen people. Even the most superficially religious tacitly agreed that God had something to do with America's development.

Colorado pioneers produced several expressions of the idea that God had chosen Americans to advance the kingdom by improvement and expansion of their civilization as may be seen in the following examples. The *Rocky Mountain News* editors wrote or copied several articles which reveal their ideas of civilization and divine purpose. In the first issue, Byers wrote, "The present age is signalized by the rapid succession of striking events in the history of divine providence." In another part of the same issue, he wrote,

> We make our debut in the far west, where ... a few months ago the wild beasts and wilder Indians held undisturbed possession--where now surges the advancing wave of Anglo-Saxon enterprise and civilization, where soon we fondly hope will be erected a great and powerful state, another empire in the sisterhood of empires.[5]

Byers clearly expected a great empire to grow up in the Far West. He seldom made a direct connection between this expectation and the coming of God's kingdom on earth. But he was not averse to printing material that did make a close connection between divine action and national progress.

Governor William Gilpin issued a Thanksgiving Day proclamation, printed in the News, which links the divine and the national.

> Immemorial usage has established among the American people the pious custom to select annually, one of the days of the closing year and dedicate it for universal prayer and Thanksgiving to Almighty God for their salvation, perpetuity and prosperity as a Christian people. I invite the people of the Colorado Territory so to elect and unanimously observe, Thursday the 28th of November inst., as a day of Thanksgiving for divine blessings to us as a people and fervent prayer for the continued existence of our greatness and harmonious Union.[6]

Gilpin was an ardent expansionist and a zealot for western development. He thought that western lands and most particularly Colorado would become the throbbing center of a mighty empire. His arguments are a curious combination of lay theology, geography, political theory, and chauvinism. As others had done before him, he predicted the natural progress of empire from East to West. Gilpin in his tract Notes on Colorado,[7] prophesied the strength and unity of a great people living on the convex surface of the North American continent, with the center of power and wealth at the peak--Colorado. Settlement, agricultural development, and mining would create a bond of unity for the world.

He based part of his geopolitics on the shape of land and part on observation of previous movements of civilizations.

He noted that on the 40th parallel of latitude and in the "isothermal line of 52 degrees of mean temperature, are located nearly all the great cities of the world, and that these lines are the center of a temperate zone, embracing four-fifths of the population and nine-tenths of the civilization of the human race." Exact definition of terms, especially "civilization," might clear up this puzzling statement. But Gilpin did not work with conceptual clarity or verbal precision. Nonetheless, his concept of civilization cannot be too far from that of his contemporaries.

He believed that great civilizations arise naturally and providentially in geographic areas where all desirable natural resources can be found. He asserted that Colorado is such a place, superior to all other points on or near the 40th parallel because the climate stimulates work, activeness, and health.

In an exhortation to westbound pioneers in 1849 and again in a speech before the British Association of Science in 1870, he spoke glowingly of the progress of civilization westward.

> The pioneer army perpetually advances, reconnoitres, strikes to the front. Empire plants itself upon the trails. Agitation, creative energy, industry, throb throughout and animate this crowding deluge. Conclusive occupation, solidity, permanence, and a stern discipline, attend every movement and illustrate every camp. The American realizes that "Progress is God." He clearly recognizes and accepts the <u>continental</u> mission of his country.[8]

He went on to explain how and why Colorado was the dominant center of this future empire. Colorado was the highest and most salubrious point in the isothermal belt.

> Within this isothermal belt, and restricted to it, the column of the human family, with whom abides the sacred and inspired fire of civilization, accompanying the sun, has marched from east to west, since the birth of time.[9]

He maintained that history proves his theory,

> This highly artificial and disciplined system of

> civilization ... is transmitted from the very dawn of antiquity, and is inherited. History is the diary of its geographical progress, of its periods of brightness and obscurity, of its struggles and its energies. When society has attained its largest numerical strength, accomplishing the highest level of intelligence and the longest duration, it is defined to be an empire. History occupies itself with the biography of these empires--their rise, culmination, and decadence. They form a succession along the undulating zone of the northern hemisphere of the globe, within the isothermal belt. They form within it a continuous zodiac from east to west. These empires are the Chinese, the Indian, the Persian, the Grecian, the Roman, the Spanish, the British, finally, the republican empire of the people of North America. These are the essential organizations which have received, held intelligently for a few centuries each, the vestal torch of civilization, perpetuated and transmitted it with more or less fidelity.[10]

Gilpin tried to create a predictive science based on geographical and historical observations. His product is tinged with chauvinism, for he hopes to justify American expansionism. He did not do so cynically, for he felt impelled by divine purpose in history.

Gilpin reiterated his claim that North America's geographic and political unity made it superior to Asia and Europe. He seemed to assume the political unity of Canada, the United States, Mexico, and the states of Central America. Without stating this assumption, he continued to extoll the virtues of North American social and political life. In North America,

> the liberties, self-government, and civilization of the people, are and have been normal and universal in principle and practice. Monarchy and military despotism have been always unknown and absent from our continent. The indestructible principles of social and political science are rescued, one by one, from the chaos and rubbish of Europe.... Rescued from the quicksands of the past, democratic-republican power, rightly understanding itself, has here set and perpetuated in the world its own indestructible foundations.[11]

Furthermore, geography favored the North American empire, which could bring peace and unity to the whole world. Europe's disunity arose because its topography is cut up by rivers and inlets from the Mediterranean Sea. In contrast, America's topography is harmonious, he explained.

> The instinct of the American people has located and erected the grand maritime cities of Philadelphia, New York, and Baltimore, where our continent receives the axis of the isothermal zone. Entering here from the east and favored by auspicious architecture of our continent, this axis of intensity traverses it athwart to the Pacific Ocean. It deviates little from the 40th degree of latitude, arching from it slightly in the middle range towards the south. Here auspicious nature unveils every propitious gift. The energy of progress, always salient upon this line, has located along it all the first selected and chief cities--Pittsburgh, Cincinnati, St. Louis, Leavenworth and Kansas [City], Denver, Salt Lake City, Virginia [City], San Francisco. Here the intrepid energies of the pioneer population have first and chiefly condensed themselves in force. But we have seen that North America is a vast amphitheatre, and is concave in configuration. Its valleys, its mountain chains, its rivers, its cordilleras, its ocean boundaries, are all and all alike longitudinal. The whole breadth of continent beneath the isothermal zone, from Cuba to Hudson's Bay, presents an undeviating harmony. This longitudinal expansion runs flush into the arctic zone, and into the equatorial zone, absolutely without any barrier or obstruction to its undulating smoothness of surface. Nature is benignant and graceful throughout her whole scheme, and is propitious in the working of her laws, and in every element.[12]

North America, which lies thus in the temperate zone, is a fit area for high human activity. "Humanity, nurtured in this affluence of divine warmth instinctively receives and cultivates discipline, elasticity, and immortal progress."[13]

Gilpin professed a doctrine similar to the milleniarism of his Puritan ancestors.[14] He predicted an age of harmony, unity and peace. As these predecessors had believed in an Age of the Spirit in the New World, so Gilpin believed in the inevitability of a golden age when the whole world would "be grouped together and fused into one universal and harmonious system of fraternal relations" when North America should become dominant. He looked forward to the abolition of war and a time when the majority of the world's people would accept the "essential teaching of Christianity in practice." (Unlike some millenialists, he did not predict the conversion of all to Christianity but only the republican majority which was to emerge.) He described his vision: "The civilized masses of the world meet--they mutually explain and understand one another--they are mutually enlightened, and fraternize to re-constitute human relations and institutions in harmony with nature and with God."[15]

In contrast to those who hoped to create the kingdom of God by reforms, Gilpin expected the kingdom to come with expansion and industrial development. Believing that God reveals truth in nature, he contended that developing the isothermal belt in North America would solve all earthly problems. Westward expansion already in progress was evidence of God's purpose and the desired goal.

> A divine light, issuing out of the obscurity of the past, shines upon our country and upon our people; it speaks out in the never silent oracles of nature, in response to which each individual heart is free to re-echo and reflect. A finite goal is unveiled to them, and distinctly seen--its possession and fruition are intelligibly revealed.[16]

The gold rushes that began expansion to the Pacific were God's way of leading men into the wilderness. The gold seekers had a divine mission to "rescue" the land "from the wilderness." The work of God seemed clear.

> This occupation of wild territory ... proceeds with all the solemnity of a providential ordinance. It is at this moment sweeping onward to the Pacific with accelerated activity and force, like a deluge of men, rising unabatedly, and daily pushed onward by the hand of God.[17]

Expansion and further development, Gilpin insisted, were a mission to which God calls the pioneers. Because they contain almost every theological justification for westward movement, his closing remarks deserve full quotation.

> The calm, wise man sets himself to study aright and understand clearly the deep designs of Providence--to scan the great volume of nature--to fathom if possible the will of the Creator, and to receive with respect what may be revealed to him.
>
> Two centuries have rolled over our race upon this continent. From nothing we have become 20,000,000. From nothing we are grown to be in agriculture, in commerce, in civilization, and in natural strength, the first among nations existing or in history. So much is our destiny--so far, up to this time--transacted, accomplished, certain, and not to be disputed. From this threshold we read the future.
>
> The untransacted destiny of the American people is to subdue the continent--to push over this vast field to the Pacific Ocean--to animate the many hundred millions of its people, and to cheer them upward--to set the principle of self-government at work--to agitate these herculean masses--to establish a new order in human affairs--to set free the enslaved--to regenerate superannuated nations--to change darkness into light--to stir up the sleep of an hundred centuries--to teach old nations a new civilization--to confirm the destiny of the human race--to carry the career of mankind to its culminating point--to cause stagnant people to be re-born--to perfect science--to emblazon history with the conquest of peace--to shed a new and resplendent glory upon mankind--to unite the world in one social family--to dissolve the spell of tyranny and exalt charity--to absolve the curse that weighs down humanity, and to shed blessings round the world!
>
> Divine task! immortal mission! Let us tread fast and joyfully the open trail before us! Let every American heart open wide for patriotism to glow undimmed, and confide with religious faith in the sublime and prodigious destiny of his well-loved country.[18]

Gilpin combined loyalty to democracy and Christianity. He tried to prove by science and history that God intends the United States to dominate the world. He justified power-seeking with a kind of altruism, for he really thought that the extension of democracy and Christianity would bring peace, prosperity, and world unity. Though he made no reference to his colonial ancestors as the children of a New Israel, his intellectual descent from them is clear. His doctrine was not theological or biblical, for he substituted pseudo-scientific arguments for the traditional scriptural exegesis. He also went beyond his ancestors, who hoped to build a purified society in a wilderness. He felt that their dream had been achieved--transacted destiny. He projected the dream to cover the whole world.

In his reflections about America's destiny, Gilpin firmly closed his eyes to a large part of reality. For example, he ignored the importance of the southern hemisphere, since his data showed that 80 percent of the population lived in the northern hemisphere. In addition, he assumed that only the white race has a significant contribution to make to civilization.

In his enthusiasm to promote the West, he overestimated the fertility of the plains and the ease of farming them. He exaggerated the supply of mineral wealth in the mountains and glossed over the technical difficulty of mining there. More than a century later, it is easy to see that he was far too optimistic about the curative powers of democracy--he could not know then that American republicanism does not always export well. Further, Gilpin made no effort to appreciate the worth of religions other than Christianity. In no way did he deviate much from popular thought, however. As a leader and a polemicist, he spoke to and for westerners, articulating their dreams and visions. His statements reveal some of the unspoken assumptions of his people. His was a statement, they felt, of noble purpose, dignifying the lives of pioneers. His vision raised their actions from the ordinary to the divinely ordained.

George Phillips, head of the Methodists' Colorado Seminary (1863-65), also worked out a statement of noble purpose for expansionism. While Gilpin's was cast largely in secular terms with references to the divine, Phillips' arguments came from scriptural interpretation. But like Gilpin, Phillips expected the United States to dominate the world and argued that such was the divine intention. He studied scripture closely and found in the prophetic and apocalyptic literature material to demonstrate the thesis that the United States is the "restored Israel."

A synopsis of his argument shows us how he, as many others in his day, combined religious and political ideas. He asks, at the outset, "whether God has any thing to do in planting us as a great nation." His answer is a strong, "Yes," for he argues that God has spoken about civil government in scripture.[19]

> The great principles of civil liberty were first taught by Jehovah to his ancient people, the Hebrews, and embodied in a form of government, known to us as the Jewish theocracy, in which the law was Divine, and the instrument of administration human.... The Hebrew Republic, for such it really was, we claim was a type of our own Government, just as the Jewish Church was a type of the Christian Church.[20]

The United States of Israel was prototypical because, Phillips argued, it was a representative government of states in a federal system, joined under a written constitution, and administered by executive, legislative, and judicial branches.[21]

But the Israelites abandoned this God-given system for the monarchy. As soon as the monarchy triumphed, prophets began predicting a "restored Israel" to come in the last time. Phillips asserted that Old Testament prophecies "clearly and unmistakably point out the United States as the restored Israel."[22] Daniel's prediction of a Fifth Empire clearly points to the United States, he continued.[23] The twelfth chapter of John's Revelation also predicts the rise and development of this country. The woman fleeing into the wilderness is the Protestant Church escaping the persecutions of the Roman Catholic Church. The man-child born there is the United States. Thus, our civil government is the child of the Church, Phillips claimed.[24] He added, "The resemblance between the great principles of Christianity and the principles of liberty, as found in our free government, is evidence that the government is the offspring of the Church."[25]

Phillips combed scripture for evidence that God created the government of the United States for a special purpose. Ingeniously, he found a prediction of the Boston Tea Party in Isaiah 33.21 and the coming of the Chinese immigrants to California in Isaiah 49.12. Other biblical references he interpreted as predictions of America's civil war and the abolition of slavery.[26] In addition to scripture, Phillips drew on history. He asserted that no true republic existed between the time of Israel and the United States.

However, great leaders kept the vision alive: for example, Milton, Cromwell, and greatest of all, George Washington and Thomas Jefferson.[27] Phillips appealed to historical interpretations when he voiced a common belief of his age:

> God seems to have kept the New World, with its vast forest and grand prairies, as the place of his Christian Israel. Here for ages the wilderness remained unbroken; kings and kingdoms rose and fell in other portions of the world, while Jehovah, in his mysterious providence, was preparing the way for the coming nation, which was not to grow up upon the ruins of another, but was to receive its birth outside of all other nations, to grow up where monarchy had never cast its dark shadow as an occupant of the country.[28]

Though scarcely convincing to the modern reader, Phillips confidently averred, "These facts of history we think clearly show that the Government of the United States was set up by the God of heaven."[29]

When Phillips thought that he had successfully analyzed the nation's past, he turned to the present and future. If God established the United States, He did so for a purpose, conferring a destiny on the people. The divine purpose was to carry an idea. "Omnipotent Providence confides to a chosen people the revelation of a great truth, a great regenerative idea."[30] This idea is the soul of the nation. The soul of the United States is the idea of liberty and equality for all people and their capacity for self-government. From this comes America's mission:

> It was the Divine will that the new nationality should keep its life covenant by expanding, by growing, in accordance with the law of its own organic life. This great fundamental, this central, this generative idea, was to be developed and promulgated. It was to be demonstrated to other governments, to all people. Our mission in this respect was important, for it was worldwide as that of the Church. We were to show that man as man has the inborn capability of self-government. God committed this high trust to us as a nation, and to none else.[31]

This present mission will end, Phillips declared, in world domination.

> Our mission, in short, as a nation, should only be accomplished when the last despot should be dethroned, the last chain of oppression broken, the dignity and equality of redeemed humanity everywhere acknowledged, republican government everywhere established, and the American flag ... should wave over every land and encircle the world in its majestic folds, then, and not till then, should the nation have accomplished the purpose for which it was established by the God of heaven.[32]

This conquest of monarchy will not come by military or diplomatic victories. The American Republic will triumph by "the power of our example."[33] Even now, Phillips asserted, "God, through the instrumentality of the Church, is preparing the world for this universal dominion of republican government. This view is in harmony with the teachings of God's Word."[34] The author was probably crediting the infant overseas mission programs with this preparatory work. Since the United States is conquering the world peacefully through the Church, he predicted that American empire, unlike any other in the history of the world, will never fall. It will be perpetual.

> As Christianity, which God gave to save the world, is to continue as long as there are men to be saved, so republican government, which God gave to govern the world, is to continue as long as there are men to govern....
>
> Surely a high destiny awaits the United States of America. That will be a glorious day for mankind, when free government shall prevail throughout the world.[35]

As in the case of William Gilpin, George Phillips' thought is imprecise, overly optimistic, and so founded on preconceptions that it distorts reality. Again like Gilpin, he rehearses convictions held by many of his contemporaries. William Clebsch comments, "The patent unoriginality of Phillips' book signifies its representing a major body of religious and nationalistic sentiment." He adds, "Neither the threads of the argument, nor the cloth of conception belonged uniquely to the author."[36]

These were lofty visions indeed for a young nation still insignificant in European and Asian eyes. We must remember that in the 1860's, American industrial and economic expansion had scarcely begun. The United States counted for little in international affairs. It is then fitting that these visionaries spoke of God's power and purpose. Their faith in God's strong arm was genuine.

Colorado's pioneers, successful in building civilized communities hundreds of miles from the line of settlement, could easily agree with Gilpin and Phillips. They gladly concurred when such leaders told them that they were fulfilling God's purpose, that God chose them to usher in a golden age for mankind, that they had a mission from heaven. Pioneer life was never easy; such rhetoric and the faith behind it, made a hard task seem worthwhile.

Such blending of religion and politics put the divine stamp of approval on secular society. If God creates civil governments to achieve His ends, then the frontiersmen were doing God's work in establishing godly communities. Thus, religion and culture intertwined. And, if the ultimate goal is to spread God's church and republicanism to the rest of the world, then their work certainly contributed to the coming of the kingdom on earth.

Visions of world unity and the coming of the kingdom did not disguise the fact that the age of unity and harmony had not yet come fully. Colorado's churchmen made little effort to bring unity to Christ's church, as we shall see in the next chapter.

NOTES

1. There is much excellent discussion of this development in American religious thought. One of the most incisive is to be found in Sidney Mead, The Lively Experiment, pp. 134-87. Others include Niebuhr, The Kingdom of God in America; Conrad Cherry (ed.), God's New Israel (Englewood Cliffs, New Jersey: Prentice-Hall, 1971); Winthrop Hudson (ed.), Nationalism and Religion in America (New York: Harper & Row, 1970); Russell E. Richey and Donald G. Jones (eds.), American Civil Religion (New York: Harper & Row, 1974).

   For reasons of clarity in discussion of this complex idea, I have formulated a working definition of religious nationalism as it seems to have existed during the Colorado pioneer period. Its adherents believed that God orders history and His actions in history so that the American republic may grow unimpeded by European intervention. Further, God intends the United States to expand and prosper until it becomes strong enough to cause the rest of the world to adopt republican governments and Christianity. Thus, Americans are a people chosen by God to inaugurate a better world, perhaps God's kingdom itself.

2. Robert T. Handy and H. Richard Niebuhr have explored the ideas of kingdom and civilization. Frederick Merk and Arthur Weinberg have given us excellent expositions of Manifest Destiny. Merk has illuminated much about Americans' sense of mission. See Handy, *A Christian America*; Niebuhr, *The Kingdom of God in America*; Merk, *Manifest Destiny and Mission in American History*; Arthur Weinberg, *Manifest Destiny* (Baltimore: Johns Hopkins University Press, 1935).

3. See Martin Marty, *Righteous Empire* (New York: Dial Press, 1970), pp. 177-209.

4. See pp. 120-28, 135-50.

5. *Rocky Mountain News*, April 23, 1859.

6. *Ibid.*, November 18, 1861.

7. William Gilpin, *Notes on Colorado* (Liverpool: Published privately, 1870).

8. *Ibid.*, p. 5.

9. *Ibid.*, pp. 17-18.

10. *Ibid.*, pp. 18-19.

11. *Ibid.*, pp. 23-24.

12. *Ibid.*, pp. 21-22.

13. *Ibid.*, pp. 22-23.

14. See Niebuhr, *Kingdom of God in America* and Cherry, *God's New Israel*.

15. Gilpin, p. 26.

16. Ibid., pp. 26-27.

17. Ibid., p. 28.

18. Ibid., pp. 50-52.

19. George Phillips, The American Republic and Human Liberty Foreshadowed in Scripture (Cincinnati: Poe & Hitchcock, 1864), p. 6.

20. Ibid., p. 10.

21. Ibid., p. 11.

22. Ibid., p. 57.

23. Ibid., pp. 85-93.

24. Ibid., pp. 94-119.

25. Ibid., p. 104.

26. Ibid., pp. 63-65, 201-203.

27. Ibid., pp. 120-21, 123.

28. Ibid., p. 62.

29. Ibid., p. 153.

30. Ibid., p. 155.

31. Ibid., pp. 170-71.

32. Ibid., pp. 172-73.

33. Ibid., p. 223.

34. Ibid., p. 232.

35. Ibid., pp. 235-36.

36. William Clebsch, From Sacred to Profane America (New York: Harper & Row, 1968), pp. 191-92.

CHAPTER 8

COOPERATION AND COMPETITION AMONG DENOMINATIONS ON THE COLORADO FRONTIER

As missionaries rushed to spread the gospel to mining camp residents, they found the work so large and the workers so few that for a short time they engaged in limited co-operative endeavors. However, the cooperative spirit did not survive the early pioneer period. Coloradans soon fell into the pattern of the rest of the nation, in which denominational competition undermined cooperative ventures. In the first few years, union meetings and services, though rare, did occur. But these ended when the several denominations established churches in the key population centers of Denver, Central City, and active mining towns. Then members of the denominations occasionally cooperated in revivals and a few social reforms, but no more than their eastern cousins.[1] An attempt to introduce the Evangelical Alliance, an early ecumenical venture, came to nothing.[2] They competed heartily with one another in establishing mission churches and schools. Hostility between the Catholic and Protestant melted somewhat. But, with few exceptions, the relationships of the denominations one to another did not change but paralleled the national trend as the frontiersmen planted churches and as preachers carried the gospel. Denominational diversity remained an established social fact; ecumenism or cross-denominational sentiment grew very little during Colorado's formative years.

The few changes in polity, noted above,[3] did grow out of the peculiar needs of the scattered settlers. Presbyterian centralization of mission efforts and a tendency toward greater congregational autonomy among Episcopalians, however, did not alter competitive patterns. In fact, the Presbyterians adopted Sheldon Jackson's scheme in order to compete more effectively. The Episcopalians' move toward greater congregational autonomy represented a desire for increased lay leadership and did not arise from any wish to work cooperatively with other denominations.

The early missionary efforts in the mining camps produced some cooperation. During 1858 and 1859, when workers were few and needs large, ministers and lay preachers of several denominations joined forces to preach. They shared pulpits in the few available buildings. People of all Protestant groups attended services led by any preacher who came to town. But as soon as society began to stabilize, early cooperation broke down and competition for members and funds returned. Coloradans cooperated best in establishing union Sunday Schools. The first, in Denver, included Methodists, Presbyterians, Congregationalists, and Episcopalians. Though it did not survive many months, it served an important purpose and illustrates some willingness to make joint efforts. Other union Sunday schools, usually cooperative Methodist-Congregationalist gatherings, appeared briefly in Boulder, Georgetown, and Central City. In each of these cases, however, the Methodists dominated and soon converted the schools into Methodist organizations.[4]

Union churches also apppeared early on, but they proved shortlived. As we have seen, Lewis Hamilton's union congregation in Central City failed after a few months. William Phipps and Harvey Mellis attempted cooperative congregations in Boulder and Georgetown. But they soon realized that the Methodists with whom they worked would swallow the tiny Congregationalist groups if the projects continued, and so they withdrew. Amos Billingsley held union prayer meetings which met with much enthusiasm, but the groups disbanded after he left the territory.[5]

Revivals and voluntary societies, in which Protestants easily crossed denominational lines in the East, provided opportunities for minimal interaction of Colorado Protestants. Even here, pioneers showed little interest in abandoning their divisions. Revivals and camp meetings attracted men and women from several denominations. But ministers did not cross lines to preach. Methodist leadership predominated, and persons converted almost invariably joined the Methodist Church. Agencies of the "benevolent empire" (American Bible Society, American Tract Society, American Home Missionary Society, American Sunday School Union, and others) had spent their force nationally by 1859. Even the A. H. M. S., which was active in Colorado, had become a Congregationalist society. Though the agents tried to initiate cooperative ventures, they did not succeed. The voluntary societies in Colorado were denominational affairs. The Episcopal Mite Society, Presbyterian aid societies, Protestant women's missionary societies, and Roman Catholic confraternities functioned but did not disturb party lines. Joint efforts occurred informally in temperance work, as we have seen.[6] But large interdenominational rallies and concerted, organized campaigns simply did not happen.

Even when clergy shared community goals, they tended to ignore one another except in instances of community disaster such as the serious flood in Denver during the summer of 1864. Then clergymen banded together to furnish relief measures to homeless citizens.[7]

Laymen of several denominations crossed boundaries more easily than their ministers. When Roman Catholics held fund raising festivals for a hospital in Central City and for a church bell in Denver, lay people from all of the churches pitched in to help. Both hospital and bell (used for civic alarms as well as calls to worship) were community assets and worthy of support.[8]

Denominational competition for members, funds, and space began to appear in Colorado by mid-1860, as more and more missionaries arrived. Presbyterian Alexander Rankin's diary reveals him to have been a keen competitor. He began by simply ignoring the work of others. In August, 1860, when Methodist, Southern Methodist, and Episcopal churches had been established in Denver, he wrote, "There are no church organizations here and not much preaching." Rankin disliked John Kehler, who held himself aloof from the temperance campaign. He also had little respect for Episcopalians generally. When Kehler preached at the funeral of J. S. Stone, Rankin noted,

> He pronounced the deceased a good man, [since] he was baptized and died in communion with the Episcopal church--rather slim evidence of true piety, I think.[9]

Congregationalist agents who arrived late in Colorado found the competition stiff and declared themselves to be at some disadvantage. The ubiquity and numerical success of the Methodists bothered them especially. Some attributed the Methodists' success to unfair tactics. Evans and Chivington, it was said, made Methodism the "court religion." Norman McLeod accused the governor and army commander of controlling government contracts and refusing to let any such contract unless the contractor joined the Methodist Church or contributed heavily to it.[10] While their allegations may have been true, Methodist success in missions arose more from efficient polity, a large supply of ministers, and dedication and persistence among the preachers. The denomination maintained its dominance long after Evans and Chivington left office.[11]

Another Congregationalist minister complained about Episcopal and Roman Catholic fund raising devices. After hearing about a festival where revelers danced until dawn, William Crawford remarked that if he could use such foul measures, he could easily collect his salary in full and on time.[12]

The Episcopalians established churches in Colorado early, as we have seen. But their numbers remained small, and when George M. Randall became the resident bishop he began looking for ways and means to compete successfully with the Methodists and Roman Catholics. In his first report to the mission board, he declared,

> We are here <u>early</u> and yet <u>late</u>; early as compared with the time when the Church has commonly entered new fields, and yet late, because others are ahead of us. The Romanists and the Methodists are here in considerable strength. Both of these bodies of Christians have schools of a high order in Denver. They have several parishes in the Territory supplied by energetic pastors.[13]

He commented that the Catholics' early arrival had helped their growth. He felt that the Catholic bishop spoke rightly when he judged his churches to be the strongest in the territory.

Alluding to the rumors of spiritual extortion quoted above, he wrote,

> The Methodists, in consequence of influences not purely ecclesiastical nor strictly religious, gained a temporary ascendance, which, but for these extraneous and extraordinary helps, they could not have attained. Present indications warrant the belief that such helps, however pleasing for the time, are not the elements of a substantial and enduring growth.[14]

The bishop proved to be wrong, however.

In spite of small numbers and funds, Randall felt that the competitive race was not lost and took hope from a relative lack of prejudice against the Episcopalians. He wrote,

> The people have come hither from almost every State in the Union. They have severed old ties, and in many instances, former religious associations. Most of them have left behind not a little of prejudices, which bound them to certain systems, and made them hostile to others which they knew nothing about. They are now the subjects of new associations; are living a new kind of life; they are pursuing a new business, and have become so accustomed to novelties that they are no longer afraid of ecclesiastical systems which they once opposed, chiefly because they did not understand them, and did not care to understand them.
>
> Many of this class do not find on this distant frontier just the shade of creed and mode of worship in which they have been educated, or else do not fancy that type of it which exists here. Such persons are in just that condition which constitutes them good material out of which to make Churchmen. In spite of their former feelings, and in contravention perhaps of their intentions, they find themselves attending our services sometimes as a sort of compromise between their conflicting opinions, sometimes as a matter of taste; and though professedly hostile to forms, yet imperceptibly yielding to the attractive dignity and Christian propriety of a liturgical service; and though they may not be in every instance very religious, yet they are godly enough to prefer a Gospel sermon to a Christless lecture or a political essay, and are inclined to select their place of worship accordingly; and so before they fairly know it, they are calling themselves Churchmen, and finally become such.[15]

Such unexpected advantage meant that work must be begun with haste and zeal. "We must," he concluded, "begin at the beginning. We must allow our enemies to teach us, and learn wisdom from the Romanists. Their priests are indeed ever in the vanguard of their missionary army, but their school teachers follow closely after." Episcopalians need to do the same, for, "[The Roman Catholics] are sure to take good care of the young of their own flock, while they exhibit a very tender solicitude for the lambs of other folds. In the larger towns before they have a church edifice they have a schoolhouse." And he warned,

> They are not content with baptizing their children, and then leaving them to grow up in ignorance, or to be taught by irreligious instructors, or by those who do not hold to their own faith. They aim to have in the new settlements of a country better schools than any other religious body can have, and thus they contrive to compel Protestants to send their children to Romish schools. This is now done in Denver. Episcopalians are sending their daughters to the Convent because it is the best school in the Territory.
>
> The people here are able and willing to pay liberal tuition. A school for girls in Denver, of a high order, with competent instructors, would be at once self-supporting.[16]

He announced his intention to enter the race for school children at once and pleaded for building funds.

He finished his report with a resounding plea to help stem the tide of competing denominations,

> Will you suffer me to go back again, singlehanded and alone, to stand there and see the immense tide of emigration pouring into this great State, as large in area as all New England and a part of New York; and behold infidelity sweeping through the land, and Romanism triumphant; and other zealous denominations spreading their systems with more or less of error; while I am powerless, because solitary, and solitary because the Church will "not come up to the help of the Lord against the mighty?" Is that to be the destiny of my Apostolic Mission? NO! NO! I don't believe it can be so. God forbid! There is too much godliness, too much of the mind of Christ in His people to allow it.[17]

He assured his audience that he had faith in their devoutness. With their help, "God will surely crown our labors with a measure of success that will gladden every heart capable of rejoicing in the triumphs of Christ and His Church."[18]

As we see from Randall's pleas, competition in schools was open and almost gleeful. The denominations also competed in building churches. Though joint occupancy of new buildings would have served, every congregation in every town and camp attempted a building. Those groups that had no building looked with considerable envy on those who had. When the Episcopalians bought the Southern Methodist chapel, the Northern Methodists were jealous.[19] When, two years later, the Methodists built a Gothic structure in Denver and solid halls for Colorado Seminary, all of the other denominations wanted the same. But none of them then had the money to do so. The Congregationalists felt especially piqued for they had no building at all. In Denver, they borrowed the Presbyterian church for a while, but they quit the building when they discovered that Presbyterians attended their services and tried to win the small number of Congregationalists over to their body. Next, they borrowed the unfinished "Baptist Basement," which they found uncomfortable. Now they redoubled their efforts to squeeze enough money out of the town for their own building. They finally succeeded but only by appealing to non-Congregationalists on the basis of civic pride. Indeed, most of the denominations did this and managed to secure large sums of money from men not of their tradition and from several who belonged to no church at all.[20]

The competition among Protestants was usually polite and often subtle. That between Roman Catholics and Protestants was neither polite nor subtle, as Bishop Randall's remarks show. But comments such as his appear quite infrequently. The virulent and outspoken anti-Catholicism of the 1840's seems to have abated by the time of the Colorado gold rush. Perhaps westward movement created more openness to genuine pluralism. Perhaps Colorado Protestants, who had little interest in Mexican Americans, willingly left that field to the Roman Catholics.

The relative lack of evidence indicative of anti-Catholicism in Colorado itself or of intense competition between Protestants and Catholics is offset by clearer evidence of distaste for Roman Catholicism among neighboring New Mexicans. Joseph C. Talbot, Episcopal bishop, and Methodist John Dyer travelled to New Mexico and wrote long reports in which they lamented the abuses of Catholicism there. They probably represent a widely held sentiment. Talbot, seeking out possible missions in the territory, found the Catholics in command and deplored it. He also found, "The uniform statements of American residents in New Mexico showed that as a whole the Mexican population is exceedingly degraded." He was shocked to find widespread concubinage,

> Priests and people are alike guilty. The present Bishop of the Roman Church, it is agreed on all hands, has done much towards a reformation of the conduct of the clergy. The old Mexican priests have been removed--some of them excommunicated and foreign priests put in their places.[21]

But Talbot was skeptical that the new priests would be much better than the old. In fact, he heard that one "has been tried for murder, and though acquainted with the law and acquitted, is believed by many to have poisoned his predecessor to secure his living."[22]

Talbot liked Bishop Lamy very much but saw much among priests and people that disturbed him. What he heard was even worse. It was said that Lamy himself had conducted a lavish funeral for a "notorious prostitute and gambler." The bishop ordered the streets swept clean and headed a grand procession. For his services, he is said to have charged a fee of $1, 597. 00.[23] This expedient for raising money appalled Talbot as did the Catholics' reputed custom of demanding fees for marriages, baptisms, and burials. The residents were appallingly poor, and many, rather than pay the money, lived together in common law without marriage, and many did not baptize their children. Those who did paid well. Talbot commented acidly when he heard a bell pealing to announce a baptism,

> No wonder they ring so merry a peal for it tells also of a handsome fee for the well-fed priest, a fee too, not willingly given but extorted with utmost cruelty of oppression from the very poorest. Children grow up unbaptized because of their parents being too poor to pay what is demanded and disowned by their mother when dead and secretly left in the Church by night that the priest may be compelled to bury them without a charge, which would deprive their parents of every worldly comfort![24]

Talbot saw some practices that were simply aesthetically distasteful to him but which he interpreted as signs of depravity. He told of a chapel that had "all the appurtenances of Romish worship and is indeed revolting to a well informed churchman." He noted,

> The ugly dolls, with tin crowns representing the Virgin and other Saints, the miserable daubs which picture our Blessed Lord, the Virgin, and the Holy Family, the tin candle sticks, the tin glitter everywhere, the box for the confessional, the super altar with its sacrarium--these are there and without doubt are valued by the people as aids in devotion not only, but as essential in public worship.[25]

Talbot concluded that "no people can need the gospel more. The question, whether they will receive it, is quite another."[26]

John Dyer, though he found little enough in common with Talbot, agreed whole-heartedly with his thoughts about Catholicism in New Mexico. Much of his narrative is so like that of Talbot that the two could be used interchangeably. He added some notes, however, that Talbot did not. He held that the Indians had become Christian only because the priests whipped them, took them prisoners, and baptized those who were "not able to resist." Dyer commented wryly, "This was missionary work."[27] Dyer presents no evidence that his statements are fact but he clearly believed them to be. Whatever his preconceptions, his own observations distressed him as much. After preaching in Santa Fe, he concluded, "They needed Yankee civilization as well as the gospel."[28]

The practices of the penitents horrified him. During Lent, men stripped to the waist, dragged heavy crosses around all day, and scourged themselves and each other with barbed whips and cactus branches. Thinking that such actions freed them of sins, the worst sinners worked the hardest. Men often died as a result of excess beating. Dyer recalled, "It was a strange sight, and I was never more astonished than to find that we had people in the United States who were so low and heathenish."[29]

Dyer thought that some improvements had been made in recent years and attributed them to the Protestants rather than to Bishop Lamy's vigorous efforts at reform.

> I learned this lesson, that the Roman Catholics were reformed more by Protestants than by any other means, in their schools and all other features of civilization. As a proof: There has been

> more improvement in the last twenty years in New Mexico among the Romanists than for three hundred years previous, when Catholicism had it all its own way.[30]

Dyer deplored the lack of education and the servile dependence of the illiterate and inexperienced on the priesthood. "The people in New and Old Mexico are not to blame for their condition so much as are their religious teachers."[31] A corrupt clergy had led the people into laxity, immorality, and ignorance. "The majority had learned no law save what priests taught them, confession and mass, payment of a portion of all they had or could raise to the Church." Worse, the church offered them "nothing to elevate them to a higher state of civilization or make them men and women in our nation."[32]

Dyer clearly felt that the church had a duty to civilize as well as Christianize. He thought that the church can and must educate the people for citizenship in the city of the world as well as in the city of God. His anger with the Catholics in New Mexico centered less on their ritualistic practices than on what he considered to be their deriliction of duty to the people in their charge.

The anti-Catholicism expressed by Talbot and Dyer, and shared by many in frontier Colorado, seems in many ways to have been as much anti-foreign sentiment as anti-Catholic sentiment. Coloradans seldom criticized the Roman Catholics in their home territory. But they were harshly critical of the Mexican-Americans and Indians of New Mexico. Though these men and women were by no means foreigners, the Coloradans regarded them as such. Even if their antipathy toward New Mexicans was not xenophobic, it certainly appears to have been a form of racism. For the Indians of New Mexico came from a different racial background than did the majority of the Colorado setttlers. Their antipathy toward other minority groups in Colorado was clear. The coming kingdom on the American frontier was not open to all.

NOTES

1. See pp. 115-28.

2. Rocky Mountain News, January 8, 1866.

3. See pp. 33, 83, 85, 90-92.

4. Nathan Thompson to Dr. Badger, April 16, 1866; William Phipps to Badger, March 4, 1867; Theodore Marsh to Phipps, April 22, 1868; Thompson to Badger, April 14, 1869, Letters, A. H. M. S. Correspondence.

5. Amos Billingsley, Journal, Colorado Magazine, Vol. XL (October, 1963), p. 246, June 13, 1861.

6. See p. 124.

7. Howlett, Life of Joseph P. Machebeuf, pp. 317-18; O'Ryan and Malone, pp. 59-61.

8. Rocky Mountain News, August 1, 10, 1863; April 12, 1865.

9. Rankin, His Diary and Letters, pp. 94, 118.

10. Crawford to Badger, July 13, 1863, February 11, 1864; McLeod to Badger, October 15, 1864, A. H. M. S. Correspondence; George Randall, First Report, p. 15.

11. Annual Minutes of the Methodist Episcopal Church, 1860-70, passim.

12. Crawford to Badger, A. H. M. S. Correspondence, November 12, 1863.

13. Randall, First Report, p. 15.

14. Ibid.

15. Ibid., p. 16.

16. Ibid., pp. 16-17.

17. Ibid., p. 23.

18. Ibid., p. 24.

19. E. J. Stanley, Life of Reverend L. B. Stateler (Nashville: Methodist Publishing House, 1916), p. 167.

20. Crawford to Badger, August 30, 1863; Crawford,

Quarterly Report, March, 1864; McLeod to Badger, October 15, 1864; G. D. Goodrich to Badger, November 3, 1865; Thompson to Badger, October 10, 1876; McLeod to Badger, December 8, 1867; February 25, 1868, A. H. M. S. Correspondence.

21. Talbot, Journal, June 25, 1863.

22. _Ibid._

23. _Ibid._, July 8, 1863.

24. _Ibid._, July 10, 1863.

25. _Ibid._, July 16, 1863.

26. _Ibid._, June 25, 1863.

27. Dyer, _Snow Shoe Itinerant_, p. 189.

28. _Ibid._, p. 190.

29. _Ibid._, p. 191.

30. _Ibid._, p. 194.

31. _Ibid._, p. 258.

32. _Ibid._, p. 241.

CHAPTER 9

MINORITY GROUPS ON THE COLORADO FRONTIER

America's Declaration of Independence asserts that all men are created equal. This eighteenth-century ideal is a bright principle upon which Americans have acted in pursuit of egalitarianism. Many have sought and won (in part) universal suffrage, education for all, and enlarged economic opportunity as manifestations of inalienable rights to life, liberty, and the pursuit of happiness. Many historians, following Turner, insist that the frontier experience contributed more to this process than any other factor in American life. The Turnerians seem justified when they assume that the frontier fostered a degree of egalitarianism among free, white men of "Anglo" heritage. But the experiences of blacks, women, Latin Americans, and Indians were different. On the Colorado frontier, the minority groups found as little freedom and as much inequality as they did everywhere in the United States.

The founders and leaders of Colorado's frontier society were all white men; most of them came fron northern European stock. They tacitly assumed white, male superiority to be normal and desirable. Indians, blacks, women, and Mexican-Americans made up a large part of the population. Most did not participate as equals with the white "Anglo" men. Each minority group has a unique story; beyond exclusion from certain rights and privileges, they shared little.

Very few blacks migrated to the Colorado Territory. In 1860, only 46 free blacks lived there. By 1870, the number had reached 456.[1] Whites in Colorado felt they had no race problem, since few Negroes lived there and "appropriate" jobs for them were plentiful. In fact, many leaders said that they favored more black migration, because the need for domestics was much larger than the supply. The territorial legislatures did not pass measures discouraging the immigration of freedmen, as some western territories did. But few actively assented when black churchmen proposed to invite colonization by displaced freedmen.[2]

The history of Negroes in frontier Colorado may be summarized briefly. Though clearly outside the cotton belt where slavery was thought an economic advantage, antislavery advocates opposed the importation of slave labor for work in the gold mines. Antislavery sentiment ran high. If any gold hunters brought slaves with them, they had left by June, 1860, when the census was taken. One witness declared several decades later that he had seen slaves at work in the Colorado mines. But no clear evidence of chattel slavery in Colorado has been found.[3]

So long as Colorado remained a part of Kansas, its free or slave status depended on the provision of the Kansas-Nebraska Act of 1854, which declared slavery banned in Nebraska and subject to popular referendum in Kansas. The bloody battle over the extension of slavery into Kansas did not touch the gold hunters. No mention of slavery appears in the constitutions of the Territory of Jefferson. Jefferson prohibited blacks from voting. However, the territorial constitution made no mention of slaves or freedmen,[4] thus allowing full civil rights.

Thus, under the territorial constitution which went into effect in 1861, black men could vote, hold office, sit on juries, and serve in the militia--at least technically. Colorado black men suffered no legal exclusion from full exercise of their civil rights under the 1861 document. Some blacks probably voted. However, in 1864, Coloradans changed their territorial constitution by referendum and excluded blacks from voting and holding office. When a group of blacks in Denver challenged this, they declared that they had voted in previous elections. White officials denied that they had. Congressmen investigating the controversy concluded that whether or not blacks had voted previously, the territory could change its law to exclude black suffrage. The exclusion prevailed for several months.

Congressmen favoring Negro suffrage could not force a change in territorial law, but they could muster enough strength to block Colorado's bid for statehood in 1864. The passage of the 15th amendment to the federal constitution extended the vote to black men; Coloradans grudgingly complied with the law.

Segregation of blacks and whites in public schools and other public places proved a vexing problem for the blacks. For several years, blacks paid taxes for schools, where they could not send their own children. Coloradans made no provision for "separate but equal" facilities. Therefore, black children had no educational opportunities unless their parents could afford the fees at private academies and could convince academy administrators to admit them. No one tried. However, black leaders challenged the injustice by petitioning Governor Alexander Cummings (1865-67). Cummings managed to correct the wrong in 1866, but only after facing down stiff opposition. Thereafter, black children could attend public schools with whites.[5]

In both matters, black leadership came from the black churches. Though sources are scant, available evidence indicates that leaders of the black congregations in Denver took the initiative in protesting legal discrimination against their people. Mr. Magee and others worked quietly and often unnoticed by whites to right obvious wrongs.[6]

Housing restrictions vexed Denver's black residents. No whites would rent to blacks. Again, with church leadership, Denver's blacks bought land and built houses. Of necessity, Denver's Negro population became propertied. Low land prices, large parcels of available land, and relatively relaxed homestead provisions allowed blacks to overcome the difficulty placed in their way by bigoted "landlords." The blacks tended to buy lots and build their homes in a cluster, partly from choice and partly because of social segregation.[7]

Exclusion from hotels, restaurants, theaters, and churches seems to have been the norm expected by whites and accepted (perhaps unhappily) by blacks. Maurice Morris, British traveler, commented that his hotel, like the town, was "conducted on the most republican principles of social equality." But no blacks could register. "The only qualification required for admission to its hospitalities," Morris observed was, "Caucasian descent; for I do not think the President of Hayti himself--the greatest man of the proscribed race I can at this moment recall--would be admitted to its fellowship."[8]

Churches probably did not exclude black members. Clara Brown, ex-slave and laundry proprietress, and others attended Methodist services in Denver. But blacks did not feel welcome in most churches. A. B. Jennings held special Sunday afternoon services for blacks in Central City and classes to instruct them in doctrine, liturgy, and scripture. Jennings' motives seem to have been charitable and his efforts laudable. But his practice did produce a kind of segregation and subtle exclusion of blacks from morning services.[9]

Separate black congregations formed in Denver and attracted nearly all of the black population as members. We do not know precisely when they were formed or who formed them.[10] We also do not know whether blacks established separate congregations because whites excluded them. Blacks soon realized that separate congregations made cohesive social action possible and allowed talented men and women to assume leadership positions. The Negro churches provided not only places of worship but also an area for politics and social life otherwise denied them by the white majority.

After black congregations formed, white churches and clergy generally ignored the black populace. The small, tightly-knit, self-sufficient groups effectively withdrew from the larger community except to challenge exclusion from polling places and schools. Their protests were peaceful, dignified, and surprisingly effective. Denver whites demonstrated that even though many opposed slavery most did not consider blacks equal or entitled to equal civil rights. But it is to the pioneers' credit that they acceded peacefully to black demands in two critical areas.

Most of the residents of southern Colorado were Mexican Americans. A fair number of people with Spanish surnames lived in Denver and Central City. In pioneer days, Colorado "Anglos" ignored this large minority group. Spanish Americans voted and attended public schools freely. Legislative members from southern Colorado and one ward in Denver had Spanish surnames. Legal notices appeared in both Spanish and English in the Rocky Mountain News. Apparently the Spanish Americans constituted an effective and recognized political force, even though white "Anglos" looked down upon their cousins in New Mexico.[10]

Most of the Mexican Americans belonged to the Roman Catholic Church. Methodists and Presbyterians made small but passing efforts to win converts among them. But Protestants had so much work among "Anglos" in the mining regions that they had little inclination to invade the heavily Roman Catholic area. Further, none of the Protestant groups had Spanish-speaking clergy.[11] Physical distance was another deterrent among missionaries in the mining regions.

While most Coloradans of the dominant race regarded blacks as inferior and Spanish Americans as foreign, they looked upon women as dependent but important members of society. However, women could not vote, hold office, serve on juries, or sign up for militia duty. Most occupations were closed to them by convention though not by law. Women who worked outside their homes could find employment only as teachers, domestics, shop assistants, and bar maids.[12]

Because of this male view, women were limited to the roles of guardians of community and individual morality. Their mere presence in a community guaranteed improved behavior. Practically speaking, the women's primary functions included bearing children, rearing and training them, and managing homes. In their roles, the women naturally helped shape the thoughts and behavior of young people. But mid-century men also credited women with similar influence on the moral behavior of adult men. In economic, political, and social matters, men assumed paternalistic control over women. In moral affairs, women acted maternally toward men. While this might be a theoretically reasonable division of labor, in practice the sexes exercised almost tyrannical powers in their separate spheres. Human freedom was limited, and neither men nor women took, or shared with each other, full responsibility for themselves.

The cause of women's rights made little headway on the Colorado frontier. Frontier individualism, innovation, and experimentation were lacking in this area. The essential conservatism led to defeat of referenda for women's suffrage, the first of which was held in 1877, and meant that innovation in the status of women was as unwelcome as innovation in church practices.

Eleanor Flexner, in her excellent study of the women's suffrage movement, states that frontier experiences broke down barriers of convention for a time. While pioneers, both men and women, labored to hack out homes in a wilderness, the artificial barriers of custom broke down; the sexes cooperated on an almost equal basis. Though the conventions returned as civilized society grew up the seed of sexual egalitarianism remained to flower later.[13] Whatever merits this hypothesis may have in other frontier regions, it does not seem to be valid for Colorado's frontier.

Women did not work in the mines, even though they worked hard to build houses, plant gardens, and so on. The rapid establishment of town and village culture around Colorado's gold mines reduced the time when women participated on an equal level. By 1860 (or before), men insisted that women exert their "gentle" influence on men and children, adorn society, dress extravagantly and uncomfortably, and add charm to the rough and tumble society.

The respectability of any public entertainment was measured by the number of women who attended. When rhapsodizing about the Denver theater, a pioneer actor capped his praise with the observation that many ladies had attended and "they wore hats!"[14] When Maurice Morris visited Denver, he commented with pleasure on how decorative the women were at church. Their dresses and bonnets led him to hope that their inward adornment matched their outward. The ladies of Central City

> are the real ornament of Central; and is it not as a tribute to them that all these jewellery and finery shops are maintained? Is it not owing to their influence that these rough places of the earth have been made to feel the power of refinement and civilization, and that the miner, instead of degenerating into a gnome or troglodyte, becomes a good citizen, imbued with all the charities of life?[15]

George Phillips summarized the prevailing attitude of most mid-century men toward women's proper role in the social process.

> The records of history, from the earliest to the latest times, testify to the efficiency of woman's influence in molding and polishing the institutions of civil society.... The edifices of human society would present but a rough exterior were it not for the polishing hand of woman.[16]

However traditional the attitude toward women might have been in most areas, in the field of education for women, Colorado pioneers were slightly in advance of their time. In an era when many objected to the education of women, Coloradans quickly established schools for girls. But the curricula indicate that the founders wished to educate the girls as the graceful guardians of culture and morality rather than as full participants in political, economic, and social life. No science, no philosophy, no history, no mathematics appear in the courses of study. Instead, music, language, domestic arts, and dancing constituted women's learning.[17] Thus educated, young women could fill their allotted functions but could scarcely move beyond the realm of home, social club, and church.

Women made up a large portion of the church-going public in Colorado as elsewhere. Within the church, they enjoyed full membership. They allied informally with clergy in their positions as guardians of community righteousness. But, paradoxically, the churchmen consistently ridiculed any feminist position, declaring moves for economic and political independence to be destructive of the home, the community, and the church. Furthermore, women did not preach, seek ordination, or serve on lay boards and vestries. Colorado church women found themselves ever in supporting roles and seem to have accepted the situation without protest.

The socially dominant group in Colorado faced no terribly vexing problems in their relations with blacks, Spanish Americans, or women. No members of these groups (regarded as inferior) seriously threatened their control of society or objected to peaceful coexistence. But Colorado's Indians did.

At first, the Indians seemed content for the whites to work the mines. But they expected that the whites would take the gold and leave. When they did not leave but began to encroach on the Indians' hunting and then to seize their land, the Indians began to fight. The whites fought back with a vindictiveness born of fear and contempt.

Many settlers and visitors recorded their low opinion of the Indians. White settlers, convinced that it is virtuous to till the soil and make the land productive, found Indian hunting and gathering cultures repugnant. Horace Greeley expressed it well when he wrote,

> The Indians are children. Their arts, wars, treaties, alliances, habitations, crafts, properties, commerce, comforts, all belong to the very lowest and rudest ages of human existence.... They are utterly incompetent to cope in any way with the European or Caucasian race. Any band of schoolboys, from ten to fifteen years of age, are quite as capable of ruling their appetites, devising and upholding a public policy, constituting and conducting a state or community, as an average Indian

> tribe. And, unless they shall be treated as a truly Christian community would treat a band of orphan children providentially thrown on its hands, the aborigines of this country will be practically extinct within the next fifty years.[18]

He agreed with westerners who loathed the Indians.

> It needs but little familiarity with the actual palpable aborigines to convince any one that the poetic Indian--the Indian of Cooper and Longfellow--is only visible to the poet's eye. To the prosaic observer, the average Indian of the woods and prairies is a being who does little credit to human nature--a slave of appetite and sloth, never emancipated from the tyranny of one animal passion save by the more ravenous demands of another.

The sight of Indians sitting idle during the height of the planting season proved the last straw. Greeley burst out: "These people must die out--there is no help for them. God has given this earth to those who will subdue and cultivate it, and it is vain to struggle against His righteous decree."[19]

Greeley explained to easterners that real Indians did not deserve the sympathy they got from those who had never been west. William Crawford, on his arrival from Massachusetts, agreed. He had expected to find the "noble savage" and had not. He wrote that his feelings had changed greatly since

> I studied the character of the ideal Indian in the works of Cooper, Irving and other novelists....[20] We who have seen live Indians know that, as a whole, they are a filthy, lazy, treacherous, vengeful race of vagabonds. It would be difficult for us to shed many tears over their demise, nor can we entertain any strong hope for their being reclaimed from the savage state and brought under the blessings of the Gospel. "Nurture will not stick" upon them. The grace of God may indeed be sufficient for them; and yet, humanly speaking, there seems to be no better destiny in store for them, than to fade away before the white man.[21]

John Dyer shared Crawford's skepticism about civilizing the Indians and Christianizing them. He believed that

Indians might be civilized but only after they had been thoroughly conquered.

> It is impossible to have a sinner converted unless he is first convicted; and it is just as impossible to tame and educate an Indian until he is subdued. My prayer is that all wars may cease and the red men of the forest may be civilized and Christianized. When this is done, will there not be cause for a jubilee? May God hasten the time![22]

In theory, three ways lay open to deal with Indian-white collisions. Whites could try to assimilate, remove, or exterminate the Indians. By 1859, few westerners wanted assimilation. Most favored removal to reservations. When this plan seemed to have failed to solve the problem, frontiersmen turned to extermination. Crawford reported that by 1865, majority opinion had swung to extermination. "There is but one sentiment, in regard to the final disposition which should be made of the Indian. 'Let them be exterminated,' people say, 'men, women, and children together.' They are regarded as a race accursed like the ancient Canaanites, and like them," he reported, "devoted of the Almighty to utter destruction." He hastened to add, "Of course, I do not myself share in such views."[23]

Though Crawford and many of his fellow clergymen did not approve of the citizens' bloodthirsty attitude, they did little or nothing to help the Indians. Many of them seem to have shared other settlers' fear of and comtempt for the Indians. Even though John Chivington, William Goode, and Sheldon Jackson served as missionaries to Indians elsewhere, they made no effort to establish missions among the Cheyennes, Arapahoes, or Utes.[24] Goode and Jackson seem to have shelved the problem; they seem to have become discouraged with Indians and turned to missions for whites. Chivington moved from reputed concern and seeming respect for the Wyandots of Kansas to hatred and vindictiveness toward Colorado's Indians. It is hard to explain this radical shift. The Kansas Indians were relatively hospitable to white missionaries and seemed ready to accept white agrarian cultural values. They were probably ready to make peace at any price after their defeat and removal from Ohio. Colorado's Indians, hitherto unmolested by white intrusions, fought back to save their lands. This may explain Chivington's change in attitude.

Whatever the cause, Chivington changed from a tolerant and helpful missionary to a vengeful military commander. In Kansas, Chivington made every effort to convince the whites that the Indians were not savages and that the two races could live together peacefully. He persuaded suspicious settlers that they had nothing to fear from the Wyandots. He fostered peaceful and friendly relations by founding a biracial Masonic lodge. He explained that the Indians' religious beliefs were quite compatible with the teachings of Christianity and that they should be nurtured in the faith and in the arts of agrarian civilization. When Chivington left this mission for another assignment, he harbored no ill-feeling or undue sense of failure and frustration, the fate of many missionaries to the Indians.[25]

But when he arrived in Colorado, he ignored the Cheyennes and Arapahoes as if they were not there at all. When the Indians moved onto reserved lands between Sand Creek and the Arkansas River, Chivington took no particular note of them. When, however, the Indians began raiding white settlements and wagon trains, Chivington became enraged. Then the commander of the volunteer regiments, he ordered the massacre at Sand Creek. By behavior, he showed hatred for the Indians. In his defense of the brutal attack, he stated repeatedly that the Indians had been hostile and dangerous, even though he had little ground for this belief. As far as we know, he did not express verbal contempt for the Indians as Greeley had done; he did not say he thought extermination was the best disposition of the Indians.[26] But his actions speak for him. This is not the place for analysis of Chivington's psychic motivation. But when a former missionary to one tribe brutally assaults other tribes and never doubts the rightness of his actions, something strange is going on. Chivington's personal aberration can be classified as monumental ambivalence, at least.

Of more importance here is the general attitude of western pioneers toward the Indians. The pioneers, convinced of their right to western lands, cheated the Indians, assaulted them inhumanely, and drove them out. Mere human greed does not explain these actions sufficiently, although rapaciousness certainly existed. The ideals of civilization, destiny, and mission described above[27] preceded and motivated much of the movement into western lands. Settlers, convinced that their migration was part of providential ordering of the kingdom of God, thought their battles against the Indians justified. As the Israelites, an earlier chosen people, had driven the Canaanites out of the promised land, so Americans drove the Indians out of the best parts of another promised land. As victorious Hebrews felt no remorse for slaughtering pagans and Baal worshippers, many westerners sustained no guilty feelings for shooting pagan buffalo hunters. That their forefathers had hoped to evangelize these pagans and improve their lot gave the westerners little pause. Missionary ventures among the Indians had been colossal failures. The Indians (with some exceptions, such as the Cherokees) did not want the Christian gospel and American patterns of civilization. The frontiersmen thus wrote the Indians off as hopeless recalcitrants and evicted them with hardly a second thought.

Many easterners reacted in horror to the westerners' cavalier treatment of native Americans. The critics shared the same vision of "choseness" but recoiled from brutal measures. Westerners retorted that easterners did not understand, that they retained illusions about the "noble savage," and, most telling, that people in comfortable eastern homes were not the ones in danger of murder, rape, and pillage at the hands of hostile Indians. In some instances, their criticism of their critics was correct. It is impossible, however, to excuse the pioneers' actions since they did a great deal more than defend themselves, as they claimed.

John Dyer wrote, nevertheless, that the western people saw their actions as self-defense.[28] The Indian wars were partly that, for the Indians did cruel and brutal deeds, too. But white settlers acted as aggressors and emerged victors. Almost no pioneer could see beyond the defensive. Their fear and their vision combined to blind them to their cruelty and prevented many of them from holding Christian compassion for the Indians.

The Christian missionaries and churches made no move to counter this phenomenon by either preaching to whites or attempting to help the Indians. On this issue, culture seems to have swallowed the gospel. Or, perhaps, Israelite examples of conquest crowded out God's command to love neighbors, even one's enemies.

Colorado pioneer civilizers seem to have had very little impulse to extend equality outside the circle inhabited by white, "Anglo" men of the broad middle class. Many were excluded from the enjoyment of frontier egalitarianism.

NOTES

1. U. S. Census, 1860, p. 547; 1870, Vol. I, pp. 4-6.

2. Harmon Mothershead, "Negro Rights in Colorado Territory," Colorado Magazine, Vol. XL (July, 1963), p. 213; James Harvey, "Negroes in Colorado," Colorado Magazine, Vol. XXVI (July, 1949), pp. 165-76, and his "Negroes in Colorado," Unpublished M. A. Thesis, University of Denver, 1948.

3. Mothershead, "Negro Rights in Colorado Territory," Colorado Magazine, Vol. XL (July, 1963), pp. 212-13; Harvey, "Negroes in Colorado," Colorado Magazine, Vol. XXVI (July, 1949), p. 169.

4. For copies of the constitutions, see Rocky Mountain News, August 13, 1859 and Marshall, Early Records of Gilpin County.

5. Mothershead, pp. 215-16.

6. Harvey, "Negroes in Colorado," Colorado Magazine, Vol. XXXVI, pp. 165-76.

7. Ibid.

8. Maurice O. Morris, Rambles in the Rocky Mountains, pp. 77-78.

9. Randall, First Report, p. 8; Breck, The Episcopal Church in Colorado, p. 32.

10. The first record of a black congregation in Denver appears in the Rocky Mountain News, April 11, 1865. The item announces services at the new "Colored Church" and lists Magee as pastor.

11. Rocky Mountain News, August 27, 1861 et passim.

12. Dyer, Snow Shoe Itinerant, pp. 196, 240.

13. See provisional, territorial, and state constitutions in Marshall, op. cit. and Rocky Mountain News, August 13, 1859.

14. Eleanor Flexner, Century of Struggle (New York: Atheneum, 1972), p. 9.

15. (Denver) Republican, October 12, 1902; see also Rocky Mountain News, October 28, 1861.

16. Morris, pp. 96, 134.

17. Phillips, The American Republic and Human Liberty Foreshadowed in Scripture, p. 136.

18. See advertisements in the Rocky Mountain News, February 18, 1865, October 18, 1865.

19. Horace Greeley, An Overland Journey, p. 151.

20. Ibid., pp. 151-52.

21. Apparently many people accepted Cooper's unrealistic descriptions of Indians as authentic and were bitterly disappointed when they met real Indians. For one who did not swallow Cooper's portrayal, see Twain's essay on Fennimore Cooper's literary crimes in Bernard De Voto (ed.), The Portable Mark Twain (New York: Viking Press, 1946), pp. 541-56.

22. Crawford to Badger, Letter, September 25, 1864, A.H. M.S. Correspondence.

23. Dyer, pp. 182-83.

24. Crawford to Badger, Letter, September 25, 1864, A.H. M.S. Correspondence.

25. Craig, The Fighting Parson, pp. 33-35; Goode, Outposts of Zion, pp. 249-75, 281-311, 323-62; Stewart, Sheldon Jackson, p. 38, 92.

26. Craig, The Fighting Parson; Clarence Lyman, "The Truth about Major John M. Chivington," ms. Western History Dept., Denver Public Library, Denver, pp. 52-61.

27. John M. Chivington, Papers, mss., Western History Dept., Denver Public Library, Denver. These writings contain no mention of his attitude toward the Indians.

28. See pp. 155-68.

29. Dyer, p. 182.

CHAPTER 10

CONCLUSIONS AND EPILOGUE

At the outset, I suggested that Colorado's pioneers set out to transport their social and religious institutions to the Rocky Mountain frontier rather than create institutions to match their new environment. Early missionaries contributed much to this effort by establishing churches which functioned as the centers of the civilizing venture. I also posed several questions. The story told in previous pages furnishes some answers. Even at the cost of some repetition and restatement, it might be useful to run through these questions and answers thematically.

What kinds of people settled this frontier?

Contemporary reports tell us that at first a large band of young, relatively poor but generally middle class, adventurous, risk-taking men began the migration in search of riches. Most had no intention of settling but planned to get rich and go home. Most had no experience in mining and did not intend to pursue it for long. They regarded their coming to the gold fields as a chance to gain fortune and adventure. They envisioned their lives as open; they could and would engage in a variety of trades before settling on a vocation. They hoped to improve their stations in life by adaptability and skill in seizing new opportunities. The gold rush was just one alluring option among several. They did not take themselves or their mining very seriously. Generally, they came, dug a while, tasted the thrill of untrammeled life in the camps; then, usually with scant fortune gained, if any, they drifted off or else turned to other opportunities in the emerging society in the region. Such men as Amos Steck, Thomas Wildman, Richard Sopris, and Richard Whitsitt are outstanding examples of the latter group.

Alongside these people, a few entrepreneurs, merchants, practicing professionals, and some of their families set out to offer goods or services in bonanza land. They came to build, to turn profits, and to bring civilization. They included town-builder William Larimer, newsman William Byers, physician Dr. Peck, actor Jack Langrishe, jurist Benjamin Hall, governor and financier John Evans.

Men and women in both of these groups had heard much about the divine task given to America--the expansion of American religion and value system to the entirety of the American continent. Most felt themselves participants in such a mission. Their immediate needs for order led them to recreate civilization on proven models, and their efforts succeeded rather well. Gold discoveries and recoveries proved disappointing, and most of the adventurers left. They were replaced by new immigrants who quickly joined the ranks of civilizers as merchants, farmers, entrepreneurs, or professionals. Though migration continued throughout the sixties, the overall population did not increase much.

By 1870, the population of Colorado had taken on quite a different cast from that of 1860--settlers had replaced adventurers and created ordered communities, a diversified economy, and a normal occupational distribution. They mined, farmed, and exchanged needed goods and services with each other. The core of the civilizers had grown to become the majority.

What kind of society did they create as they planted civilization in the wilderness?

As the character of the pioneer population changed, so did the society. At first, transient gold diggers hastily grouped together in mining camps. So eager were they to dig gold that they tended only their most immediate needs. These included shelter, food, and a modicum of order. The result was helter-skelter towns of little beauty and alarming impermanence together with *ad hoc* codes of mining law. Lonely, isolated, cut off from most institutions of order and identity, many of the gold diggers drank too much, fought, and brawled. Among the adventurers were some social misfits who engaged in criminal activity. To protect themselves from this criminal element, miners formed vigilance committees or people's courts. However, beyond these informal measures, the early miners (with the exception of a few civilizers) made little attempt to create permanent machinery for justice, peace, and comfort. But the civilizers did much. They organized town companies, created territorial government, chartered town governments, elected officers, passed laws, built schools, organized churches, and formed lodges, literary societies, and ladies aid groups. In a parallel way, they attended to their several vocations: building, selling, cultivating the land, digging ditches, practicing professions and crafts, waiting table, driving wagons.

In about mid-1861, the surface gold ran out; the amateur miners left, to be replaced by professionals hired by large eastern-owned companies. Meanwhile, farmers came to till the cheap land. Townsmen sold them goods and services. Gradually, settlers found maintenance of order and enforcement of laws much, much easier. As they improved their dwellings and built more nearly permanent structures, the mining camps and Denver became self-sustaining communities resembling the towns of the Midwest, from whence so many of the settlers came. They formed clubs, aid societies, Sunday schools, literary leagues, debating societies, and lodges for companionship and the encouragement of moral order. Newspapers, theaters, and other institutions came quickly and as society stabilized, they were liberally patronized by townsmen. The social structures of the gold rush towns closely resembled those in most American communities. Laws, civil ordinances, and territorial governmental structure differed hardly at all. Once the transients had departed, these institutions functioned smoothly.

Did the pioneers and their institutions change in the new environment?

Very little. The settlers' aims were predicated on the notion that existing institutions must be carried to remote regions as nearly intact as possible. Though, as we have seen, a few technological innovations were necessary, social and cultural structures transported well. But the Coloradans created a society in which certain traits of social character were more obvious than had been the case in some other parts of the country. Visitors frequently commented on the egalitarianism of frontier society. Stripped of mannered society at first, the distinction of rank vanished. The sense of equality and freedom among the classes probably arose from an economic circumstance in the pioneer era; although there were few great fortunes, almost no one lived in poverty. After the first days of the gold rush, when unemployment plagued some of the unlucky gold hunters, almost anyone willing to could work.

Another peculiar circumstance of frontier life marked Colorado society. In rough camps, polished manners, fine clothes, and elegant language seemed incongruous, and these were consequently dropped. Even with the rise of town life and its "niceties," life-styles in Colorado remained informal.

Life in the rough environment seemed to produce a noticeable degree of individualism. The open economic and vocational setting made such individualism and independence easier to gain and sustain. But ordered society required that these traits exist within the framework of established forms. So, for the civilizers, excesses of all sorts were interdicted. For example, "individualism" did not imply any right to infringe on the prevailing standards of moral behavior, which included temperance, Sabbath observance, and family loyalty--even if occasional lapses occurred.

In some areas, the pioneers faced new problems that required innovation and ingenuity. The most important changes were made in mining and farming technique. However, political, social, cultural, and religious institutions changed little.

All this pertains to "mainstream people," and tendencies. There were, however, several groups of outsiders--the Indians, the Spanish Americans, and the blacks. The last found problems much as they found them in the rest of the country. Except for the Indians, the minorities lived peacefully with the dominant group.

What role did churches and missionaries play in the formation of Colorado society?

The first and most important task of the missionary to the gold fields and towns was to carry the gospel and to create a worshipping community. Missionaries and churches helped people overcome loneliness and established places of worship. A corollary was, of course, to draw the unchurched into a visible institution. In these efforts, the missionaries followed patterns laid down from the very beginnings of the expansion of American Christianity.

A second task was the creation of a sense of community in the midst of social chaos. The clerics and churches acted as a desperately needed social adhesive and offered the stability of tradition and identity. Before the formation of territorial government, the churches were the main stable organizations. As such, the churches functioned as signs of permanence. Buildings were symbolic; but it was the very presence of organized congregations open to all that conveyed the sense of stability and security. In a society where agencies of order--courts, legislatures, law enforcement officers--led a precarious existence, as they did under the provisional government, the function of relatively stable church bodies was greater than it was in groups securely governed and possessing a sense of continuity. And yet, the settlers knew how to survive with _ad hoc_ institutions. And they were confident that Congress would act soon. Chaos was not their future. But the churches functioned as a social adhesive and as a reminder of the settlers' goals.

Even after this phase ended, the place of churches in Colorado's history had been fixed by the pioneer experience. It has been said that the function of a church is to comfort the afflicted and afflict the comfortable. In those early days, no one was comfortable. So the churches acted accordingly. Not until the railroad came were fortunes made. With this development, the function of the church did not change much. When the large laboring force needed clerical support, the old patterns remained and few ministers joined the cause of the exploited labor. The church leaders tended, after 1870, to serve the comfortable more effectively than they served the afflicted.

The ministers acted as ceremonial leaders on important celebratory occasions. They baptized, married, and buried people. They opened legislative sessions and public assemblies with prayer. They did the same at festival times, especially on the Fourth of July. In so doing, the clerics acted only as they would have acted in any established American community.

They sometimes entered into community projects, such as drilling the militia in emergencies, serving as officials in public schools, and participating in lodge activities. They instituted some civic projects, especially in education. Again, these functions did not set them apart from their brother ministers "back East."

Third, the clergy acted as moral authorities, reinforcing the efforts of the civilizers and attempting to reform those recalcitrants who disturbed social order. In reform, the lay civilizers joined them. At first, the missionaries labored conjointly with a small core of settlers to enforce some standard of behavior. They sought to do so by the liturgical devices and preaching services. They also tried revivals and reform crusades.

The ministers worked not only in the contexts of their churches but also in the auxiliary institutions. The relation of church and society was close, but the age old problems of accommodation faced the clergy of Colorado as they have faced missionaries in many times and places. Even in this mission field where church and society pursued many of the same goals, problems arose. In the early camps and in the towns, civil disorder, social dislocation, and materialism required cultural change or churchly accommodation. Accommodation seemed out of the question. Thus, it became the task of the missionaries to impose moral order, to help create communities of concern to alleviate the loneliness of social dislocation, and to create plausible alternatives for fortune seekers. In partnership with lay civilizers, they succeeded in the first aim. Together with their congregations, they achieved the second. In the third, they failed and accommodated to the prevailing materialism of the civilizers, even though they were rid of a part of the problem after the early gold diggers left. The accommodation seemed reasonable, since the most successful merchants filled prominent positions as lay leaders, since churches depended on them for support, and since the entrepreneurs upheld standards of morality with vigor and zeal.

Ironically, the social conservatism, which seemed necessary at first, hampered missionaries in their abortive attempts to redirect the energies of their flocks from material to spiritual well-being. Dependence on lay leaders made it virtually impossible for church leaders to act except in accordance with the culture at large. Moral leadership depended on lay support.

The frontier clerics played the role of conserver because they acted as conveyors of tradition and traditional values. This applied not only to doctrinal matters but also to questions of morality and social value. As ministers of the gospel, they sought to win allegiance to a way of life, based on traditions accumulated over many centuries. In moral instruction and the transmission of tradition, the ministers shared their tasks with laymen, who included educators, newsmen, and civil leaders. The morality taught by all was roughly the same--a practical ethical code designed to make ordered and pious life possible for those who chose it. This meant that a minimum standard of good and orderly behavior was required of all. The traditions transmitted by clergy and laymen differed in some respects. Clergy were charged with exhortation and instruction in the Christian tradition; laymen took on instruction in American democratic tradition. Both preached morality.

In the sphere of moral instruction, significant interaction of church and society took place. Interaction and parallel action often occurred as the agencies of order, including the churches, consolidated the gains made by early civilizers. The interaction was often subtle--a mutual reinforcement of goals and aspirations. But the shared aims acted as a social adhesive, a basis for fellowship, and a source of inspiration in a difficult task--taming a wilderness and imposing civilization on its inhabitants.

How did westward movement change the churches' patterns of action and thought?

Changes in the structure of the missionary churches were slight. The Methodist and Roman Catholic polities had evolved such an efficient missionary machine that no changes were necessary. The Presbyterians and Congregationalists faced the problem of western space. Their decentralized polities made mission efforts difficult to coordinate. Both groups were reluctant to form temporary and very small congregations. This reluctance hampered their missionary effectiveness. The Presbyterians bowed to the needs of the time and place by finally appointing a missions superintendent who acted as the Methodist presiding elder did. The Congregationalists toyed with adopting a similar policy but decided against it. Changes in missionary polity were few. Internally, the churches of Colorado changed little. That is, the pioneer ministers carried the gospel, their understanding of it, and their modes of worship to the frontier intact. And it remained so throughout the pioneer period and beyond.

EPILOGUE

Though the story of the pioneers in Denver and its environs ends in 1870, with the coming of the railroad and the more direct linkage of Colorado with eastern America, a brief look at further developments adds to the arguments presented and suggests fields for further study. The social picture of Colorado in the 1870's (and thereafter) is a portrait of middle class society. Everything became much larger, and social diversity began to appear. Surprisingly, the expansion and diversification did little to change the institutional and cultural patterns established in the sixties. The completion of railroad connections to Denver, followed soon by a network of rails to the mines, led to vast increases in population, mineral and agricultural production, and all the components of civilized living. Two more major mineral discoveries (Leadville in 1879 and Cripple Creek in 1891) plus a host of smaller ones, contributed to this amazing growth. The opening of mines for other useful minerals also proved of vast economic importance. But these booms created towns and communities patterned on Denver. The civilization process was extremely rapid. Churches and schools arose even faster than in and around Denver, for missionaries and teachers lived a few miles away rather than seven hundred or more miles to the east. So these gold rushes were different. This is not to minimize the excitement and wildness but only to indicate that the circumstances that made the Denver gold rush unique socially and religiously did not exist there.

One major change occurred in the years of industrial and mineral growth. The egalitarianism (limited as it was to white men) and social homogeneity of frontier Colorado waned. A few entrepreneurs began to make large fortunes, and the laboring force began to receive proportionately lower wages and fewer of the benefits of "prosperity." The laboring force contained more foreign immigrants, and the population of the towns became more nationally and racially diverse. But the sense of optimistic egalitarianism remained among middle class Colorado men. Religious and social patterns were set by this group. Especially in the churches, where mercantile vestries and trustees set the trends, very little altered, even though the population and its class complexion had changed a great deal. Despite important economic and social shifts, the social and religious institutions continued to serve the dominant middle class and did not change. They simply grew.

Much of this conservatism resulted from churchly accommodation to prevailing thought patterns. As pioneers conquered the wilderness and made the desert blossom, they began to lose the vividness of their sense of a transcendent God and of the providential nature of their errand in the wilderness. After 1870, vastly improved technology, increased prosperity, and better understanding of the physical world through scientific research increased confidence and seemed to affirm the near autonomy of humanity. As Americans in Colorado began to turn from a vision of the Kingdom of God in the future to a vision of the present evolution of the Kingdom of God on earth, a few favored social reform to hasten the day, but most felt that the present society needed no changes. Among the church people of Colorado, most held the latter position. Except for a brief fling with Progressivism in which Coloradans elected a Progressive governor, more to benefit silver legislation than to bring social reform, Coloradans did not participate in that wave of political reformism.

Religiously, the Coloradans conformed to the older patterns as better ones and denied the need to foster a sense of social responsibility in Colorado's churches. There were exceptions, of course. But on the whole, Coloradans retained the religious and social patterns established during the pioneering period as adequate to their needs and reflective of their thought. The increased sense of human autonomy led ultimately to secularism. But these are matters for further research and interpretation. The point needing reinforcement here is that the patterns laid down during the pioneer era were not new. The frontiersmen were not utopians. As the pioneer period ended, the patterns continued to meet social needs. The frontiersmen and their descendants clung to them longer than their eastern cousins, because urbanism did not create such severe problems as it did in larger eastern cities. The Coloradans saw little need to develop new forms when the old ones continued to work well.

But growth and development after 1870 brought changes to Colorado. Denver's population soared from about 4,000 in 1870, to about 12,000 in 1872. The explosive growth continued throughout the decade, and the city's populace numbered well over 35,000 in 1880. In the next two census years, Denver's inhabitants numbered 106,713 and 133,859 respectively. The statewide population climbed steadily. From 39,864 in 1870, it zoomed to 194,327 in 1880, 413,249 in 1890, and 539,700 in 1900.[1] To serve the needs of these people, new stores, offices, schools, and churches appeared. Churches multiplied rapidly and easily, since the organization of the main denominations was well established by 1870. In 1870, 770 Methodist members and probationers lived in the territory. Two years later, 1,277 of the same denomination did.

In 1880, the number was 3,318, in 1890, 8,293. Not only did the totals increase, but the material prosperity did, too. In 1870, Methodists owned thirteen churches in Colorado valued at over $75,000; by 1872, buildings numbered twenty-three, with a probable value of over $113,000. In 1880 and 1890, churches numbered thirty-six and seventy, with property values of $109,257 and $892,094 respectively. Once the period of frontier isolation had passed, the denomination could and did send more ministers to serve the growing flocks. The number of appointments for the territory and state totalled seventeen in 1870, twenty-two in 1872, nearly forty in 1880, and over seventy in 1890.[2]

Though the Methodists outnumbered the other Protestants, the pattern of expansion described applied to other Protestant groups. The growth of the Roman Catholic population and expansion of its ecclesiastical properties and personnel was even more dramatic. By 1890, the Catholics composed more than half of the total church membership. 47,111 of 86,837 church members declared themselves Roman Catholic. The Methodists enrolled 10,850, the Presbyterians 6,968, the Baptists 4,944, the Episcopalians 3,814, the Congregationalists 3,217, and the Disciples 2,400.[3]

Though the proportion of Protestants one to another remained about the same, there were some other changes in denominational patterns. A large number of small denominations established themselves in the area after 1870. Some were ethnic churches brought by European immigrants; some were splinter groups; some were new. By 1900, these included the Free Methodist, Wesleyan Methodist, Reformed Presbyterian, Reformed Episcopal, Church of Christ, Unitarian, Universalist, German Reformed, Evangelical United Brethren, seven branches of the Lutheran tradition, Seventh Day Adventist, Church of the Nazarene, Assembly of God, Pillar of Fire, Christian Scientist, Russian Orthodox, Quaker, Mennonite, Church of the Latter Day Saints or Mormon, Reorganized Church of Jesus Christ of the Latter Day Saints, Jewish, Plymouth Brethren, Christadelphian, and Spiritualist groups.[4]

Religious diversity reflected a greater social diversity. The predominantly white, Anglo-Saxon society of 1860 had been changed by the influx of other national groups. While in 1860, the 2,666 foreign born residents made up less than eight percent of the populace, in 1870, 6,599 Coloradans were foreign born and constituted slightly over twenty-two percent of the people. In 1880 and 1890, the percentage remained about the same but numbers increased. In 1880, 39,790 and in 1890, 83,990 Coloradans had been born abroad. As the decades advanced more and more of these people came from southern and eastern Europe rather than from northwestern Europe and Canada.[5]

Economically, Colorado just grew. Mining, farming, railroad construction, and related industry expanded. Production in mining continued to climb, and more mining was done in material other than gold and silver. Gold sales soared from $3,015,000 in 1870, to $28,762,036 in 1900. Silver extraction increased from 496,988 fine ounces in 1870, to 20,335,512 in 1900. In 1870, miners produced 183,000 pounds of copper; in 1900, they produced 7,826,815 pounds. Lead and coal production increased dramatically over the three decades.[6]

City growth fluctuated. Although Denver grew steadily, some of the towns waned. Central City and other boom towns declined as newer mineral fields proved more productive. Railroad termini created temporary boom towns. Most of them shrivelled when the railroad moved on, but some main stations became permanent towns. In spite of the social dislocation occasioned by expansion, the social patterns laid down during the sixties remained the norm for many, if not most. Indication of the retention of pioneering attitudes in matters religious may be obtained from study of the responses of leading clerics to important social and religious issues of the day. As labor troubles began to erupt in the Colorado mines in the 1890's, few of the clergy felt the need to arouse the social consciousness of their congregations. Few felt the need to create innovative ministries to serve the unique needs of the working people. One dissenting evangelical was horrified that only she alone of Leadville's many ministers preached to striking miners during an especially bitter strike in 1896.[7] Only Congregationalist ministers Thomas Uzzell, Charles Uzzell, and Myron Reed established city missions for working persons and their families.[8] All were figures of controversy and political involvement. But little of their preaching was genuinely heard beyond a narrow circle of loyal adherents. Coloradans generally did not seek to answer or respond to the era's challenge to the churches' programs of social action. This may have arisen from excessive concern to retain established patterns or from a balanced judgment that the churches met the needs of most of the people. The purpose of this paper is not judgment of these actions but illustration of the retention of pioneering attitudes in religious and social matters.

In much the same ways, Colorado's religious leaders also sought to maintain patterns of thought which had proved useful in subduing the wilderness. In the face of the era's challenge to the churches' systems of thought, they assumed a defensive posture. Almost all of the ministers rejected historico-critical biblical studies, Darwin's theories of evolution and natural selection, and related applications of scientific methods to many areas of thought.

Three prominent clerics, Methodist Bishop Henry White Warren, Episcopal Bishop John Franklin Spalding, and Episcopal Dean Henry Martyn Hart reacted negatively on these issues. As resident leaders of their denominations, they represented a large portion of church opinion. In lectures and sermons, they inveighed against modern biblical criticism and theories of evolution.

Bishop Warren ridiculed the action of natural selection--with a curious twist. In speaking of man's ideals, he asserted that, by "natural selection," man selects idols and not the true God.[9] He wrote, "Throw natural selections and natural law to the winds in making your conclusions. There was a supernatural selection and selector. There must have been an infinite thinker."[10] Though he misapplied the theory of biological natural selection, he made his antipathy to such notions clear, as he elsewhere berated scientists for seeking to discover natural laws. In opposition to such theories, he declared that the Bible is a self-authenticating authority and far more reliable than scientific speculation.

Warren contended that biblical miracles are authentic while Spinoza's pantheism, Hume's skepticism, rationalism in all forms, and contemporary biblical scholarship are not. His main complaint about biblical critics was that they "took clear things and muddled them."[11] He attacked by simple rejection. We may see an example of his style in his answer to Thomas Huxley, when Huxley declared, "We agnostics deny ... as immoral the doctrine that there are propositions which men ought to believe without logical scientific evidence." Warren replied,

> He is as wrong as the old astronomers were in saying the sun went round the world ... Mr. Huxley's logical and scientific standards would banish

> the whole realm of morals at one fell swoop.... The life of scientific theory is ephemeral; life of Christian certainties as durable as man.[12]

The bishop flatly denied that scientific investigations, conclusions, or methods could be valid or useful. He, as many of his generation, sought to deal with the challenges of science to the church's ways of thought by invoking his own authority and hoping to discredit his challengers. Henry Martyn Hart, Dean of St. John's Cathedral, was more temperate. He wrote, "The Darwinian theory still awaits proof."[13] But he clearly did not expect that a reasonable proof would be forthcoming. In his arguments against the documentary hypothesis and the ideas of multiple redaction, he was not so calm. He declared,

> It has always been the endeavor of our great Adversary to throw doubt and disrepute upon the exact meaning of the Word of God.... There can be little doubt that the weakening of the authority of religion, which is characteristic of our modern society, is due to the widespread attack of Higher Criticism upon the literalness of the Biblical statements.[14]

John F. Spalding rehearsed some of the same themes as he defended his belief in the literal interpretation of the Bible. He referred to contemporary rationalist thought as folly. And he felt threatened by it. He lectured,

> A growing spirit of rationalism ... is defended by writers of no mean ability. It allies itself with science and philosophy. It is popularized in current literature, which abounds in unwarrantable assumptions, discrediting the Bible in its supposed relations to science, the authenticity of the Sacred Books, the substantial accuracy of Bible History. The uninstructed are asked to sit in judgment on questions in the solution of which trained abilities and the deepest research are necessary. Nothing is too sacred to be questioned. No authority is too high to be brought into doubt and practical contempt. Man is infinitely exalted. The infallibility of reason is substituted for the infallibility of the Bible. All possible problems of nature and spirit, profane and sacred, are rashly decided. God in man, rather man himself, becomes man's Teacher, Guide, and Saviour.[15]

These few examples show how conservative clergymen resisted challenges to their established patterns of thought.

These brief considerations suggest themes for further investigation. It would be interesting to know how the pioneers' legacy of social conservatism influenced later generations in the Far West. Given the presence of a few theological and ecclesiastical liberals and the majority's conservatism, it would be instructive to examine the tension that almost certainly surrounded the liberals. It would be interesting to study the rise of small churches and splinter groups. Public or mainstream reactions to these groups would provide much insight into the social character of the population. One wonders whether Protestant Coloradans maintained their friendliness with Catholic Coloradans, as the latter increased in number and national diversity. The rise of the labor movement, the churches' relations to the laborers, and the laborers' reactions to mainstream Colorado society would make a fascinating study.

Another intriguing possibility is comparison of Colorado's frontier social patterns with those of other frontiers. It would be interesting to know whether Colorado's mining frontier communities were like or unlike other mining frontier societies and whether they resembled communities with agricultural or ranching economies. The study of society and churches in the trans-Mississippi West needs further and more comprehensive consideration for contemporary understanding of the relation of culture and religion.

NOTES

1. United States Department of Interior, Bureau of the Census, Abstract of the Twelfth Census, 1900, pp. 100, 32-33.

2. Annual Conference Minutes of the Methodist Episcopal Church, 1870, pp. 155-56; 1872, pp. 222-23; 1880, pp. 317-18, 205, 206; 1890, 287, 429.

3. United States Department of Interior, Bureau of the Census, Compendium of the Eleventh Census, 1890, Part II, pp. 265-66.

4. Ibid., Martin Rist, "History of Religion in Colorado," LeRoy R. Hafen (ed.), Colorado and Its People,

Vol. II (New York: Lewis Historical Pub. Co., 1948), pp. 205, 210, 214-24.

5. United States, Census 1890, Part II, p. 600; Part I, p. 472.

6. Hafen, Colorado and Its People, Vol. II, pp. 691-93.

7. Molly Alma White, Looking Back from Beulah (Bound Brook, N. J.: Pillar of Fire, 1909), pp. 282-83.

8. Hopkins et al., The Bible and the Gold Rush, pp. 69-70, 136-38, 143-46.

9. Henry White Warren, The Bible and the World's Education (New York: Hunt & Eaton, 1892), p. 71.

10. Ibid.

11. Ibid., pp. 125-29.

12. Ibid., pp. 163-64.

13. Henry Martyn Hart, The Tragedy of Hosea and Nineteen Other Sermons (London: Skeffington & Son, 1908), p. 79.

14. Ibid., p. 71.

15. John Franklin Spalding, The Church and Its Apostolic Ministry (Milwaukee: Young Churchman Co., 1887), pp. 10-11; see also his "The Evidential Value of Miracles," Charge to the Colorado clergy, Denver: 1894.

APPENDIX A

ESSAY ON THE SOURCES

The secondary sources on Colorado religious history deserve critical examination. The several denominational histories provide valuable source materials. Though the data collected are invaluable, certain limitations make a fresh interpretation helpful. First, denominational works tend to focus rather narrowly on the activities of single groups without consideration of the ways in which the secular and ecclesiastical overlapped or examination of the ways in which the members of various churches viewed one another. Second, these scholars tend to triumphalism; they tell success stories of ever larger congregations and buildings without much reflection on the social roles of the clergy and church people. The growth of churches on this frontier was rapid; the enterprise of planting congregations was enormously successful. But there is more to the story, as we have seen. Third, the authors tell us a great deal about the clergy and almost nothing about the laity. Source materials dictate this one-sidedness; it is difficult to avoid. Nonetheless, one can know something of the work of important lay leaders, and these leaders deserve consideration.

A brief survey of the important secondary works may help those interested in pursuing this subject further. A seminal work is Martin Rist's article, "History of Religion in Colorado."[1] This essay is the product of thorough and comprehensive research in primary documents collected by Rist. Here one gleans not only data but clues for more extensive research. Rist chooses materials to emphasize rapidity of growth and important beginnings. Thus, his work is a useful basis for more investigation and interpretation. Three doctoral dissertations on Colorado Methodism by Rist's students expand his research and follow his method.[2]

William O'Ryan and Thomas Malone wrote The History of the Catholic Church in Colorado in 1889, when much of the state was still frontier.[3] The authors participated in the pioneering venture and reflect the values of the frontiersmen.

Although O'Ryan and Malone also chronicle the establishment and growth of several parishes and schools, most of the book is a memorial tribute to Bishop Joseph P. Machebeuf, who died during the year of publication.

William Howlett's biography of Machebeuf, published nearly twenty years later, is a better source.[4] Howlett worked under Machebeuf for several years. The book is intimate biography which does not sacrifice historical objectivity. One of the sources is a collection of Machebeuf's letters to his family in France. As far as the remaining data can be checked against other sources, Howlett's work is reliable. It has some interpretative limitations--he omits discussion of Protestant, Indian, and Spanish reactions to Roman Catholics', activities.

A strength of this book, unusual in such studies, is Howlett's care to describe some aspects of the social setting in which missionaries worked. His description is not thorough but it makes for lively reading. An engaging feature of this book is the balance between personal and institutional history. Though told about the erection of church, school, and hospital buildings, the reader need not sift through many pages of minor details to learn about the men and women who used the buildings.

In his history of Presbyterianism in Colorado and Utah, Andrew Murray attempts to place the history of his denomination in historical context.[5] Murray proposed to study the interaction of faith and culture. The book is an update of his doctoral dissertation which Murray classified as an American success story. Unfortunately, he changed the character of the work hardly at all when he added a final chapter in which he asserts a number of things for which he gives little or inappropriate evidence. His study suffers from imbalance; he focusses too much on Sheldon Jackson, whose abundant papers are important. But Murray uses evidence from Jackson's papers to support generalizations about other missionaries in other eras.

Robert L. Stewart wrote a biography of Sheldon Jackson that is really more useful than Murray's more recent work. As with Howlett's book, we find a close personal and ecclesiastical relationship between the author and his subject.[6] Stewart demonstrates a degree of hero worship, shares Jackson's presuppositions about the nature of missions. One such assumption was that the precepts of American Protestantism represented the form of the gospel best suited to save the world. In spite of its limitations, this biography is a useful source.

Two works dealing with the spectacular career of John Milton Chivington exaggerate the facts to make a good story better.[7] The first, an unpublished manuscript by Clarence Lyman, a journalist whose wife was a descendant of Chivington, includes many family legends. Reginald Craig later published a book reportedly based on Lyman's manuscript. Craig's work suffers some of the same flaws of exaggeration and overdramatization. He uses some additional sources successfully. His main purpose is to vindicate Chivington's reputation. The main emphasis is, of course, on Chivington's controversial role in the Sand Creek affair. Despite the drawbacks, both works are quite useful if one is careful to check their data against other sources.

Issac Beardsley's study of Methodism in Colorado is a collage of writings by pioneer Methodists and conference records.[8] Though it lacks unity and coherence, the data are valuable primary sources.

No one has published a history of Baptist missions and churches, perhaps because source materials are scant. Eugene Parsons wrote a brief preliminary study and compiled a short article for a popular Colorado periodical. The data are useful but meager.[9]

Walter S. Hopkins and several colleagues studied Congregationalism in Colorado.[10] The result is a series of chapters based on the American Home Missionary Society's correspondence. The authors have also made use of some newspapers and local congregational histories. The study focusses on the foundings and avoids too much emphasis on the bricks and mortars of the buildings. But the authors lose sight of the laity. They make little attempt to relate religious history to social history and fail to note Congregationalists' relations with other Christians. The authors mention the formative union of churches but gloss over the import of these cooperative ventures.

Allen D. Breck has written a thorough chronicle of the official action of Episcopalians in the territory and state.[11] Breck, professor of history at the University of Denver, has chosen to limit his work to conventions, convocations, and other such matters because sources are plentiful. But in so doing has left out a highly significant part of the picture. There are fugitive sources dealing with the lives and labors of resident clergy and laity. Nevertheless, Breck's work directs one to these, and the data he presents are highly useful.

As helpful as the secondary sources are, it seems clear that a comprehensive study of all denominations within the cultural context is important to the understanding of the roles of Christians in the formation of this frontier society.

There are abundant primary sources dealing with missionaries and churches in frontier Colorado. Although the authors of the works discussed consulted some of them, they do not analyze and interpret them adequately. Several collections are in Denver. The manuscript collection in the Colorado State Historical Society Library contains John Kehler's diary and letters, Francis Byrne's papers, and Bethuel T. Vincent's papers. The library owns a complete file of the Rocky Mountain News. The Western History Department of the Denver Public Library is an excellent and well ordered collection. Its holdings include the manuscript record of St. John's, the diaries of Jacob Adriance, the record book of his mission, John M. Chivington's miscellaneous papers, and an index to the Rocky Mountain News, partial before 1865 and complete after that year. The archival collection of Methodist materials at Iliff School of Theology is excellent but was uncatalogued at the time of my visit. The materials were, however, arranged in a logical manner. This is Martin Rist's collection and shows how thoroughly Rist knows the sources. Record books for most Methodist churches of the pioneer era are there. Short diaries by George Richardson and William Howbert are helpful. The Episcopal diocesan office holds reports of missionary bishops, annual reports, episcopal addresses, and records of St. Paul's, Central City, and St. Mark's, Black Hawk. The Chancery Office of the Roman Catholic archdiocese holds William Howlett's manuscripts--a parish-by-parish history of the diocese and his reminiscences, some of which date from the period under study.

In Austin, Texas, the Episcopal Church Historical Society has J. C. Talbot's papers. A valuable archival source is the Colorado correspondence file of the American Home Missionary Society, located at the Amisted Research Center at Dillard University in New Orleans, Louisiana. These letters contain detailed information on the affairs and progress of all denominations as well as the Congregational. They also describe the field very well.

Many primary sources are available in printed form. Most of these are included in the footnotes accompanying the text and are listed alphabetically in the bibliography appended to this essay.

The primary sources present a kaleidoscopic view nearly factually complete but without coherence. Interpretation requires the ordering of the data and assessment of their place in the social history of Colorado. Some interesting questions, such as those discussed in the final chapter, arise as one looks over the sources. Answers begin to emerge as one analyzes the material.

Valid interpretation requires critical assessment of the reliability of primary data. Any careful history of the American West involves a special critical problem, for westerners love to tell tall tales, and many historians accepted early ones as fact. Most of the tales contain a grain of truth and capture the tone and character of the era. Often when assessing a good tale, one is tempted to say with Mark Twain that if it isn't true, it ought to be. Analysis of tall tales is like analysis of other historical data and often proves that the truth is as entertaining as the story. Several critical tools help. These bear a striking resemblance to the techniques developed by biblical critics. This is not surprising when one remembers that the biblical scholars are engaged in the historical examination of primary sources of great importance to a community's sense of identity and worth.

The first task is to decide the purpose for which the author tells his story. William Gilpin wrote most of his books to promote western railroads. Many of his glowing predictions and some of his data are then suspect. John Chivington wrote an account of his part in the battle of Sand Creek, hoping to salvage his reputation. His work is often unreliable. Diaries, not meant for publication, are usually first rate sources if they contain any data of interest. Usually ministers used diaries to keep their church records straight and to keep track of sermons preached. Neither of these purposes led the authors to distort their facts, though ambitious churchmen sometimes misrepresented the membership of their churches. Otherwise, the narrative data, observations and opinions, and attitudes recorded are highly personal. Amos Billingsley and Alexander Rankin revealed much of themselves in their diaries. John Kehler, whose journal is shorter and more businesslike, did not.

Letters to friends and families in the East are not so straightforward. The writers wanted to tell their loved ones of the exciting events of westward passage and life. Often their descriptions are accurate and may be verified by cross-checking among the various sources. But sometimes, a son writing home played down the wild and wooly character of his new home or inflated the business opportunities there, as did Thomas Wildman when he wrote to his parents in Connecticut. Missionaries writing to supporting agencies sometimes exaggerated the poverty of the region or the prospects for growth in order to get sufficient people and money to do their job properly.

After assessing the purpose of the work, scholars must bring to bear on the data all the information they can about the general social, political, cultural, and economic circumstances in which the author lived. Once they understand the milieu, they must learn how the author reacted to it. They can then recognize some of the presuppositions and assumptions of the writer.

Before scholars can tell the story contained in the data, they must check the truth of the statements made. Where possible, all facts should be checked in several primary sources. Some discrepancies will be found. To choose the best source, one must examine them for several clues. A work written by someone present at the event, soon after, is likely to be the most accurate, unless the author has some reason to distort the facts. Several stylistic quirks are revealing. If a writer reports long conversations for which there is no other record and does so in detail, he is probably working with an imaginative reconstruction. Generally, people do not record details of dress, speech, mannerism, mood, and other subtle components of an interaction. If an account contains these and has been written very long after the event, it is well to be suspicious. The details may be absolutely accurate but likely are not. Strangely, people who do not record much of their surroundings may make accurate and detailed accounts of the weather or landscape, if it is new to them.

Awareness of the problems of critical scholarship leads one to a concentrated and chronic suspicion of everyone's accounts. But the tradition is rich in reality and deserves to be treated with scholarly care and respect for those who lived out the story.

NOTES

1. Rist, "History of Religion in Colorado," Hafen (ed.), Colorado and Its People, pp. 199-224.

2. Kenneth Metcalf, "The Beginnings of Methodism in Colorado," Th.D. dissertation, Iliff School of Theology, 1948; Lowell Swan, "A History of Methodism in Colorado, 1863-1876," Th.D. dissertation, Iliff School of Theology, 1951; Templin, "A History of Methodism in Denver, 1876-1912."

3. William O'Ryan and Thomas Malone, The History of the Catholic Church in Colorado (Denver: C. J. Kelley, 1889).

4. Howlett, The Life of Rt. Rev. Joseph P. Machebeuf.

5. Murray, Skyline Synod.

6. Stewart, Sheldon Jackson.

7. Clarence Lyman, "The Truth about Colonel John M. Chivington"; Craig, The Fighting Parson.

8. Beardsley, Echoes from Peak and Plain.

9. Parsons, "History of Colorado Baptists"; "Mother of Churches"; "Baptist Progress and Achievement in Colorado," The Trail, Vol. XVI (July, 1924), pp. 3-16.

10. Hopkins et al., The Bible and the Gold Rush.

11. Breck, The Episcopal Church in Colorado.

APPENDIX B

INTERPRETIVE PERSPECTIVES AND CONCEPTS

Much of the work in American church history treats of themes explored in this book; however, modifications of some of the theories may be in order. Surveys and monographs in the field concentrate almost exclusively on events occurring east of the Mississippi River. Perhaps historians assume that normative development took place only in the eastern regions. Probably they assume that western development paralleled eastern and, therefore, requires little attention. But even though westerners consciously imitated eastern styles and conscientiously transplanted American culture in the West, this very process created rather distinctive social and religious patterns. The effort to reproduce American life in the wilderness produced a conservatism which nearly stifled ecclesiastical innovation and rendered the churches powerless in the face of altered social circumstances toward the end of the nineteenth and at the start of the twentieth centuries.

Western historians have for many decades tried to explain the social patterns of the West as a result of adaptation of people and their institutions to the harsh physical environment and lack of orderly, established society on the frontier. Frederick Jackson Turner, the father of western frontier historiography, suggested that what is uniquely American was forged in the crucible of frontier experiences. He hoped by his emphasis upon the frontier, to correct an over-emphasis upon European origins in the study of American history. Turner's theories, therefore, deal with the whole of American history rather than with western history exclusively.[1]

Turner's theses are complex and not easily summarized. However, central to his studies and those of many of his followers is the suggestion that leading American characteristics such as individualism, innovativeness, optimism, egalitarianism, and progressivism resulted as much from the Americans' encounters with frontier wildernesses as from the influence of European Enlightenment thinkers, seminal democratic experiences in the Germanic forests, and other European casual factors. Extensive investigation into frontier history led Turner to conclude that westward expansion produced a climate conducive to adaptation in the eastern lands behind the frontier line rather than on the frontier itself. He suggested that each region, having been frontier, displayed a degree of openness to innovation created during the frontier era but which did not produce such change until some years after the frontier had passed.[2]

Turner's hypotheses led many American historians to study western history and to reflect on the significance of the frontier experience for American history. Much of their work supports Turner's theories. Some, of course, does not.[3] Still other historians have suggested modifications of Turner's generalizations. Of the last, one of special interest for church historians is T. Scott Miyakawa's study of the roles of four Christian groups in the formation of frontier society.[4] Miyakawa concludes that frontiersmen, influenced by these churches, did not develop significant individualism but rather stressed discipline and community effort, because only a disciplined group could cope with the wilderness. Thus, he argues that the frontier did not produce individualism, as Turner and some of his followers seem to say.

The foregoing study of the roles of churches and clergymen in frontier Colorado suggests that the frontier did not foster much innovation in religious institutions either. Early pioneers in Colorado generally made no changes in transplanted institutions, especially social and religious institutions. In the case of Colorado's churches, this early conservatism carried over into the post-pioneer period and actually discouraged innovation.

In addition to specialized studies, general studies of American church history raise some interesting points about the development of religion on American frontiers. Outstanding American church historians generally agree that the frontier experience, among other things, led American Christians to construct a religious system characterized by voluntarism and denominationalism and, therefore, different from European religion. In this connection, they suggest some themes also treated in this paper. A brief description of their ideas and how they relate to my work may be helpful.

Sidney Mead has made some penetrating observations.

Mead concludes that American churches became highly adaptable in response to changing environments in the new frontier land.[5] Mead takes care to avoid any form of environmental determinism, however, by reminding his readers that the adaptations were firmly grounded in inherited tradition. The free churches on the frontiers grew out of the colonial churches transplanted from Europe. The rise of denominationalism and the development of flexible mission policies are striking examples of the adaptations to which Mead refers. However, people living in settled areas and not on frontiers made the changes. The encounter with the wilderness necessitated some new forms, but the frontiersmen did not create them. They developed in the East. In the case of Colorado, ecclesiastical adaptation did not occur, for it was not needed.

William W. Sweet's investigations of the religion of the frontier tend to support the theory that frontier experiences led Americans to alter their religious forms.[6] His work deals with frontiers settled before 1840, almost all east of the Mississippi. In this setting, he observes that ministers developed revivalism, the Methodist polity, and other adaptations to meet the needs of scattered frontier communities. His interpretation is pertinent for the times and places which he studied. For the Far West, they do not pertain. Revivalism, as he describes it, had become institutionalized and almost liturgical by the time of the Colorado gold rush. Where revivalism had been an adaptation to a new environment, though based on New England and British models, in Colorado and other western areas, revivalism was an established form. The innovations which Sweet explores did not occur during the pioneering process west of the Mississippi.

An interesting study of American Protestantism is Martin Marty's Righteous Empire.[7] He describes the thought and action common among Protestants in the early decades of the nineteenth century and concludes that their unifying vision was a dream of expanding Protestant morality and democratic freedom of inquiry to all. Late in the century, the Protestant majority split into two parties--1) the evangelical, premillenial, conservative and 2) the socially-concerned, post-millenial, liberal. At about the same time, many Protestants began to find their imperial vision insufficient--even in the midst of seeming success. The story of Christian expansion in pioneer Colorado falls neatly into Marty's larger plot, even though he does not consider this region. His reliance upon other secondary works precludes this, as does his seeming assumption that what occurred east of the Mississippi is normative for the rest of the country. Despite this exclusion, he discusses themes of importance for the Far West--revivalism, reform, and theological reflection. All of these depended on the Protestant conviction that conversion would lead to empire of the good and godly. Put another way, Protestant imperialists tried to create empire by conversion and to sustain it by making people good. This interpretation is a very useful one. My data reinforce rather than challenge it. However, the experiences of Colorado frontiersmen lead me to modify it somewhat. Marty contends that Protestantism dominated the righteous empire. In Colorado, rapid Roman Catholic missionary activity made Catholicism an important force. On the Colorado scene, though the Protestants and Catholics remained suspicious of one another, they pursued the same goals with many of the same measures, and since the field was so large, they seldom collided. This gave the impression of a lessening of hostility, which may have been just that. This friendly coexistence requires examination in Colorado and wherever else it may have arisen. Marty's focus on Protestantism cannot be faulted, since this is his chosen subject. But his insistence on Protestant dominance may be questioned. Much of what he treats as strictly Protestant was in the American Roman Catholic tradition, too.

In his large and admirable survey of American religious history, Sydney Ahlstrom appropriately reminds his readers that frontier is process rather than region.[8] His discussion of frontier religion centers on the expansion of gospel preaching into the trans-Appalachian region before 1840 and isolates as most important the revivalism and primitivism of the Baptists, Methodists, and Disciples. He notes, in agreement with Sweet, that these groups sought innovation in a conserving sense--return to more nearly ancient Christian forms. His description of frontier religion and its processive development stops too short in space and time. He implies that what happened in Kentucky, Tennessee, and the Old Northwest set the pattern for all the rest. As we have seen, this simply was not so in Colorado. Coloradans did not borrow patterns from the southern frontiers but from the village cultures of upstate New York and the Midwest.

Conrad Cherry's excellent collection of primary sources illustrating civic religion in America points up national convictions that Americans are or have been especially chosen by God to create, sustain, and expand a way of life marked by freedom and superior morality.[9] His selections and interpretive introductions make it clear that nineteenth century Americans attributed national uniqueness to providential design. One recognizes these attitudes in the pioneers studied here. The civilizers felt destined by the Almighty to take American civilization to an almost empty land. They felt justified in their maltreatment of the Indians. They felt sure that God intended to maintain the Union during the Civil War so that America could expand even more.

Cherry makes an implicit distinction which he might have pursued further. He notes the presence of both spiritual religion and civil religion. At times, the two are quite distinct. In times of war, expansion or explosive social change, the advocates of civil religion tend to adopt symbols from churchly or biblical religion in order to justify their actions. Arguments from providential design to justify American expansionism provide examples. At such times, the two types of religion overlap, intermingle, and influence one another. Critics feel that this ties Christianity too closely to the existing social order, robs the church of its prophetic role, and diminishes its moral authority. In pioneer Colorado, the cooperation of Church and society in subduing the wilderness was fruitful and mutually beneficial for both. Early patterns lingered after their period of usefulness and tended to tie the churches to the mercantile establishment. This meant that the ministries to the poor and the workingmen faltered and churchly concern for social justice did not develop very fully.

Cherry's insights into the rhetoric of expansion are provocative. He notes that "the magnitude and rich natural resources of the western American wilderness strengthened the conviction that Americans were the chosen people."[10] He observes that while earlier generations conceived of their chosen status as conferring a special task, the expansionists felt that God favored Americans for their achievement of their western mission. His selections illustrate an increasing loss of the sense of divine transcendence. They include works of Lyman Beecher, Walt Whitman, Albert Beveridge, and John O'Sullivan. His choices may illustrate the leading roles played by laymen in the shift from a conception of providential task under a transcendent God to manifest destiny with its emphasis on human autonomy.

An excellent work dealing with Christian symbols

and ideals is Robert T. Handy's analysis of the ideal of Christian commonwealth in America.[11] He contends that church and culture formed a unifying and workable partnership during the nineteenth century. The goal was the Christianization of society through individual piety and reform. Handy limits his investigations to the visions of Protestant evangelicals. His limits expose him to the same criticism directed earlier at Marty. However, Handy's insights are important for this study. The Colorado pioneers shared the vision but with a twist. They hoped to transport American civilization; churches and missionaries were to be agents of the process. The Colorado pioneers seemed concerned to make religion a vital part of their civilization but seemed less interested in making their society Christian than in keeping it orderly with the moral authority of the church. They hoped that Christian precepts would dominate the realm of manners and morals but had little interest in leavening the loaf of commerce with Christianity.

Handy concludes that evangelical leaders reversed priorities in the course of the nineteenth century. Instead of emphasizing Christianity as the key to civilization, they concentrated too heavily on the process of civilization and drifted into a religion of culture. My reading and analysis lead me to believe that this reversal of priorities had occurred before the time Handy indicates.[12] This is especially true of laymen. Dependent on lay leadership and support, the clergy followed rather soon. Handy bases his conclusion on the utterances of eastern clergymen bound up in the abolition crusade. When the Civil War began, they turned their attention to other matters in which the shift of priorities, which I think occurred before 1859, became apparent.

William A. Clebsch's discussion of the problems of the secularization of American society and the profanation of sacred values is most important.[13] His work is an interesting exposition of the problems of success. His thesis is that the clergymen of the nineteenth century successfully convinced Americans of the need to educate and reform so well that they moved these goals into the secular sphere. Much of Clebsch's evidence shows that secular Americans adopted the goals of the religious and tried to achieve them by secular means. Thus, it was the very partnership of lay persons and clergy mentioned in this essay that led to the profanation of education and reform. The hypothesis might be restated: the lay people and clergy shared goals; the structure of American society was such that the laity often succeeded better than the clergy in achieving their common goals; secular educators, reformers, and moralizers began to become more important than their clerical partners. The restated thesis fits my evidence as well as Clebsch's.

All of these works have been enormously helpful in formulating my own thesis about the roles of missionaries and churches in frontier Colorado. The modifications suggested apply to that frontier. It is possible that they apply also to other portions of the Far West, but further investigation is necessary if this is to be considered.

NOTES

1. Turner, The Frontier in American History, pp. 1-38, 269-359.

2. Billington, Frederick Jackson Turner, pp. 444-471.

3. Taylor, The Turner Thesis; Billington, America's Frontier Heritage.

4. Miyakawa, Protestants and Pioneers.

5. Sidney Mead, "The Rise of the Evangelical Conception of the Ministry in America," in H. Richard Niebuhr and Daniel D. Williams (eds.), The Ministry in Historical Perspective (New York: Harper, 1956), pp. 207-49; The Lively Experiment, pp. 107-08.

6. William W. Sweet, Religion on the American Frontier (New York: Henry Holt & Co., 1931-46); The Story of Religions in America (New York: Harper, 1930); Methodism in American History; Revivalism in America.

7. Marty, Righteous Empire.

8. Ahlstrom, A Religious History of the American People.

9. Cherry (ed.), God's New Israel.

10. Ibid., p. 111.

11. Handy, A Christian America: Protestant Hopes and Historical Realities.

12. Handy's periodization needs some explanation, which he does not provide adequately. Why 1859 should be a dividing line, he does not say.

13. Clebsch, *From Sacred to Profane America.*

APPENDIX C

I. STATISTICS OF THE POPULATION OF COLORADO, 1860 AND 1870[1]

Race

	1860	1870
White	34, 231	39, 221
Black	46	456
Tribal Indian	6, 000*	7, 300
Non-tribal Indian	--	180
Oriental	--	7
Aggregate non-Indian	34, 277	39, 864
Aggregate	40, 277	47, 164[2]

Sex

	1860	1870
Males	32, 654	24, 820
Females	1, 577	15, 044

Age

	1860		1870
0-9	770		9, 515
10-14	298	(10-15)	3, 885
15-19	1, 015		
20-29	18, 143		
30-39	10, 806		
40-49	2, 210	(16-59)	25, 717
50-59	409		
60 and over	93		747
Age unknown	533		--

National Origin

	1860	1870
Native born	31, 611	33, 265
Foreign born	2, 666	6, 599
One parent foreign born	--	10, 707
Both parents foreign born	--	9, 347

*Approximate.

Specific National Origin

	1860	1870
British America	684	753
British Isles	1,135	3,397
England	352	1,358
Ireland	624	1,685
Scotland	120	188
Wales	38	165
Great Britain (unspecified)	1	1
German states and Austria	576	1,507
France	103	209
Scandinavian countries	55	297
Mexico	25	129
Switzerland	25	140
Holland	16	17
Poland	11	49
Belgium	11	11
Italy	6	16
Sandwich Islands	2	1
West Indies and Atlantic Islands	2	7
Africa	1	--
Portugal	1	--
Asia	--	1
Russia	1	10
Spain	1	5
South America	1	11
Bohemia	--	15
China	--	7
Hungary	--	2
India	--	2
Europe (unspecified)	10	--

Sectional Origin (within the U. S. A. and Territories)

	1860	1870[3]
New England	3,644	1,788
Middle Atlantic States	5,975	4,753
Midwest	13,271	7,227
South	4,413	2,160
Trans-Mississippi West and Southwest	4,010	17,223
Unknown or at sea	298	24

Occupation

	1860	1870
Agriculture	220	6,462
Professional and Personal Services	1,608	3,625
Trade and transport	1,374	2,815
Mining and Manufacturing	23,539	4,681
Mining	22,086	2,200
Manufacturing	1,453	2,481

II. STATISTICS OF MEMBERSHIP AND EDIFICES OF THE METHODIST EPISCOPAL CHURCH IN COLORADO, 1860-1870[4]

	Members	Probationers	Local Preachers	Sunday Schools	Students
1860	27	35	1	--	--
1861	348	43	17	7	212
1862	159	33	14	6	233
1863	255	32	15	9	409
1864	no report				
1865	214	15	8	7	556
1866	234	97	10	11	676
1867	398	126	13	13	885
1868	454	107	11	13	754
1869	498	147	11	21	1,290
1870	589	181	18	28	1,555

	Buildings	Value
1860	--	--
1861	3	$ 1,800.00
1862	1	200.00
1863	1	2,100.00
1864	no report	no report
1865	2	22,500.00
1866	3	25,000.00
1867	5	27,700.00
1868	8	28,100.00
1869	12	65,900.00
1870	16	85,500.00

III. STATISTICS OF COLORADO CHURCHES IN 1870[5]

	Organizations	Buildings	Sittings	Property Value
Baptist	5	4	855	$11,090.00
Christian	2	--	--	--
Congregational	4	4	1,050	28,200.00
Protestant Episcopal	9	8	2,000	46,040.00
Methodist Episcopal	14	13	3,815	50,800.00
Presbyterian	6	5	1,200	21,800.00
Roman Catholic	14	13	8,575	49,300.00

IV. MINISTERS RESIDENT IN COLORADO 1858-1870[6]

Name	Denomination	Active Years Resident	Places Resident
Vincente S. Montaño	Roman Catholic	1858-60	Conejos
*Jacob Adriance	Methodist Episcopal	1859-62	Denver, Golden/Boulder, Central City
Rev. Hammond	Methodist Episcopal	1859-60	Denver
P. Porter	Methodist Episcopal, South	1859	Central City
Lewis Hamilton	Presbyterian (New School)	1859-81	Denver, Central City, Bergen Park, St. Vrain, Burlington, and Evans
Mr. Wood	Baptist	1859	Central City
*Jospeh P. Machebeuf	Roman Catholic	1860-89	Denver
*Jean B. Raverdy	Roman Catholic	1860-89	Denver, Central City
Jose M. Vigil	Roman Catholic	1860-66	Conejos
*William Howbert	Methodist Episcopal	1860-63	Tarryall/Hamilton, Blue River/Breckenridge, Colorado City/Canon City, Pueblo
*John M Chivington	Methodist Episcopal	1860-61	Denver (Presiding Elder)
Landon Taylor	Methodist Episcopal	1860	Denver
Rev. Bradford	Methodist Episcopal, South	1860-62	Denver
*John H. Kehler	Protestant Episcopal	1860-76	Denver, Army Chaplain
*Alexander T. Rankin	Presbyterian (Old School)	1860	Denver
Sylvester W. Lloyd	Methodist Episcopal	1861-62	Colorado City, Denver
J. W. Caughlin	Methodist Episcopal	1861-62	Boulder/Golden
William A. Kenney	Methodist Episcopal	1861-62	Denver
William H. Fisher	Methodist Episcopal	1862-63	Central City, Pueblo/Canon City

*See Appendix D for more biographical data.

Name	Denomination	Active Years Resident	Places Resident
Oliver A. Willard	Methodist Episcopal	1862-66	Denver (Presiding Elder), Golden, Empire
*Amos S. Billingsley	Presbyterian (Old School)	1861-62	Denver
D. H. Petefish	Methodist Episcopal	1862-63	Central City, Boulder
Charles King	Methodist Episcopal	1862-66	Boulder/Golden, Black Hawk, Empire/Georgetown
Baxter C. Dennis	Methodist Episcopal	1862-63	Denver (Presiding Elder), Golden
Horace B. Hitchings	Protestant Episcopal	1862-68	Denver
Issac A. Hagar	Protestant Episcopal	1862	Denver
Alanson R. Day	Presbyterian (Old School)	1862-7	Denver, Boulder
George W. Warner	Presbyterian (New School)	1862-	Central City
George C. Betts	Methodist Episcopal	1863	Denver
Thomas A. Smith	Roman Catholic	1863-66	Central City
W. B. Slaughter	Methodist Episcopal	1863-64	Southern Colorado (Presiding Elder)
George Richardson	Methodist Episcopal	1863-67	Denver, Empire
*John L. Dyer	Methodist Episcopal	1863-87	South Park (Presiding Elder), Colorado City, Laurette, Lincoln, Fairplay/Dayton, Divide, Montgomery, Evans, Platteville, Ft. Lupton, Monument, Alma, Breckenridge, Denver
Francis Granger	Protestant Episcopal	1863-65	Central City
William O. Jarvis	Protestant Episcopal	1863	Empire, Gold Dirt, Idaho Springs

Name	Denomination	Active Years Resident	Places Resident
*William Crawford	Congregational	1863-67	Central City
*Bethuel T. Vincent	Methodist Episcopal	1864-	Central City, Black Hawk, Nevada, Denver (Presiding Elder)
George S. Phillips	Methodist Episcopal	1864-65	Denver
Oscar P. McMains	Methodist Episcopal	1864-71	Central City, Black Hawk, Burlington, Nevada, Colorado City, Pueblo, Excelsior, Rock Bridge
C. H. Kirkbride	Methodist Episcopal	1864-70	Nevada, Boulder, Pueblo, Colorado City
Alvin B. Jennings	Protestant Episcopal	1864-69	Central City
George Rice	Presbyterian	1864-70	Idaho Springs
Theodore D. Marsh	Presbyterian	1864-67	Central City, Black Hawk
C. M. Campbell	Presbyterian (Old School)	1864-	Valmont, Boulder, Upper St. Vrain, Denver
B. M. Adams	Baptist	1863-64	Canon City
Walter McD. Potter	Baptist	1864-65	Denver
Almond Barelle	Baptist	1864-	Central City
Norman McLeod	Congregational	1864-65; 1867-69	Denver
John Gilland	Methodist Episcopal	1865	Oro City
William W. Baldwin	Methodist Episcopal	1865-68	Black Hawk, Valmont, Burlington (Presiding Elder)
William M. Smith	Methodist Episcopal	1865-74	Denver (Presiding Elder), Golden, South Park, Canon City
*George M. Randall	Protestant Episcopal	1865-73	Denver - Missionary Bishop
William A. Fuller	Protestant Episcopal	1865-67	Nevadaville

Name	Denomination	Active Years Resident	Places Resident
J. B. McClure	Presbyterian	1865-67	Denver
George D. Goodrich	Congregational	1865-67	Denver
Harvey Mellis	Congregational	1865-66	Empire
Nathan Thompson	Congregational	1865-75	Boulder
Jonathan Blanchard	Congregational	1865	Denver
J. DeBlieck, S. J.	Roman Catholic	1866-	Denver, Central City
P. J. Munnecom	Roman Catholic	1866-	Trinidad
Michael Rolly	Roman Catholic	1866-71	Conejos
George Murray	Methodist Episcopal	1866-70	Canon City/ Colorado City, Georgetown, Arkansas R. District (Presiding Elder)
William H. Phipps	Congregational	1866-69	Empire /Georgetown
Samuel Shepard	Baptist	1866-	Denver
Ira D. Clark	Baptist	1866-67	Denver
Fr. Faure	Roman Catholic	1867	Denver
William F. Warren	Methodist Episcopal	1867-	Fairplay, South Park City, Colorado City
George H. Adams	Methodist Episcopal	1868-	Central City, Greeley
W. A. Amsbury	Methodist Episcopal	1867-68	Georgetown/ Empire
*Francis Byrne	Protestant Episcopal	1867-1904	Nevadaville, Denver
*Cortlandt Whitehead	Protestant Episcopal	1867-71	Black Hawk, Georgetown
Frank Winslow	Protestant Episcopal	1867-68	Empire, Georgetown
William J. Lynd	Protestant Episcopal	1867-76	Golden
Albert F. Lyle	Presbyterian	1867-68	Black Hawk
B. F. Brown	Cumberland Presbyterian	1867	Canon City
Edward P. Tenney	Congregational	1867-69	Central City
Fr. O'Keeffe	Roman Catholic	1868	Denver
John L. Peck	Methodist Episcopal	1868-70	Denver
George S. Adams	Presbyterian	1868-	Black Hawk, Pueblo

Name	Denomination	Active Years Resident	Places Resident
Ambrose Y. Moore	Presbyterian	1868	Denver
Edward P. Wells	Presbyterian (New School)	1868-75	Denver
Alexander M. Averill	Baptist	1868-69	Denver
Fr. Percevault	Roman Catholic	1869-	San Luis, Costilla
Louis Merle	Roman Catholic	1869-76	Walsenburg
Thomas McGrath	Roman Catholic	1869-	Denver, Golden, Georgetown
Fr. Guyot	Roman Catholic	1869	Georgetown
George W. Swift	Methodist Episcopal	1869-	Big Thompson, Cache La Poudre, Ralston/Clear Creek
Jesse Smith	Methodist Episcopal	1869-	Ralston/Clear Creek, Fairplay/Granite
Issac H. Beardsley	Methodist Episcopal	1869-	Georgetown
W. D. Chase	Methodist Episcopal	1870-	Central City
Edward C. Brooks	Methodist Episcopal	1870-	Greeley
George Wallace	Methodist Episcopal	1870-	Black Hawk, Nevada
F. C. Millington	Methodist Episcopal	1870-	Golden
J. R. Moore	Methodist Episcopal	1870-	Big Thompson, Cache La Poudre
T. Harwood	Methodist Episcopal	1870-	La Junta, Elizabethtown
Joseph M. Turner	Protestant Episcopal	1870-72	Central City
Samuel Edwards	Protestant Episcopal	1870-73	Pueblo, Georgetown, Empire, Golden
Gustavus W. Mayer	Protestant Episcopal	1870-71	Georgetown
Samuel J. French	Protestant Episcopal	1870-	Denver
H. E. Hamilton	Presbyterian	1870-72	Black Hawk
*Sheldon Jackson	Presbyterian	1870-80	Supt. of Missions, Denver
W. Y. Brown	Presbyterian	1870-73	Denver
Thomas E. Bliss	Congregational	1869-73	Denver
S. F. Dickenson	Congregational	1870-	Central City
Lewis Raymond	Baptist	1870-71	Denver

NOTES

1. United States Census, 1860, pp. 546-49; 1870, Vol. I, pp. 3, 299, 328-42, 723.

2. Census enumerators of 1860 and 1870 did not include statistics for non-tribal Indians, except for approximate number living within the bounds of Colorado. Thus, all tables except general population tabulate only whites, blacks, Orientals, and Indians assimilated into or living in non-tribal society.

3. The 1870 census figures in this table do not agree. Of a total 33,265 native born, the origins of only 33,175 are listed.

4. Annual Conference Minutes of the Methodist Episcopal Church, 1860, p. 48; 1861, p. 41; 1862, p. 24; 1863, p. 131; 1864, p. 242; 1865, p. 130; 1866, p. 122; 1867, p. 141; 1868, p. 166; 1869, pp. 148-49; 1870, pp. 156-57.

5. United States Census, 1870, Vol. I, p. 531. Unfortunately, the Census of 1870 does not include actual membership statistics.

6. Information tabulated here is drawn from a very large number of sources noted throughout the paper. Space does not permit listing of them all. However, those used most include Annual Conference Minutes of the Methodist Episcopal Church, 1858-1870; Breck, The Episcopal Church in Colorado; Hopkins, et al., The Bible and the Gold Rush; Howlett, Life of Machebeuf; Parsons, "History of Colorado Baptists"; Cooper, Our Presbytery of Denver.

7. Incomplete date entries indicate residence after 1870.

APPENDIX D

BIOGRAPHICAL DATA

Biographical data on several key church leaders[1] are helpful in demonstrating what kinds of church people came to Colorado in the pioneer era. In this sampling, a look at birthplaces indicates that more pioneers migrated from the Midwest and Middle Atlantic states than from New England, the South, or Europe.[2] Of this group (not all of the birth-places are known), seven came from the Midwest, seven from the Middle Atlantic region, four from New England, four from the South, and five from Europe (three from Ireland, two from France).

Investigation of the places from which the pioneers migrated to Colorado tells a different story. Ten pioneers were already living in the West, seven in the Midwest, four in New England, four in the Middle Atlantic region, two in the South and one in Europe. Thus, many of the churchmen had already been westward bound pioneers.

Further analysis shows that some of the migrants were young but they were not uniformly so. Eight clerics and three lay leaders were thirty or under when they moved to Colorado. Ten clergy and five laymen were over thirty. Since the vast majority of all migrants were under thirty, many in our group were well above the average age.

Analysis of racial origins shows that all but one of the leaders were white. There was one black, no Orientals, and no Mexican Americans among the key leaders. Only one woman appears in the sample.

Biographical data on only the missionaries show that several had college and seminary training. Of the seventeen men sampled, eight had both college and seminary training; three had gone to college but not to seminary; six had had no formal higher education. The high proportion of formally educated missionaries in this small sample suggests that frontier preachers were generally better educated than tradition indicates.

A breakdown of education by denomination shows Methodists to have received little formal education. Roman Catholic, Episcopal, Presbyterians, Congregationalists, and Baptists were, with one exception, formally educated. Among those not formally trained we find five Methodists and one Episcopalian. Two Presbyterians and one Episcopalian had gone to college only. Two Roman Catholics, one Congregationalist, one Presbyterian, one Baptist, and two Episcopalians, and one Methodist had both college and seminary degrees.

JACOB ADRIANCE (Methodist minister) was born in upstate New York in 1835. Apprenticed as a carpenter, he felt a call to preach in the West. In 1857, he moved to Nebraska, where he came under William Goode's tutelage. Goode set him on a reading course and assigned him a circuit. Adriance accompanied Goode on his survey of the Pike's Peak area and stayed on, under special appointment. In 1860 and 1861, Adriance passed his examinations, and his bishop ordained him. In 1862, he located and left Colorado for the East.[3]

THOMAS BAYAUD (Episcopal layman and merchant) arrived in Denver in 1859. He acquired large portions of present down-town Denver. A vestryman of St. John in the Wilderness, Bayaud contributed land and money to his church. Bayaud was among the founders of the union Sunday School.[4]

AMOS BILLINGSLEY (Presbyterian minister) was born in Ohio, in 1818. He studied at Washington and Jefferson College, in Washington, Pennsylvania, and was ordained in 1854. He served congregations in Pennsylvania and Nebraska before he moved to Denver in 1861. He worked in Denver and the mountain camps for a little over a year. After his time in the mountains, Billingsley became an army chaplain. When the war ended, he went south to found a school for freedmen. He spent the rest of his life in the South.[5]

CLARA BROWN (Methodist and former slave) travelled to the gold rush after earning her own emancipation. She ran a laundry, reputedly clearing enough to purchase freedom for several members of her family.[6]

FRANCIS BYRNE (Episcopal priest) was born in Ireland in 1807, came to America as a soldier. He served in Jamaica, where he became interested in education and the ministry.

After his discharge he remained in Jamaica as an agent of the English Church Missionary Society. In 1850, he was ordained deacon. He left the island for Massachusetts in 1854. George Randall convinced him to transfer to Colorado in 1867. He was parish priest in several mining towns until 1871, when he became superintendent of Jarvis Hall, diocesan school for boys. In 1873, he returned to parish work, at which he remained until his death in 1906. [7]

WILLIAM N. BYERS (journalist) was born in Ohio in 1831. At 19, Byers moved to Iowa, where he worked as a government surveyor. From 1852 to 1854, he surveyed land in Washington, Oregon, and California. In 1854, he went to Nebraska. He settled in Omaha, which consisted of one house when he arrived. He spent five years in Nebraska, where he served as alderman and territorial legislator. In 1859, he bought a printing press and joined the gold rush to Colorado. Two days after he got to Denver, he published the first edition of the Rocky Mountain News, printed on brown wrapping paper. The News, still in publication, quickly became the leading newspaper in the territory. He edited and wrote much of the copy for many years. Byers participated vigorously in Colorado's civic life. He served as postmaster, and his name appears on boards of trustees for Colorado Seminary, Denver's library association, and many other cultural committees. [8]

JOHN MILTON CHIVINGTON (Methodist minister) was born in Ohio in 1821. He grew up in a rural, frontier setting. Encouraged by a visiting revivalist, he began the home-study course for ordination. In 1844, he was licensed to preach and spent some years preaching in Illinois and Missouri. He then moved to Kansas, where he served as missionary to the Wyandot Indians. His next charge, in Missouri, brought him into the antislavery movement. In 1857, Chivington became the presiding elder of the Omaha district. Later he served the same post in Nebraska City. In 1860, he was assigned as presiding elder of the Denver district. When he joined the army in 1861, he resigned his pastorate but continued to do lay preaching. After his army time, he became a freighter and continued to preach. He is said to have taken supply charges on two subsequent occasions. [9]

DAVID C. COLLIER (Episcopal layman), Denver lawyer and later editor of the Central City Register, participated in many of Colorado's civilizing ventures. He supported temperance, order, education, and cultural achievement in his paper. An

Episcopalian, he served on vestries of St. John in Denver and St. Paul in Central City.[10]

WILLIAM CRAWFORD (Congregationalist minister), born in Massachusetts in 1835, studied at Leicester Academy, Amherst College, Union Theological Seminary, and Andover Theological Seminary. After graduation in 1860, he served congregations in Maine, Missouri, and Massachusetts. In 1863, he accepted a call from the American Home Missionary Society to establish a congregation in Central City, Colorado. He worked there until 1868, when he returned East.[11]

SAMUEL CURTIS (Episcopal layman), Denver merchant, served as member of a constitutional convention and city treasurer. He participated in Episcopal church activities.[12]

JOHN LEWIS DYER (Methodist minister), born in 1812, in Ohio, spent all of his life on one frontier or another. As a farm youth, he received minimal education but rich revival religious schooling. In 1831, he and his family moved west to Illinois, where he married and began farming. Around 1837, he underwent a spiritual crisis and emerged convinced that he must preach the gospel. Soon thereafter, he began his ministerial career, armed with an exhorter's license signed by famous frontier evangelist Peter Cartwright. In 1844, he moved his family to Wisconsin, where he lost his wife. He turned to lead prospecting for a time. While thus engaged, he served as a local preacher and began perfecting his evangelistic technique. Soon the presiding elder assigned him to a regular circuit. Dyer became proficient as a preacher and as a leader of revivals. In 1855, his bishop ordained him as elder. In 1861, worn out by his hard work and victim of some eye disease, Dyer decided to take a vacation in the Rocky Mountains, where his son had gone mining. His vacation turned into a life's work in the Colorado mining camps. He served as a circuit rider in Colorado until his death.[13]

JOHN EVANS (Methodist layman), born in Ohio in 1814, attended preparatory school in Philadelphia, Pennsylvania, and medical school in Cincinnati, Ohio. After his graduation in 1838, he practiced in Illinois and Indiana, where he crusaded for humane care of mental patients. In 1845, he began teaching at the new Rush Medical College in Chicago. Evans' abundant energies led him to work in public education and land speculation as well. His financial adventures proved successful, and Evans was a very wealthy man by 1862, when

Abraham Lincoln appointed him as the territorial governor of Colorado. After his short term as governor, he remained in Colorado and developed land and railroads. His philanthropy in education and churches was widespread.[14]

WILLIAM GILPIN (Presbyterian layman) was born in Pennsylvania in 1822. He studied three years in England and then returned to attend the University of Pennsylvania. Appointed a West Point cadet by Andrew Jackson, he earned a second lieutenant's commission in 1836 and fought for three years in the Seminole War in Florida. When his request to be sent to the Pacific Coast was denied, he resigned from the army and moved to St. Louis, Missouri, where he practiced law and acted as secretary of the state's general assembly. In 1843, he joined one of John Charles Fremont's exploring expeditions. The party collected data on western topography and resources for Congressional advocates of western expansion. Gilpin became a zealous expansionist in the course of this trip across the Rocky Mountains to Oregon. He published a report of the expedition, which received wide circulation. For several years, he acted as a lobbyist and publicist for the expansionists. Abraham Lincoln appointed him the first territorial governor of Colorado. Gilpin served from 1861 to 1862 and was ousted for his inept handling of the territory's tiny public monies. He remained in Colorado, where he engaged in ranching and politics.[15]

OSCAR J. GOLDRICK (schoolmaster and journalist) was born in Sligo, Ireland, in 1833. He studied at the University of Dublin, and after his emigration to the United States, at Columbia College in New York. Later, he moved to Ohio, where he taught school and sold books. At the height of the Colorado gold rush in 1859, he arrived in Denver, where he established a private academy. Goldrick had a hand in founding several cultural organizations in Denver: the union Sunday School, the public library, the public schools.[16]

WILLIAM H. GOODE (Methodist minister), born in Ohio in 1807, later studied classics and law in Indiana. Though admitted to the bar in 1828, he renounced law for the minstry. Goode was licensed to preach in 1835 and admitted on trial to the Indiana Conference in 1836. His ordination complete by 1840, he served as head of an academy, circuit rider, and missionary to the Choctaw Indians. From 1854-59, he was presiding elder in Nebraska. In 1859, he surveyed the Colorado gold regions for his church and returned to a settled pastorate.[17]

WILLIAM HOWBERT (Methodist minister) was born in Virginia but moved to Ohio to remove his children from the influence of the slave system. He became a vigorous abolitionist. In 1860, while serving a charge in Iowa, he decided to vacation in Colorado. He traveled with a party of gold seekers but parted with them as soon as he reached Denver. He accepted a charge for a congregation in Hamilton and continued as an active minister until his location in 1863. He farmed for a few months and died shortly after his retirement.[18]

SHELDON JACKSON (Presbyterian missions superintendent) was born in 1834, in upstate New York. He studied at Union College in Schenectady, New York. In 1855, he entered Princeton Seminary, where he acquired enthusiasm for foreign missions. Unable to get a position as overseas missionary, he took a charge to the Choctaw Indians in 1858. He moved to Iowa, several years later, and began active work in domestic missions. In 1869, he secured his position as missions superintendent and spent the next ten years planting churches in the Rocky Mountains. In 1880, he moved to Alaska, where his missionary adventures made him a folk hero.[19]

JOHN KEHLER (Episcopal priest), born in Maryland in 1797, grew up in Maryland and Virginia. He became a Lutheran minister like his father. In 1841, he requested ordination in the Protestant Episcopal Church. After completing a course of readings, Kehler was ordained. He acted as pastor in Maryland and Virginia for 18 years. In 1860, he migrated to Denver, where he founded St. John in the Wilderness and served as army chaplain. He retired after the war but remained active as substitute preacher for many years.[20]

JOHN S. (JACK) LANGRISHE (Episcopal layman), theatrical entrepreneur and actor, was born in Ireland in 1824. He began his acting career as a child actor in Dublin. He migrated to the United States in his teen years and lived for a time in New York, where he played roles as an Irish comic and reported for Horace Greeley's Tribune. Early in the 1850's, he began to play the towns along the Missouri River. On tour, he met Jeannette Allen, an actress from Lockport, New York, and married her. The couple formed a company and toured the river circuit and new settlements in Kansas. In 1860, they moved on to Colorado, where they built theaters in all the towns and many of the mining camps. The company migrated all over the Rocky Mountain mining region but regarded

Central City and Denver as their homes. In the latter years of the century, Jack and Jeannette moved to a small mining town in Idaho, where Jack died in 1890. Jeannette survived him for almost two decades.[21]

WILLIAM LARIMER (Presbyterian layman), born in 1809, grew up in Pennsylvania. He operated a freight company until 1845, when he became major of the Pennsylvania Volunteer Sixth Regiment. In 1848, he became brigadier general and, in 1852, major general. Shortly after Congress opened the Kansas-Nebraska Territory for settlement, Larimer resigned his commission, moved to Nebraska, and began town-building. He founded Larimer City, Nebraska, and La Platte, Nebraska. In 1858, he moved to Leavenworth, Kansas, whence he and a group of associates journeyed to the Colorado gold fields in November. Larimer was Presbyterian and headed an effort to establish a church in Denver. Though remembered as Denver's founder, Larimer returned to Kansas after only a few months' residence in Denver.[22]

JOSEPH PROSPER MACHEBEUF (Roman Catholic priest and bishop), born in Riom, France, in 1812, received his primary education at an academy directed by the Brothers of Christian Schools. He studied classics at the College of Riom and theology at a Sulpician Seminary in Monteferrand, near Clermont. Ordained in 1836, he took a charge at nearby Cendre. In 1839, he left France for the United States. His first post was as traveling missionary in frontier Ohio. When his friend Jean B. Lamy became vicar apostolic of New Mexico, Machebeuf joined him and became his vicar general. During the Colorado gold rush, Lamy sent Machebeuf to establish Catholic parishes. In 1867-68, Colorado became a vicariate apostolic, and Machebeuf was elevated as vicar. Bishop Machebeuf remained in Colorado until his death in 1889.[23]

A. F. PECK (Episcopal layman), physician and dentist, attended New York Medical College. He practiced in Denver from 1859 to his death. Peck was active in politics and civic affairs. He also served as an Episcopal vestryman.[24]

GEORGE MAXWELL RANDALL (Episcopal priest and bishop), born in 1809, in Rhode Island, studied at Brown University and the Theological Seminary of New York. After his graduation and ordination in 1838, he took a charge in Massachusetts. Randall took leadership in educational and civic improvement ventures, worked as a Mason, and edited the

Christian Witness and Church Advocate. He was elected as bishop of Colorado and Parts Adjacent in late 1865 and took up his duties in 1866. He remained in Colorado until his death in 1874.[25]

ALEXANDER T. RANKIN (Presbyterian minster) was born in 1803, grew up in Tennessee with his ten brothers and sisters. Rankin graduated from Washington College with high honors in 1826. He held pastorates in Ohio, Indiana, and New York. In 1859, he toured Kansas for the Presbyterian missionary society. That summer, he traveled to Denver to survey the gold regions. He returned to his home in New York after a few months' work in Denver and the mining towns.[26]

JEAN B. RAVERDY (Roman Catholic priest), born in 1831, in Rhiems, France, studied philosophy and theology at the College of Chalons. He left for the United States just after his ordination and worked in New Mexico for one year. In 1860, he accompanied Jospeh Machebeuf to Colorado, where he remained until his death in 1889.[27]

RICHARD SOPRIS (Congregationalist layman), born in Pennsylvania in 1813, apprenticed as a carpenter. After his marriage, he moved to frontier Indiana in order to make his fortune in canals and railroads. In 1858, he caught gold fever and went to Colorado. He helped found Auraria and was elected to the Kansas territorial legislature. In 1860, he moved his family to Denver. He served in the volunteer regiment during the Civil War. The Sopris family farmed and prospered. Richard Sopris was a prominent leader in Colorado. He served as sheriff of Arapahoe County, mayor of Denver, and organizer of the state agricultural society. He and his family contributed time and energy to the Congregational Church in Denver.[28]

AMOS STECK (Episcopal layman), native of Pennsylvania, was educated in Philadelphia. He caught gold fever in 1849 and went to California. Within a few months, he returned to Pennsylvania. Soon, however, he went to Wisconsin, where he became a miller. Early in 1860, he moved to Denver and became a successful lawyer. He held several public offices including member of the legislature, mayor of Denver, and judge of Arapahoe County. Steck also served as vestryman for St. John in the Wilderness.[29]

LEWIS N. TAPPAN (merchant and soldier) arrived in Denver

in 1858 or 1859. He helped establish the union school. His real estate and trading ventures prospered. A founder of Colorado City, he also engaged in town-building as a profitable enterprise. Tappan was one of the few Coloradans to defend Indian rights in the Sand Creek affair.[30]

BETHUEL T. VINCENT (Methodist minister), born in Alabama in 1834, graduated from Garrett Biblical Institute in Evanston, Illinois. He held a pastorate in Illinois and moved to Central City, Colorado, in 1863. He served several terms as presiding elder of the Denver district and did much to build the Sunday school program in the territory.[31]

CORTLANDT WHITEHEAD (Episcopal priest and bishop), born in New York in 1842, studied at Phillips Andover and Yale. He graduated from seminary in Philadelphia, in 1867, and went directly to a mission in Colorado. He tended parishes in Black Hawk and Georgetown until he left the territory in 1871. He returned to Pennsylvania, where he later became Bishop of Pittsburgh.[32]

RICHARD E. WHITSITT--spelled WHITSETT in some sources--(Episcopal layman) was born in Ohio in 1829. At 24, he migrated to Missouri, where he became a merchant. When the Kansas-Nebraska Territory opened the next year, he moved to Kansas, hoping to make his fortune in land dealing. When couriers brought gold samples from Cherry Creek to Leavenworth, Whitsitt joined William Larimer's town-building expedition. He chose to settle in Denver and became an important civilizer. He served as secretary, treasurer, and donating agent of the Denver Town Company. During the Civil War, he was adjutant general of the territory. In 1863 and 1864, he was an elected member of the territorial council (the upper house of the legislature). In 1866 and 1867, he served on the Denver City Council. Twice, he held the office of territorial auditor. He was a vestryman of St. John in the Wilderness and donated land and money to his parish.[33]

THOMAS G. WILDMAN (Episcopal layman), native of Connecticut, graduated from Yale in 1859. He then migrated to Denver, where he and his brother Augustus intended to make their fortunes in real estate and insurance. Both men served on St. John's vestry.[34]

NOTES

1. These people were chosen as a sample because the

information available about them is relatively abundant and reliable. The sample is too small to do more than suggest characteristics of migration. Nevertheless, correlation with census statistics indicates that the characteristics of this small group are much the same as the characteristics of the population at large.

2. New England includes Maine, New Hampshire, Vermont, Massachusetts, Connecticut, and Rhode Island. Middle Atlantic states are New York, Pennsylvania, and Delaware. The South includes Virginia, North Carolina, South Carolina, Georgia, Alabama, Florida, Mississippi, Louisiana, Arkansas, Tennessee, and Kentucky. The Midwest includes Ohio, Illinois, Iowa, Indiana, Wisconsin, and Minnesota. The West, then, included Missouri, Kansas, Nebraska, Texas, California, and the Territories.

3. Adriance, Diaries, 1859-62; Effie Burrill, "Rev. Jacob Adriance, Pioneer Colorado Minister," Colorado Magazine, Vol. XIII (March, 1936), pp. 58-62.

4. Breck, The Episcopal Church in Colorado, pp. 5, 8, 12, 17, 276, 277.

5. Donald F. Danker and Paul D. Riley, introduction to Amos Billingsley, "Journal, 1861-62," Colorado Magazine, Vol. XL (Oct., 1963), pp. 241-42.

6. Metcalf, "The Beginnings of Methodism in Colorado," p. 200.

7. Francis Byrne, Papers, mss., Colorado State Historical Society, Denver, Colorado.

8. Vickers, History of the City of Denver..., pp. 339-40; William N. Byers, "The Newspaper Press of Colorado 1884" ms., Bancroft Collection, photocopy at University of Colorado, Boulder, Colo.

9. Chivington Papers, Western History Dept., Denver Public Library, Denver, Colorado; Craig, The Fighting Parson; Lyman, "The Truth about Colonel John M. Chivington."

10. Breck, pp. 5, 8, 276-77.

11. Hopkins, The Bible and the Gold Rush, pp. 123-24.

12. Breck, pp. 7, 8, 278, 279.

13. Dyer, Snow-shoe Itinerant.

14. Vickers, pp. 412-15; McMechen, Life of Governor Evans.

15. Karnes, William Gilpin: Western Nationalist; Vickers, pp. 435-40.

16. Vickers, p. 451; Nolie Mumey, Professor Oscar J. Goldrick and his Denver (Denver: Sage Books, 1959).

17. Goode, Outposts of Zion.

18. Irving Howbert, Biographical Sketch of His Father, ms., Iliff School of Theology, Denver, Colorado; Memories of a Lifetime ...

19. Stewart, Sheldon Jackson.

20. Kehler, Diaries; Breck, pp. 4-8, 9, 13-15, 23-25, 67, 276-79.

21. Cochran, "Jack Langrishe ..."

22. Larimer, Reminiscences, pp. 8-10.

23. Howlett, Life of Machebeuf.

24. Breck, p. 8.

25. William S. Perry, The Episcopate in America (New York: The Christian Literature Co., 1895), p. 167; Vickers, pp. 565-66.

26. Nolie Mumey, Introduction to Alexander T. Rankin, His Diary and Letters, p. 7.

27. Howlett, Life of Machebeuf.

28. Vickers, pp. 572-73.

29. Vickers, pp. 587-88.

30. Metcalf, p. 200.

31. Martin Rist, "B. T. Vincent," ms., Iliff School of Theology, Denver, Colorado.

32. Breck, pp. 39-41, 283-84.

33. Vickers, p. 631.

34. Thomas G. and August Wildman, Report from Colorado: The Wildman Letters, 1859-1865 (Glendale, Calif.: Arthur H. Clark Co., 1961).

BIBLIOGRAPHY

PRIMARY SOURCES

Manuscripts

Adriance, Jacob, Diaries, 4 Vols., 1859-62, mss., Western History Dept., Denver Public Library, Denver, Colorado.

American Home Missionary Society Papers, Colorado File, mss., Amistad Research Center, Dillard University, New Orleans, La.

Byers, William N., "The Centennial State," 1884, ms., Bancroft Collection, Photocopy at University of Colorado, Boulder.

________, "History of Colorado," ms., Bancroft Collection, Photocopy at University of Colorado, Boulder.

________, "The Newspaper Press of Colorado," 1884, ms., Bancroft Collection, Photocopy at University of Colorado, Boulder.

Byrne, Francis, Diary and papers, mss., State Historical Society of Colorado, Denver.

Chivington, John M., Letter, 1862, ms., Western History Dept., Denver Public Library, Denver.

Chivington, Sarah, Letter, 1892, ms., Western History Dept., Denver Public Library, Denver.

Denver-Boulder Presbytery, Women's Missionary Society Minute Books, 1881-89, mss., Colorado State Historical Society, Denver.

Howbert, Irving, Biographical Sketch of His Father, 1909, ms., Iliff School of Theology, Denver.

Howbert, William, Diary, 1860, ms., Iliff School of Theology, Denver.

Howlett, William, "Recollections of My Life and Reflections on Times and Events during It," 1933, ms., Chancery office, Archdiocese of Denver, Denver.

Kehler, John H., Diaries, 1859-65, 1872-74, mss., Colorado State Historical Society, Denver.

________, Letter, 1871, ms., Colorado State Historical Society, Denver.

Minute Book of the Bishop and Chapter of the Cathedral of St. John the Evangelist of Denver, Colorado, 1880-92, ms., Diocesan office, Denver.

Minute Book, St. John's Episcopal Cathedral, 1860-74, ms., Western History Dept., Denver Public Library, Denver.

Parish Records of St. Mark's Episcopal Church, Black Hawk, Nov. 1867-June, 1870, ms., Diocesan office, Denver.

Parish Records of St. Paul's Episcopal Church, Central City, Jan. 1876-1939, ms., Diocesan office, Denver.

Parish Register, St. Paul's Episcopal Church, Central City, 1860-1954, ms., Diocesan office, Denver.

Parish Register, St. Paul's Episcopal Church, Central City, 1867-74, ms., Diocesan office, Denver.

Pendleton, Jonathan Mabbitt, "A Colorado '58er; Across the Plains in Half a Wagon," ms., Colorado State Historical Society, Denver.

Records of the Convocations of Clergy of the Missionary Jurisdiction of Colorado and Parts Adjacent, 1866-1900, ms., Diocesan office, Denver.

Records of Membership of Auraria and Denver City Mission, within the bounds of the Kansas-Nebraska Conference of the Methodist Episcopal Church, 1859-65, ms., Western History Dept., Denver Public Library, Denver.

Richardson, George, Diary, 1861-64, ms., Iliff School of Theology, Denver.

Sayre, Hal, Interview, May 21, 1921, ms., Colorado State Historical Society, Denver.

Sensabaugh, Oscar Fitzgerald, "Recollections," 1951, ms., Mrs. John Goode, Dallas, Texas.

Spalding, Elizabeth, "Memoirs of Bishop and Mrs. Spalding," ms., Colorado State Historical Society, Denver.

Spaulding, Sarah Griswold, "Personal Recollections of the Early Days of St. John's in the Wilderness and Wolfe Hall," ms., Colorado State Historical Society, Denver, Colorado.

Steck, Amos, Untitled manuscript about Colorado's Early Episcopalians, ms., Colorado State Historical Society, Denver, Colorado.

Stone, Wilbur F., "General View of Colorado," 1884, ms., Bancroft Collection, photocopy at University of Colorado, Boulder, Colorado.

Talbot, Joseph Cruikshank, Diaries, 1858, 1862-65, mss., Church Historical Society, Austin, Texas.

________, Journal, Summer, 1863, ms., Church Historical Society, Austin, Texas.

________, Letters to the Church Missionary Society, 1860-65, mss., Church Historical Society, Austin, Texas.

Vincent, Bethuel T., Letters, 1868-72, 1892-98, mss., Colorado State Historical Society, Denver, Colorado.

________, Miscellaneous Addresses, mss., Colorado State Historical Society, Denver, Colorado.

________, Reports of the Presiding Elder of the Denver District, Methodist Episcopal Church, mss., Colorado State Historical Society, Denver, Colorado.

Warren, Henry White, Notebook of sermon titles, ms., Iliff School of Theology, Denver, Colorado.

Books

Babcock, C. Merton (ed.). *The American Frontier: A Social and Literary Record*. New York: Holt, Rinehart, Winston, 1955.

Baird, Robert. Religion in America. New York: Harper Torchbooks, 1970. (Orig. pub. in 1856).

Barney, Libeus. Early Day Letters from Auraria: Letters Reminiscent of Pioneer Days in the West. Bennington, Vt., Bennington Banner, 1859-60. Denver: Published privately, 1907.

Beardsley, Issac Haight. Echoes from Peak and Plain: Tales of Life, War, Travel, and Colorado Methodism. Cincinnati: Curtis & Jennings, 1898.

Billingsley, Amos S. Life of George Whitefield, Prince of Pulpit Orators with Specimens of His Sermons. New York: John B. Alden, 1889.

Bird, Isabella L. A Lady's Life in the Rocky Mountains. Norman: University of Oklahoma Press, 1960. (Orig. pub. in 1879).

Bowles, Samuel. Our New West: Records of Travel. Hartford: Hartford Publishing Co., 1869.

Brady, Cyrus Townsend. Recollections of a Missionary in the Great West. New York: Charles Scribner's Sons, 1900.

Bryce, James. The American Commonwealth, 2 Vols. New York: G. P. Putnam's Sons, 1959. (Orig. pub. in 1888).

Cherry, Conrad (ed.). God's New Israel. Englewood Cliffs: Prentice-Hall, 1971.

Chivington, John M. To the People of Colorado: Synopsis of the Sand Creek Investigation. Denver: Printed privately, 1865.

Colorado Business Directory and Annual Register. Denver. Published privately, 1875.

The Colorado Council Journal of the Protestant Episcopal Church. Denver: Published privately, 1874-1886.

Conner, Daniel Ellis. A Confederate in the Colorado Gold Fields. Norman: University of Oklahoma Press, 1970.

Denver Directory. Denver: Published privately, 1873.

DeSmet, Pierre-Jean. Life, Letters and Travels. New York: Francis P. Harper, 1905.

Dyer, John Lewis. The Snow-Shoe Itinerant. Cincinnati: Cranston & Stowe, 1890.

Ellis, John Tracy (ed.). Documents of American Catholic History. Milwaukee: Bruce Publishing Co., 1956.

Finney, Charles G. Lectures on Revivals of Religion. New York: Leavitt, Lord, & Co., 1835.

General Convention Journal of the Protestant Episcopal Church, U. S. A. Published privately, 1865.

Gilpin, William. Notes on Colorado. London: Published privately by Witherby & Co., 1870.

Goode, William H. Outposts of Zion. Cincinnati: Poe and Hitchcock, 1864.

Greeley, Horace. Autobiography or Recollections of a Busy Life. New York: E. B. Treat, 1872.

_______. An Overland Journey. New York: C. M. Saxton, Barker & Co., 1860; reprinted in 1966 by University Microfilms, Ann Arbor, Michigan.

Gunn's Map and Hand Book of Kansas and the Gold Mines. Pittsburgh: Published privately, 1859.

Hafen, Mary Ann. Recollections of a Handcart Pioneer of 1860. Denver: Printed privately, 1938.

Hafen, LeRoy R. (ed.). The Colorado Gold Rush. Glendale: Arthur H. Clark Co., 1941.

_______. Overland Routes to the Gold Fields, 1859, from Contemporary Diaries. Glendale: Arthur H. Clark Co., 1942.

_______. Pike's Peak Gold Rush Guidebooks of 1859. Glendale: Arthur H. Clark Co., 1941.

_______. Ruxton of the Rockies. Norman: University of Oklahoma Press, 1950.

Hall, Frank. *History of the State of Colorado.* Chicago: Blakely Publishing Co., 1890.

Hambleton, Chakley J. *A Gold Hunter's Experience.* Chicago: Published privately, 1898.

Handbook for the Kansas-Pacific Railway. St. Louis: Published privately, 1870.

Hart, Henry Martyn. *Priests: Whence They Are: What They Are.* Denver: Published privately, 1912.

———. *Recollections and Reflections.* Denver: Published privately, 1917.

———. *The Tragedy of Hosea and Nineteen Other Sermons.* London: Skeffington & Son, 1908.

Hedges, William H. *Pike's Peak or Busted! Frontier Reminiscences.* Evanston, Ill.: Branding Iron Press, 1954.

Howbert, Irving. *Memories of a Lifetime in the Pike's Peak Region.* New York: G. P. Putnam's Sons, 1925.

Hoyt, Edward J. *Buckskin Joe, Being the Unique and Vivid Memoirs of E. J. Hoyt, Hunter-Trapper, Scout, Soldier, Showman, Frontiersman, and Friend of the Indians, 1840-1918.* Lincoln: University of Nebraska Press, 1966.

The Illustrated Miners Hand Book and Guide to Pike's Peak. St. Louis: Published privately, 1859.

Kingsley, Charles. *His Letters and Memories of His Life.* New York: Charles Scribner's Sons, 1887.

Larimer, William and W. H. H. Larimer. *Reminiscences.* Lancaster, Pa.: New Era Printing Co., 1918.

Legard, Allayne Beaumont. *Colorado.* London: Chapman & Hall, 1872.

McGuffey, William H. *New Fifth Eclectic Reader.* Cincinnati: Winthrop B. Smith & Co., 1857.

———. *New Sixth Eclectic Reader.* Cincinnati: Sargent, Wilson & Hinkle, 1857.

McPherson, George Wilson. A Parson's Adventures. New York: Yonkers Book Co., 1925.

Marshall, Thomas Maitland (ed.). Early Records of Gilpin County, Colorado, 1859-61. Boulder: University of Colorado Press, 1920.

Minutes of the Annual Conferences of the Methodist Episcopal Church, Vols. used, 1858-1872. New York: Carlton & Porter, Carlton & Lanahan, Nelson & Phillips, 1858-72.

Minutes of Annual Conferences of the Methodist Episcopal Church, South. Nashville: Southern Methodist Publishing House, 1878.

Morris, Maurice O'Connor. Rambles in the Rocky Mountains with a Visit to the Gold Fields of Colorado. London: Smith, Elder & Co., 1864.

On the Frontier or Scenes in the West. Boston: Massachusetts Sabbath School Society, 1864.

Outler, Albert (ed.). John Wesley. New York: Oxford University Press, 1964.

Phillips, George S. The American Republic and Human Liberty Foreshadowed in Scripture. Cincinnati: Poe & Hitchock, 1864.

Pitzer, Henry L. (recorded by his son, Robert C. Pitzer). Three Frontiers. Muscatine, Iowa: Prairie Press, 1938.

Randall, George M. First Report of Bishop Randall of Colorado to the Board of Missions of the Protestant Episcopal Church. New York: Sanford, Harroun, & Co., 1866.

Rankin, Alexander Taylor. Alexander Taylor Rankin: His Diary and Letters; A Pioneer Minister Who Fought Lawlessness with Religion on the Prairies of Eastern Kansas and in the Frontier Settlement of Denver Where Life Was Harsh and Brutal. Ed., Nolie Mumey. Boulder: Johnson Publishing Co., 1966.

Redpath, James and Richard J. Henton. Handbook to the Kansas Territory and the Rocky Mountain Gold Region. New York: J. H. Colton, 1859.

Richardson, Albert D. Beyond the Mississippi. Hartford: American Publishing Co., 1867.

Rocky Mountain Directory and Colorado Gazetteer. Denver: S. S. Wallihan & Co., 1871.

Salpointe, Jean B. Soldiers of the Cross. Banning, Calif.: St. Boniface's Industrial School, 1898.

Sanford, Mollie. Mollie: The Journal of Mollie Dorsey Sanford in Nebraska and Colorado Territories, 1857-1866. Lincoln: University of Nebraska Press, 1959.

Schaff, Phillip. America. Cambridge, Mass.: The Belknap Press of Harvard University Press, 1961. (Orig. pub. in 1855).

Segale, Blandina. At the End of the Santa Fe Trail. Milwaukee: Bruce Publishing Co., 1948.

Spalding, John F. The Bishop's Annual Addresses to Convocations of the Colorado Clergy. Denver: Published privately, 1874-1900.

________. Annual Reports of the Missionary Bishop of Colorado, to the Domestic and Foreign Missionary Society, 1874-1900. Denver: Published privately, 1874-1900.

________. The Colorado Mission. Denver: Published privately, no date.

________. "Congregationalism in the Church," American Church Review, April 6, 1876. Reprinted as a Pamphlet, published privately, no date.

________. The Church and Its Apostolic Ministry. Milwaukee: The Young Churchman Co., 1887.

________. Encouragements for Mission Work in Colorado. Denver: Published privately, 1890.

________. The Evidential Value of Miracles. Denver: Published privately, 1894. Bishop's charge to the clergy, 1894.

________. Letter on Missions. Denver: Published privately, 1878.

________. The Threefold Ministry of the Church of Christ. Milwaukee: The Young Churchman Co., 1887.

Sweet, William W. (ed.). Religion on the American Frontier. 4 Vols. New York: Henry Holt & Co., 1931, 1936, 1939, 1946.

Talbot, Ethelbert. My People of the Plains. New York: Harper & Brothers, 1906.

Taylor, Bayard. Colorado: A Summer Trip. New York: G. P. Putnam & Son, 1867.

Taylor, Landon. The Battle Field Reviewed. Chicago: Published privately, 1881.

Tice, J. H. Over the Plains and on the Mountains. St. Louis: Industrial Age Printing Co., 1872.

Tocqueville, Alexis de. Democracy in America. New York: Mentor, 1956. (Orig. pub. in 1841-43).

Townshend, Richard Baxter. A Tenderfoot in Colorado. London: Butler & Tanner, 1923.

Tuttle, Daniel S. Reminiscences of a Missionary Bishop. New York: T. Whittaker, 1906.

United States. Dept. of the Interior. Bureau of the Census. Compendium of the Seventh Census. Washington: A. O. P. Nicholson, 1854.

________. Population of the United States in 1860. Washington: Government Printing Office, 1864.

________. Statistics of the Population of the United States at the Ninth Census, 1870. Vol. I. Washington: Government Printing Office, 1872.

________. Statistics of the Population of the United States at the Tenth Census, 1880. Vol. I. Washington: Government Printing Office, 1883.

________. Compendium of the Eleventh Census, 1890. Washington: Published privately, no date.

________. Abstract of the Twelfth Census, 1900. Washington: Government Printing Office, 1902.

Vail, Henry. A History of the McGuffey Readers. Cleveland: Burrows Brothers, Co., 1911.

Vickers, W. B., et al. History of the City of Denver, Arapahoe County, and Colorado. Chicago: O. L. Baskin & Co., 1880.

_______. History of Clear Creek and Boulder Valleys, Colorado. Chicago: O. L. Baskin, 1880.

Villard, Henry. Memoirs, 1835-1900, 2 volumes. New York: Houghton, Mifflin & Co., 1904.

_______. The Past and Present of the Pike's Peak Gold Regions. Princeton: Princeton University Press, 1932. (Orig. pub. in 1860).

Warren, Henry White. The Bible in the World's Education. New York: Hunt & Eaton, 1892.

_______ and S. M. Merrill. Discourses on Miracles. Chicago: Jennings & Pye, 1902.

Wells, Edward P., et al. Historical Sketch of the Central Presbyterian Church and the Twenty-Third Avenue Presbyterian Church, Denver, Colorado. Denver: Published privately, 1891.

Wharton, J. E. History of the City of Denver. Denver: Byers & Dailey, 1866.

White, Arthur Kent. Some White Family History. Denver: Pillar of Fire, 1948.

White, Mollie Alma. Looking Back from Beulah. Bound Brook, N. J.: Pillar of Fire, 1909.

Wildman, Thomas G. and Augustus. Reports from Colorado: The Wildman Letters, 1859-1865. Glendale, California: Arthur H. Clark Co., 1961.

Willard, Frances. Glimpses of Fifty Years. New York: Source Book Press, 1970. (Orig. pub. in 1889).

Willard, James F. and Colin B. Goodykoontz (eds.). Experiments in Colorado Colonization, 1869-1872. Boulder: University of Colorado Press, 1926.

Young, Francis C. Echoes from Arcadia. Denver: Published privately, 1903.

Periodicals

Adriance, Jacob, Letter, The Trail, Vol. IV (Jan., 1912), p. 24.

________, Letters, Northern Christian Advocate, (Jan. 25, 1860), p. 13; (Feb. 1, 1860), p. 17.

Anderson, George C., "Touring Kansas and Colorado in 1871; The Journal of G. C. A. Partane, May 16-June 7, 1871," Kansas Historical Quarterly, Vol. XXII (Autumn, 1956), pp. 193-219.

Armor, John B. (as told to LeRoy R. Hafen), "Pioneer Experiences in Colorado," Colorado Magazine, Vol. IX (July, 1932), pp. 146-50.

Ashley, Susan Riley, "Reminiscences of Colorado in the Early Sixties," Colorado Magazine, Vol. XIII (Nov., 1936), pp. 219-30.

Billingsley, Amos, "Journal, 1861-62," Colorado Magazine, Vol. XL (Oct., 1963). pp. 241-70.

Bliss, Edward, "Denver to Salt Lake City by Overland Stage in 1862," Colorado Magazine, Vol. VIII (Sept., 1931), pp. 190-97.

Chivington, John M., "Footprints of Methodist Itinerants in Colorado," Rocky Mountain Christian Advocate (Sept. 26, Oct. 24, Oct. 31, Nov. 7, 1889), p. 2 (in all issues cited).

Coffin, Morse H., Letter, The Trail, Vol. IV (Jan., 1912), p. 24.

Crawford, William, "Colorado as Seen by a Home Missionary, 1863-68," Colorado Magazine, Vol. XII (March, 1935), pp. 60-69.

Espinosa, J. Manuel (ed.), "The Opening of the First Jesuit Mission in Colorado," Mid-America, Vol. XVIII (Oct., 1936), pp. 272-75.

Hall, Frank, "Early Recollections," The Trail, Vol. XV (Oct., 1922), pp. 12-14.

Jackson, George A., "Diary, 1858-59," Colorado Magazine, Vol. XII (Nov., 1935), pp. 201-214.

Lambert, Julia, "Plain Tales of the Plains," The Trail, Vol. VIII (Jan., 1916), pp. 9-12; (Feb., 1916), pp. 5-13; (March, 1916), pp. 5-11; (April, 1916), pp. 5-13; (May, 1916), pp. 5-13.

Miege, John B., Letters, Mid-America, Vol. XVIII (Oct., 1936), pp. 267-71.

Seymour, Bennett E. (as told by Mary Grace Wall), "Recollections of Early Colorado," Colorado Magazine, Vol. XVI (May, 1939), pp. 106-10.

Talbot, Joseph C., "Journal of the First Missionary Bishop of the Northwest: Joseph Cruikshank Talbot," Historical Magazine of the Protestant Episcopal Church, Vol. XVII (March, 1948), pp. 60-105.

Winne, Peter, "Historical Gleanings," The Trail, Vol. VIII (June, 1915), pp. 5-17; (Aug., 1915), pp. 5-17; (Sept., 1915), pp. 5-18; (Oct., 1915), pp. 5-23; (Nov., 1915), pp. 5-23; (Jan., 1916), pp. 12-20; (April, 1916), pp. 17-24.

Newspapers

Register, Central City, 1862-70.

Rocky Mountain News, Denver, 1859-1870.

Collections of Newspaper Clippings

Clipping Files, Western History Dept., Denver Public Library, Denver, Colorado.

Dawson Scrapbooks, State Historical Society of Colorado, Denver, Colorado.

Warren, Henry White, Scrapbooks of newspaper articles by him, Iliff School of Theology, Denver, Colorado.

SECONDARY SOURCES

Unpublished Manuscripts

Howlett, William, "The Diocese of Denver," ms., Chancery Office, Archdiocese of Denver, Denver, Colorado.

Lyman, Clarence A., "The Truth about Colonel John M. Chivington," ms., Western History Department, Denver Public Library, Denver, Colorado.

Parsons, Eugene, "History of Colorado Baptists," 1923, ms., Colorado State Historical Society, Denver, Colorado.

________, "A Mother of Churches, the First Baptist Church, Denver," ms., Colorado State Historical Society, Denver, Colorado.

Rist, Martin, "B. T. Vincent," ms., Iliff School of Theology, Denver, Colorado.

________, "A Century of Colorado Methodism," Address, 1959, ms., Iliff School of Theology, Denver, Colorado.

Wetherell, W., "History of the Reverends John M. and Isaac Chivington in Their Relationship to the Early Methodist Episcopal Church in Kansas and Nebraska," Western History Dept., Denver Public Library, Denver, Colorado.

Dissertations and Theses

Bailey, Alvin K., "The Strategy of Sheldon Jackson in Opening the West for National Missions, 1860-80," Ph. D. dissertation, Yale University, 1948.

Cochran, Alice C., "Jack Langrishe and the Theater of the Rocky Mountain Mining Frontier," M. A. thesis, Southern Methodist University, 1968.

Gieseler, Carl A., "The History of the Colorado District of the Missouri Synod Lutheran Church," Th. D. dissertation, Iliff School of Theology, 1947.

Goslin, Thomas S., "Henry Kendall and the Evangelization of a Continent," Ph. D. dissertation, University of Pennsylvania, 1948.

Harvey, James, "Negroes in Colorado," M. A. thesis, University of Denver, 1948.

Metcalf, Kenneth E., "The Beginnings of Methodism in Colorado," Th. D. dissertation, Iliff School of Theology, 1948.

Murray, Andrew, "A History of Presbyterianism in Colorado," Th. D. dissertation, Princeton Theological Seminary, 1947.

Peek, George H., "A Story of the Protestant Episcopal Church in Colorado," M. A. thesis, Colorado State College, Greeley, 1948.

Olsen, Olaf S., "A History of the Baptists of the Rocky Mountain Region," Ph. D. dissertation, University of Colorado, 1952.

Perrigo, Lynn, "Life in Central City, Colorado, as Revealed by the Register, 1862-1872," M. A. thesis, University of Colorado, 1934.

________, "A Social History of Central City, Colorado, 1859-1900," Ph. D. dissertation, University of Colorado, 1936.

Rainsford, George M., "Dean Henry Martyn Hart," M. A. thesis, University of Denver, 1963.

Swan, Lowell B., "A History of Methodism in Colorado, 1863-1876," Th. D. dissertation, Iliff School of Theology, 1951.

Sylvest, Edwin E., "Motifs of Franciscan Mission Theory in Sixteenth Century New Spain, Province of the Holy Ghost," Ph. D. dissertation, Southern Methodist University, 1970.

Templin, J. Alton, "A History of Methodism in Denver, 1876-1912," Th. D. dissertation, Iliff School of Theology, 1956.

Thompson, Thomas G., "The Cultural History of Colorado Mining Towns, 1859-1920," Ph. D. dissertation, University of Missouri, 1966.

Books

Abbott, Carl. Colorado: A History of the Centennial State. Boulder: Colorado Associated University Press, 1976.

Addison, James T. The Episcopal Church in the United States, 1789-1931. New York: Charles Scribner's Sons, 1951.

Ahlstrom, Sydney. A Religious History of the American People. New Haven: Yale University Press, 1972.

Arieli, Yehoshua. Individualism and Nationalism in American Ideology. Cambridge: Harvard University Press, 1964.

Armstrong, Maurice, et al. The Presbyterian Enterprise. Philadelphia: Westminster Press, 1956.

Athearn, Robert G. The Coloradans. Albuquerque: University of New Mexico Press, 1976.

Atherton, Lewis. Main Street on the Middle Border. Bloomington: Indiana University Press, 1954.

Bancroft, Caroline. Gulch of Gold: A History of Central City, Colorado. Denver: Sage Books, 1958.

Bancroft, Hubert H. History of Nevada, Colorado, and Wyoming, 1540-1888. San Francisco: The History Co., 1890.

Barth, Gunther. Instant Cities: The Urbanization of San Francisco and Denver. New York: Oxford University Press, 1975.

Bartlett, Richard A. The New Country: A Social History of the American Frontier, 1776-1890. New York: Oxford University Press, 1974.

Beaver, R. Pierce. All Loves Excelling: American Women in World Mission. Grand Rapids: William B. Eerdmans, 1968.

Beesley, Claude A. The Episcopal Church in North Texas. Wichita Falls: Published privately, 1952.

Berthoff, Rowland. Social Order and Disorder in American History. New York: Harper & Row, 1971.

Billington, Ray Allen. The American Frontier Thesis: Attack and Defense. Washington: American Historical Association, 1971.

_______. America's Frontier Heritage. San Francisco: Holt, Rinehart, & Winston, 1966.

_______. The Far Western Frontier, 1830-1860. New York: Harper, 1956.

_______. The Protestant Crusade, 1800-1860. New York: Rinehart, 1938.

_______. Frederick Jackson Turner. New York: Oxford University Press, 1973.

Brauer, Jerald C. Reinterpretation in American Church History. Chicago: University of Chicago Press, 1968.

Breck, Allen D. The Episcopal Church in Colorado, 1860-1963. Denver: Big Mountain Press, 1963.

Brown, Dee. Bury My Heart at Wounded Knee. New York: Bantam Books, 1971.

Bucke, E. S. (ed.). The History of American Methodism. New York: Abingdon Press, 1964.

Burleson, Hugh L. The Conquest of the Continent. New York: Domestic and Foreign Missionary Society, 1911.

Burns, Edward M. The American Idea of Mission: Concepts of National Purpose and Destiny. New Brunswick, N. J.: Rutgers University Press, 1957.

Cather, Willa. Death Comes for the Archbishop. New York: A. A. Knopf, 1927.

Clark, Robert D. The Life of Matthew Simpson. New York: Macmillan, 1956.

Clark, Joseph B. Leavening the Nation: The Story of American Home Missions. New York: Baker & Taylor, 1903.

Clebsch, William A. American Religious Thought: A History. Chicago: University of Chicago Press, 1973.

________. From Sacred to Profane America: The Role of Religion in American History. New York: Harper & Row, 1968.

Clemens, Samuel (Mark Twain, pseud.). Roughing It. Hartford: Holt, Rinehart and Winston, 1962. (Orig. pub., 1872).

Cogley, John. Catholic America. New York: Dial Press, 1973.

Conrad, Howard L. "Uncle Dick" Wooten: The Pioneer Frontiersman of the Rocky Mountain Region. Chicago: W. E. Dibble & Co., 1890.

Cooper, Arthur B. The Story of Our Presbytery of Denver, 1870-1950, Including Earlier Days in the Rockies. Denver: Published privately, 1950.

Craig, Reginald S. The Fighting Parson: The Biography of Colonel John M. Chivington. Los Angeles: Westernlore Press, 1959.

Crooks, George. The Life of Bishop Matthew B. Simpson. New York: Harper, 1890.

Cross, Whitney R. The Burned-over District. Ithaca: Cornell University Press, 1950.

Current, Richard N. and John A. Garraty. Words that Made American History. Boston: Little, Brown & Co., 1965.

Dale, Edward E. Frontier Ways: Sketches of Life in the Old West. Austin: University of Texas Press, 1959.

De Onis, Jose (ed.). The Hispanic Contribution to the State of Colorado. Boulder: Westview Press, 1976.

Donnelly, Thomas C. (ed.). Rocky Mountain Politics. Albuquerque: University of New Mexico Press, 1940.

Dorsett, Lyle. The Queen City: A History of Denver. Boulder: Pruett Press, 1977.

Douglas, Winfred. The Diocese of Colorado and Its First Bishop and Dean. Denver: Published privately, 1936.

_______. Henry Martyn Hart. Denver: Published privately, 1938.

Durkheim, Emile. Elementary Forms of the Religious Life. New York: Free Press, 1965. (Orig. pub. in English, 1915).

Ellis, John T. American Catholicism. Chicago: University of Chicago Press, 1969.

Elson, Ruth Miller. Guardians of Tradition: American Schoolbooks of the Nineteenth Century. Lincoln: University of Nebraska Press, 1964.

Engelhardt, Zephyrin. Missions and Missionaries of California. San Francisco: J. H. Barry Co., 1908-1915.

Faulk, Odis B. Land of Many Frontiers. New York: Oxford University Press, 1968.

Ferguson, Charles. Organizing to Beat the Devil. New York: Doubleday, 1971.

Fetler, John. Pike's Peak People. Caldwell, Idaho: Caxton Printers, 1966.

Fischer, Christiane. Let Them Speak for Themselves: Women in the American West, 1849-1900. Hamden, Connecticut: Archon Books, 1977.

Fisher, Vardis and Opel L. Holmes. Gold Rushes and Mining Camps of the Early American West. Caldwell, Idaho: Caxton Printers, 1968.

Flexner, Eleanor. Century of Struggle. New York: Atheneum, 1973.

Foster, C. Z. An Errand of Mercy. Chapel Hill: University of North Carolina Press, 1960.

Foxhoven, Omer Vincent. The City of God in the City of Gold. Published privately, 1952.

Garraghan, Gilbert. The Jesuits in the Middle United States, 3 Vols. New York: America Press, 1938.

Garrison, Winfred Ernest. Religion Follows the Frontier: A History of the Disciples of Christ. New York: Harper & Row, 1931.

Goodykoontz, Colin B. Home Missions on the American Frontier with Particular Reference to the American Home Missionary Society. Caldwell, Idaho: Caxton Printers, 1939.

Golden Anniversary of the Highlands Methodist Church, Denver: Published privately, 1942.

Greever, William. The Bonanza West. Norman: University of Oklahoma Press, 1963.

Grimsted, David. Melodrama Unveiled, 1800-1850. Chicago: University of Chicago Press, 1968.

Hafen, LeRoy R. (ed.). Colorado and Its People, 4 Vols. New York: Lewis Historical Publishing Co., 1948.

________. Colorado: The Story of a Western Commonwealth. Denver: Peerless Publishing, 1933.

Hall, Frank. History of the State of Colorado. Chicago: Blakely Printing Co., 1890.

Handy, Robert T. A Christian America: Protestant Hopes and Historical Realities. New York: Oxford University Press, 1971.

________. A History of the Churches in the United States and Canada. New York: Oxford University Press, 1976.

Hill, Alice Polk. Colorado Pioneers in Picture and Story. Denver: Brock-Haffner Press, 1915.

Historical Sketch of Central Presbyterian Church, Denver, Colorado. Denver: Published privately, 1911.

History of the Calvary Baptist Church of Denver, Colorado, 1881-1931. Denver: Published privately, 1931.

Hofstadter, Richard and Seymour Lipset (eds.). Turner and the Sociology of the Frontier. New York: Basic Books, 1968.

Hollenback, Frank R. Henry White Warren: A Prince of the Church. Denver: Published privately, 1934.

Hollingsworth, Harold M. and Sandra L. Myres (eds.). Essays on the American West. Arlington: University of Texas Press, 1969.

Hollon, W. Eugene. Frontier Violence: Another Look. New York: Oxford University Press, 1974.

Hopkins, Walter S., et al. The Bible and the Gold Rush: A Century of Congregationalism in Colorado. Denver: Big Mountain Press, 1963.

Horgan, Paul. Lamy of Santa Fe. New York: Farrar, Straus, and Giroux, 1975.

Horner, John W. Silver Town. Caldwell, Idaho: Caxton Printers, 1940.

Howlett, William J. Life of the Right Reverend Joseph P. Machebeuf. Pueblo, Colorado: Franklin Press, 1908.

Jacknick, Sidney. Early Days on the Western Slope of Colorado. Denver: Carson-Harper Co., 1913.

James, Theodore B. The First Hundred Years, 1863-1963, Valmont Community Presbyterian Church. Valmont, Colorado: Published privately, 1963.

Jeffrey, Julie Roy. Frontier Women: The Trans-Mississippi West, 1840-1880. New York: Hill and Wang, 1979.

Jones, William H. The History of Catholic Education in the State of Colorado. Washington: Catholic University of America Press, 1955.

Karnes, Thomas L. William Gilpin, Western Nationalist. Austin: University of Texas Press, 1970.

Kelsey, Harry E. Frontier Capitalist: The Life of John Evans. Denver: State Historical Society of Colorado, 1969.

Kemper, Clarence. The Story of Old First or Seventy Five Years of the First Baptist Church of Denver. Denver: Published privately, 1938.

Larsen, Lawrence H. *The Urban West at the End of the Frontier*. Lawrence: Regents Press of Kansas, 1978.

Latourette, Kenneth S. *History of the Expansion of Christianity*, 7 Vols. New York: Harper & Row, 1937-45.

Leete, Frederick D. *Methodist Bishops, Personal Notes and Bibliography*. Nashville: Parthenon Press, 1948.

Lemassena, R. A. *Colorado's Mountain Railroads*, 5 Vols. Golden, Colorado: Smoking Stack Press, 1963-68.

McAvoy, Thomas T. *A History of the Catholic Church in the United States*. Notre Dame: Notre Dame University Press, 1969.

McGiffert, Michael. *The Higher Learning in Colorado: A Historical Study, 1860-1940*. Denver: Sage Books, 1964.

McLoughlin, William G. *Modern Revivalism*. New York: Ronald Press, 1957.

McManamin, Hugh L. *The Pinnacled Glory of the West*. Denver: Smith-Brooks Co., 1912.

McMechen, Edgar C. *Life of Governor John Evans*. Denver: Wahlgreen Publishers, 1924.

________. *The Shining Mountains, Colorado*. Denver: Denver Public Library, 1935.

Manross, William W. *The Episcopal Church in the United States, 1800-1840*. New York: Columbia University Press, 1938.

Marty, Martin E. *Righteous Empire: The Protestant Experience in America*. New York: Dial Press, 1970.

Marx, Leo. *The Machine in the Garden*. New York: Oxford University Press, 1964.

Maynard, Theodore. *The Story of American Catholicism*. New York: Macmillan, 1943.

Mead, Sidney. *The Lively Experiment*. New York: Harper & Row, 1963.

________. "The Rise of the Evangelical Conception of the

Ministry in America," in H. Richard Niebuhr and Daniel Day Williams (eds.). The Ministry in Historical Perspective. New York: Harper & Bros., 1956, pp. 207-49.

Merk, Frederick. History of the Westward Movement. New York: Knopf, 1978.

________. Manifest Destiny and Mission in American History. New York: Vintage Books, 1963.

Metcalf, P. Richard (ed.). The American People on the Western Frontier. West Haven: Pendulum Press, 1973.

Miller, Perry. Errand into the Wilderness. New York: Harper Torchbooks, 1956.

Minoque, Anna C. Loretto: Annals of the Century. New York: The America Press, 1912.

Mitchell, James. The Life and Times of Levi Scott. New York: Phillips & Hunt, 1885.

Miyakawa, Scott. Protestants and Pioneers: Individualism and Conformity on the American Frontier. Chicago: University of Chicago Press, 1964.

Mode, Peter G. The Frontier Spirit in American Christianity. New York: Macmillan, 1923.

Mumey, Nolie. History of the Early Settlements of Denver. Glendale, California: Arthur H. Clark Co., 1942.

________. Professor Oscar J. Goldrick and His Denver. Denver: Sage Books, 1959.

Murray, Andrew. The Skyline Synod. Denver: Golden Bell Press, 1971.

Nash, Gerald D. The American West in the Twentieth Century: A Short History of an Urban Oasis. Albuquerque: University of New Mexico Press, 1977.

Nash, Roderick. Wilderness and the American Mind. New Haven: Yale University Press, 1967.

Newman, Albert H. A History of the Baptist Churches in the United States. New York: Charles Scribner's Sons, 1915.

Niebuhr, H. Richard. The Kingdom of God in America. New York: Harper Torchbooks, 1957. (Orig. pub. in 1939).

Norwood, Frederick A. The Story of American Methodism. Nashville: Abingdon Press, 1974.

Nothing Is Long Ago: A Documentary History of Colorado, 1776-1976. Denver: Denver Public Library, 1976.

O'Ryan, William F. and Thomas H. Malone. History of the Catholic Church in Colorado. Denver: C. J. Kelley, 1889.

Paul, Rodman. Mining Frontiers of the Far West, 1848-1880. Albuquerque: University of New Mexico Press, 1974.

________ and Richard W. Etulain. The Frontier and the American West. Arlington Heights: A. H. M. Publishing Corporation, 1977.

Paxson, Frederic Logan. The Last American Frontier. New York: Macmillan, 1915.

Perry, William S. The Episcopate in America. New York: Christian Literature Co., 1895.

Phares, Ross. Bible in Pocket, Gun in Hand. Garden City: Doubleday, 1964.

Phelan, John L. The Millennial Kingdom of the Franciscans in the New World. Berkeley: University of California Press, 1970.

Portrait and Biographical Record of the State of Colorado. Chicago: Chapman Publishing Co., 1899.

Rickard, Thomas A. The Romance of Mining. Toronto: Macmillan of Canada, 1944.

Rist, Martin, "History of Religion in Colorado," in Leroy R. Hafen (ed.). Colorado and Its People, Vol. II. New York: Lewis Historical Publishing Co., 1948, pp. 199-224.

________, "Methodism Goes West," in E. S. Bucke (ed.). The History of American Methodism, Vol. II. New York: Abingdon Press, 1964.

Sanford, Charles L. The Quest for Paradise: Europe and the American Moral Imagination. Urbana, Illinois: University of Illinois Press, 1961.

Savage, W. Sherman. Blacks in the West. Westport, Connecticut: Greenwood Press, 1976.

Schaefer, Lyle L. Faith to Move Mountains: History of the Colorado District of the Lutheran Church, Missouri Synod. Denver: Published privately, 1969.

Schoberlin, Melvin. From Candles to Footlights. Denver: Old West Publishing Co., 1941.

Seventy-fifth Anniversary of the Sheldon Jackson Memorial Church, Fairplay. Published privately, 1947.

Seymour, George F. Memorial Sermon in Memory of the Rt. Rev. Joseph C. Talbot. Indianapolis: Frank H. Smith, 1883.

Shelton, Don. Heroes of the Cross in America. New York: Literature Dept., Presbyterian Home Missions, 1904.

Shinn, Charles G. Mining Camps: A Study in American Frontier Government. New York: Alfred A. Knopf, 1948. (Orig. pub. in 1885).

Sibell, Muriel. Cloud Cities of Colorado. Denver: Smith-Brooks Printing Co., 1934.

________. Ghost Cities of Colorado. Denver: Smith-Brooks Printing Co., 1933.

Sketches of Colorado. Denver: Western Press Bureau, no date.

Smiley, James. History of Denver. Denver: Times-Sun Publishing Co., 1901.

Smith, Duane A. Colorado Mining: A Photographic History. Albuquerque: University of New Mexico Press, 1977.

________. Rocky Mountain Mining Camps. Bloomington: Indiana University Press, 1967.

Smith, H. Shelton. Changing Conceptions of Original Sin: A Study in American Theology Since 1750. New York: Charles Scribner's Sons, 1955.

Smith, Henry Nash. Virgin Land: The American West as a Symbol and Myth. New York: Vintage Books, 1957.

Smith, Timothy L. Revivalism and Social Reform: American Protestantism on the Eve of the Civil War. New York: Harper Torchbooks, 1965.

Spencer, Elma D. Russell. Green Russell and Gold. Austin: University of Texas Press, 1936.

Sprague, Marshall. Colorado: A Bicentennial History. New York: W. W. Norton & Co., 1976.

Stanley, E. J. Life of the Reverend L. B. Stateler: A Story of Life on the Old Frontier. Dallas: Publishing House of the Methodist Episcopal Church, South, 1916.

Stauter, Patrick C. One Hundred Years in Colorado's Oldest Parish. Denver: St. Cajetan's Press, 1958.

Steffen, Jerome O. (ed.). The American West: New Perspectives, New Dimensions. Norman: University of Oklahoma Press, 1979.

_______ and David Harry Miller (eds.). The Frontier: Comparative Studies. Norman: University of Oklahoma Press, 1977.

Stewart, Robert L. Sheldon Jackson: Pathfinder and Prospector of the Missionary Vanguard in the Rocky Mountains and Alaska. New York: Fleming H. Revell Co., 1908.

Stone, Irving. Men to Match My Mountains. Garden City: Doubleday, 1956.

Stone, Wilbur F. History of Colorado. Chicago: S. J. Clarke Publishing Co., 1918.

Strout, Cushing. The New Heavens and New Earth: Political Religion in America. New York: Harper & Row, 1974.

Sweet, William W. Methodism in American History. New York: Abingdon Press, 1961.

_______. Revivalism in America. New York: Abingdon Press, 1944.

________. The Story of Religions in America. New York: Harper Bros., 1930.

Taylor, George R. (ed.). The Turner Thesis. Boston: D. C. Heath, 1956.

Trinity Methodist Church, Denver, One Hundredth Anniversary. Denver: Published privately, 1959.

Turner, Frederick J. The Frontier in American History, New York: Henry Holt & Co., 1920.

Tuveson, Ernest L. Redeemer Nation: The Idea of America's Millennial Role. Chicago: University of Chicago Press, 1968.

Twitchell, Ralph E. The Leading Facts of New Mexican History, 4 Vols. Cedar Rapids, Iowa: The Torch Press, 1912.

Ubbelohde, Carl. A Colorado History. Boulder: Pruett Press, 1965.

________. A Colorado Reader. Boulder: Pruett Press, 1962.

Utley, Robert M. Frontiersmen in Blue: The United States Army and the Indian, 1848-1865. New York: Macmillan, 1967.

________. Frontier Regulars: The United States Army and the Indian, 1866-1891. New York: Macmillan, 1977.

Weber, Max. The Protestant Ethic and the Spirit of Capitalism. New York: Charles Scribner's Sons, 1930.

Webb, Walter P. The Great Frontier. Austin: University of Texas Press, 1951.

________. The Great Plains. New York: Grosset & Dunlap, 1931.

Weinberg, Arthur K. Manifest Destiny: A Study of Nationalist Expansion in American History. Baltimore: Johns Hopkins University Press, 1935.

Weisberger, Bernard A. They Gathered at the River. Chicago: Quadrangle Paperbacks, 1958.

West, Elliott. The Saloon on the Rocky Mountain Mining Frontier. Lincoln: University of Nebraska Press, 1979.

White, Greenough. An Apostle of the Western Church: Memoir of the Right Reverend Jackson Kemper and His Contemporaries. New York: Published privately, 1900.

Wister, Owen. The Virginian. New York: Grosset & Dunlap, 1902.

Wolf, Robert B. History of the Rocky Mountain Synod of the Evangelical Lutheran Church in America. Published privately, 1941.

Wright, Louis B. Culture on the Moving Frontier. New York: Harper Torchbooks, 1961.

Articles in Periodicals

Athearn, Robert G. "The Fifty-Niners: Colorado's First Great Gold Rush," American West, Vol. XIII (Sept.-Oct., 1976), pp. 22-25.

Baur, John E. "The Health Seeker in the Westward Movement," Mississippi Valley Historical Review, Vol. XLVI (June, 1959), pp. 91-110.

Burg, B. Richard. "Vigilantes in Lawless Denver, the City of the Plains," Great Plains Journal, Vol. VI (Fall, 1966), pp. 68-84.

Burrill, Effie L. "Rev. Jacob Adriance, Pioneer Colorado Minister," Colorado Magazine, Vol. XIII (March, 1936), pp. 58-62.

Cochran, Alice. "Jack Langrishe and the Theater of the Mining Frontier," Colorado Magazine, Vol. XLVI (Fall, 1969), pp. 324-37.

________. "Jack Langrishe's Mining Town Theaters," Montana, the Magazine of Western History, Vol. XX (April, 1970), pp. 58-69.

Finkelstein, Barbara J. "The Moral Dimensions of Pedagogy: Teaching Behavior in Popular Primary Schools in Nineteenth Century America." American Studies, Vol. XV

(Fall, 1974), pp. 79-89.

Fitzgerald, Mary Paul. "A Jesuit Circuit Rider," Mid-America, Vol. XVIII (1936), p. 184.

Flynn, A. J. and LeRoy R. Hafen. "Early Education in Colorado," Colorado Magazine, Vol. XII (Jan., 1935), pp. 13-23.

Gilbert, Benjamin F. "Pike's Peak or Bust: A Summary of the Colorado Mining Rushes," Journal of the West, Vol. IV (Jan., 1965), pp. 21-26.

Goodfriend, Joyce D. and Dona K. Flory. "Women in Colorado Before the First World War." Colorado Magazine, Vol. LIII (Summer, 1976), pp. 201-28.

Gower, Calvin W. "Kansas Territory and the Pike's Peak Gold Rush: Governing the Gold Region," Kansas Historical Quarterly, Vol. XXXII (Autumn, 1966), pp. 289-313.

Harvey, James. "Negroes in Colorado." Colorado Magazine, Vol. XXVI (July, 1949), pp. 165-74.

Larson, T. A. "Women's Role in the American West." Montana: The Magazine of Western History, Vol. XXIV (Summer, 1974), pp. 3-11.

Mothershead, Harmon. "Negro Rights in Colorado." Colorado Magazine, Vol. XL (July, 1963), pp. 212-23.

Noel, Thomas J. "The Multifunctional Frontier Saloon, 1858-1876." Colorado Magazine, Vol. LII (Spring, 1975), pp. 114-36.

O'Connor, Thomas F. "Bishop Machebeuf." Colorado Magazine, Vol. XII (July, 1935), pp. 130-39.

Parsons, Eugene. "Baptist Progress and Achievement in Colorado." The Trail, Vol. XVI (July, 1924), pp. 3-16.

________. "Some of Colorado's Churches." The Trail, Vol. XV (Aug. 1922), pp. 3-11.

Paxson, Frederic L. "The Territory of Colorado." American Historical Review, Vol. XII (Oct., 1906), pp. 53-65.

Perrigo, Lynn. "Law and Order in Early Colorado Mining

Camps." Journal of American History, Vol. XXVIII (June, 1941), pp. 41-62.

Peterson, Richard H. "The Frontier Thesis and Social Mobility on the Mining Frontier." Pacific Historical Review, Vol. XLIV (February, 1975), pp. 52-67.

Schlissel, Lillian. "Women's Diaries on the Western Frontier." American Studies, Vol. XVIII (Spring, 1977), pp. 87-100.

Smith, Duane. "The Golden West." Montana, The Magazine of Western History, Vol. XIV (July, 1964), pp. 2-19.

Smith, Timothy. "Protestant Schooling and American Nationality, 1800-1850." Journal of American History, Vol. LIII (1966-67), pp. 679-95.

Tyack, David. "The Kingdom of God and the Common School." Harvard Educational Review, Vol. XXXVI (1966), pp. 447-69.

Willard, James F. "Sidelights on the Pike's Peak Gold Rush, 1858-59." Colorado Magazine, Vol. XII (Jan., 1935), pp. 3-13.

INDEX